Scott,

Thank you so much
for your support a
the work you do! We
need all the warriors
we can get!"

Angel

And he called me
Angel

Angel Meyers

THE STORY OF A
HUMAN TRAFFICKING SURVIVOR

authorHOUSE®

AuthorHouse™
1663 Liberty Drive
Bloomington, IN 47403
www.authorhouse.com
Phone: 1 (800) 839-8640

Published by AuthorHouse 2/2/2015

ISBN: 978-1-4969-6729-9 (sc)
ISBN: 978-1-4969-6727-5 (hc)
ISBN: 978-1-4969-6728-2 (e)

Library of Congress Control Number: 2015901524

Note From The Author

This book was written to honor and give reverence to all the souls lost to Human Trafficking. And so that you, the reader, can get an understanding of why some children can't "just get out" of this situation on their own. The most frequently asked questions of a trafficking victim is "Why did you stay? Why didn't you get help?"

I was trafficked for sex as a teen and it is not as simple as it seems. This is a billion dollar industry and it will not be overcome easily. The traffickers have increased in numbers and so have the victims. Statistics say hundreds of thousands are currently being trafficked, there are many more than we are aware of.

Sex Trafficking isn't alone, in Labor Trafficking people are forced to work to earn small amounts of food. Humans die in both of these industries. Trafficking will not stop until more is done about the demand for humans, whether it be for sex or labor. No demand, means no need for traffickers to exist.

Please, read my story and find out what happens on the inside. Learning about trafficking betters your chances of recognizing the signs of trafficking so you can protect the one's you love.

Some names/locations in this book have been changed to protect others. Please excuse the language, it was necessary to express the culture of the lifestyle. Some conversations may not be exact in original wording, but all of the stories are real.

Contents

~Chapter 1~

Two 20's for a 40

Memories, something most people try to hold on to, those are things I've tried to forget. I only have a hand full of memories of the old house out in the country in Arkansas. I can remember a silver Christmas tree that I thought was very weird, going to see the new house in town when I was around 4 or 5yrs old, and the day Mom killed the Dog. We had a black dog, and one day the dog bit me on the hand. I don't remember why the dog bit me but I remember momma changing the bandages and the healing part. I guess because it hurt more after than it did in that moment. What I do remember most though is Momma walking down the dirt driveway. You see, our house was down a long country road that ran between endless cotton fields. The driveway to the road was a dirt path lined with several trees and filled with tire grooves that led you to the house. She was walking with a quick determined pace because she was real upset. She had the dog by the collar dragging it along with her. In the other hand she had a gun, it was long and black, a rifle. I watched mom rush down the driveway until she disappeared between the trees. A few seconds later I heard it. "Pow!" I knew exactly what it was, I was used to guns. My dad and uncles frequently shot clay plates they sent flying through the air with a slingshot. What I didn't know before that moment was that guns were used to kill, let alone my mom would use one to kill. The dog had bit me and she killed it. All 6 of us kids cried for our dog. Mom helped us give our dog a proper burial and we all lined up to say our goodbyes. Our only brother was at the head and the five of us girls followed in order. It was a very sad day. I thought about it for years after. My mom killed our dog because of me. Being one of the middle children I was often forgotten about, but not that day. That day she wanted to protect me so much that she killed that dog, our dog. I remember that the most. And moving, I remember moving. The six of us were growing up and we were moving into town so this meant neighbors, school, and most of all friends. My Aunt had come by and was asking about the new house in town. I was excited to move so when my aunt was telling mom she was going to see the new house I wanted to go. Number one I loved riding in a car and number two I would do anything to go to town. I ran into the living room "Aunt Janell, Aunt Janell I wanna go, I wanna go, please take me with you." I begged. She smiled and looked at my mom, "can she go?" Mom quietly said yes so I went to town with Aunt Janell and got to see it all by myself, no other kids. We rode through Main Street, there was a drugstore, department store, barbershop, and a couple of other buildings all connected in a row. Our new house was Just a few blocks from the downtown area, and as small as the town was everyone's house was a few blocks away. We moved there a couple of days later. The house was big and white and was technically three stories to us kids because we counted the scary attic. There was a big wrap around porch and a big ole beehive inside the wall of the house when we first got there. My dad and some others got rid of the bees; of course, we kept the honey. In town, there were two stores to get food from, one we called Reba Bland's, and the other was the Black's. The Black's store was Just down the road from the big house we moved into in town. We had a big garden in the back for vegetables and Dad would sometimes hunt or fish for our meat. I remember going froggin with him. He would take these pitch forks on long poles and spike them down into the water from a bridge above. Those frogs were huge, and they taste Just like chicken. After dinner I would try to be the one who got to lay on mom's chest while we watched the science fiction shows my dad liked. I remember laying on her chest and hearing her heart beat. I would try to listen for mine as well to see if our hearts beat the same. I would slow my breathing to try to match her breathing. I thought, well, if I come from her, I should be in rhythm with her. I would work at trying to stay in her rhythm, sometimes I could make it work, but most times we were slightly off. She would talk and it was like having your ear up to a speaker with a bit of a muffled sound. I would hope that she would talk during the show just so I could hear the inside muffled sound. Those were the days…it was exactly what you would think small town living would be.

There were good memories in that town, but it didn't end that way. It was famously touted throughout the family that dad had proclaimed to mom. "When you turn 40, I'm trading you in for two 20's." It was a joke, to us, but it wasn't to him. He meant it and he did it, he traded mom in for two girls who were not quite in their 20's but they were in our family, my mom's blood kin. Yep, that's what I said. Two blood nieces! Yea, not good, I knew then and know now how "not good" that was. Mom's mood changed when that happened. She used to be happy, now she was just there. I never seen her cry but I watched her face fade away over the pain day by day. My cousin showed off their relationship before they even began the divorce. That added more pain and less momma. Very shortly after that our big ole white house burned to the ground, the only thing still standing was the freezer that was in the dining room. We had to move to a house several blocks away and when we did… dad didn't. Mom was never the same afterwards, being his wife was all she knew. They met when she was finishing out her teen years. She was raised in the country in the cotton fields and went from there to Dad's house. She only finished 6th grade. According to her, Grandpa wanted them to learn to read, write, and do arithmetic, then go to the cotton fields. Her family slowly migrated to Oklahoma leaving her there in Arkansas mostly alone. The sister she had there wasn't exactly on her side, she had moved there only because Dad convinced her to come back. With no one and nothing to stabilize her, I personally think mom had a mental breakdown. It was only weeks later when mom met her new boyfriend, and he didn't come alone. She'd never had any other relationships besides Dad. She had no clue what was coming at her. "The twins" Dan and Ron quickly became the disciplinarians of the house. They were much younger than she was, she had traded off for two twenties as well. I don't know if she intended for it to be that way but it was. She had done the same thing to Dad that he did to her. Only thing was, they weren't doing anything to each other. They were doing something to us kids but they were too busy in their own worlds to realize it. Mom had gotten things together to go to night classes at the high school to get her GED so she could get work to take care of us kids. She'd never had to have an outside job before, she had a job, and it was called "Mom!" She'd never been away from us either. This was the first time she would need to be away but it was important. How could she take care of 6 kids with no education? So she went to school and when she did, the twins began babysitting / molesting all six children in some way, shape or form. Ron had taken Amanda for himself and Dan had the rest of us to his self. I didn't fully understand what was going on, but I knew deep in my soul it was wrong, it felt wrong, as wrong as wrong could be. I waited for mom to step in and do something. She didn't know at first but after a few weeks I told her about Shelia having to go to the bathroom with Ron and her telling us stories about it. Dad was told by others in town that the twins were living with us and according to mom, he was steaming mad. I was glad someone told him and was waiting for the moment when he would walk through the door and stop all of this since mom was ignoring the existence of it. He never showed up. It was only a day or so later that mom told us to pack a bag. She said to put a few suits of clothes and some underwear in a bag. I thought we were going to a friend's house or the church for a camp of some kind.

Each of us grabbed a hand full of things and we waited for mom's friend to show up. When it was time to go mom was acting strange. She was looking out of the windows and acting all nervous. When the car pulled up she opened the door and hurried us all out to the car. We threw our bags in the trunk and got in the backseat. "Get down, get down!" mom yelled to us. We had no clue why but we got down as low as we could. After driving for a while on the highway she said we could get up. We looked out the windows and there were nothing but cotton fields all around. We started going through a town and pulled up to a building with a lot of windows. We filed out of the car and into the building mom went to the counter while we found seats. We were there for hours and it wasn't hard to figure out that it was a bus station. Mom finally told us that we were headed to Memphis, Tennessee. We got on the bus when it was our turn. It was fun at first but after a while that long drive wore us down. It was night time when we pulled up in Memphis TN. We had just gotten off the bus when I looked up to see a very familiar face. I froze right where I was. "How was the ride?" was the first thing he said. I couldn't say anything back, it was Dan and Ron. Clearly they had planned with mom to meet us here in Memphis. Why were they here? Why was she going to let this start happening again? We walked with them several blocks away from the bus station. When we got to the tall buildings we went inside one. Mom got a hotel room and we went up the elevator to the room. Mom went back down and told Dan the room number for him to come up later so the hotel didn't know there were so many people in the room. We only lasted a week or so there and Dan didn't let a day go by without some kind of contact with me. The only income was the twins going to the blood bank and they could only do that once each. Mom went to the legal aid office and they paid to put us back on the bus. Now we were on our way to Oklahoma. This is where I met my grand-parents and other family members. It was great, at first, until mom let the twins join us in Oklahoma. The molestation began again the night they arrived. We were living in a small shack of a house near the fair grounds that my uncle owned. My Aunt didn't like that Dan and Ron had come

5

to Oklahoma and it wasn't long after that we moved. We moved in with old man Letcher that mom did side jobs with. We were only supposed to stay for a little while, just long enough for mom to find another place. I guess it was easy for the old man to see what Dan had begun so he followed suit. I had gotten sick and my mom sent me to sleep in his bed. I thought it was to take care of me, it was for a whole other reason. This is when I really began to wonder if being touched and messed with was just a part of getting older. I hadn't spent much time at other's houses to observe because we were always grounded even though we did what we were supposed to. And we moved every couple of months. It was Dan's way of keeping us from being close enough to anyone to tell on him. So I didn't know if this was happening to my friends too and I didn't want to ask. We eventually moved to, what we called "Little Mexico" a neighborhood just south of downtown Oklahoma City. The house we moved into was not quite done, some of the walls were gone on the inside. You could see through to all the rooms in the front. There were the outside boards and that was it. The landlord gave us stacks of sheetrock for the twin's to put up in exchange for the deposit and first month's rent. We were in that house for a while. It didn't take but a few months for the landlord to catch on to what the twins were doing, just like Letcher did. He started taking us with him to help with paint jobs in the summer. He would buy us all lunch and that was payment enough for us. We would work all day to get that burger and fries. I didn't like being around him. I knew what he wanted. I couldn't get home fast enough. I didn't ever want to go with him. When he would come over I would go hide in the room and act sick. Mom would make us go because it was free food and a break for her. But it wasn't a good place for us to be. That part didn't matter much. Through the years it became more evident that everyone knew what was going on. We had several visits from the state but they always left us there. They would talk to mom and she would tell them it was all lies between sisters over an ex-husband. She knew it was going on, the lies were hers, not theirs.

One day most of us were in the living room watching TV, Dan was in his recliner when all of the sudden he began to shake violently. Mom Jumped up and started unbuttoning his pants. I didn't know what was going on, I thought she was going to do CPR on him or something. I was very confused when I saw lean toward him. Unfortunately I knew exactly what she was about to do. Before she could get to him he slapped her so hard that she flew back on the floor. He screamed at her "A young girl, it has to be a young girl!" Evidentially at some point he had to have told mom that if he were to fall into a "seizure" that the only remedy was to get a BJ. Later this version of instructions was confirmed. Apparently he left out the part about it not being her that could "get him out of it". My sister told one of my aunts about it so the state was called again. After another visit with the Welfare workers, we had to move. They had been given reports that we were being touched inappropriately and living in a condemned house. It wasn't condemned but it wasn't far from it either. So for spring break of 84', we got to move instead of rest. We were moving in a small car so we had to take several trips, and some of it, we were walking it over. The houses were only a few blocks from each other. I had rode back with Dan to the house to get some more things. I hated being alone with him. He always took advantage of that and today was no different. I reluctantly walked in the house with heavy feet. I wished that one of my steps would crash through the old floor and swallow me up. I wanted to disappear into a hole like Alice in Wonderland did. I stepped harder each step and nothing happened. There was nothing I could do anyway. He had made it clear through the years that he would not hesitate to burn us alive in our beds if we told what he did. He had set the house on fire a few times to make sure we knew he was serious. I didn't want to be the reason my whole family was dead so I did what he demanded. In the middle of it I heard a noise at the door. I looked over my shoulder and locked eyes with mom. I'm sure my eyes bugged out of my head. I don't know exactly what I looked like but my first thought was "Save me!" She was standing in the door looking at us through a 3-4 inch crack in the door. The look that she had on her face was one I will never forget. She looked at me as if I were stealing her boyfriend. There was no help in her eyes, there was only jealousy. I didn't understand why she was looking at me that way. I didn't want to do this, I didn't want any part of this, why didn't she know that? Why didn't she believe me? She seen it with her own two eyes many times but would never admit that it was happening and we were there again. She walked away, I couldn't see anything but her face and the way she was looking at me. The way she turned her back and walked away, leaving me there with him. After, we gathered some more things and went to the other house. I wanted to talk to her, I wanted to ask her why she looked at me like that. What did it mean? What was she saying to me? But Mom wouldn't speak to me or look at me. I tried to talk to her and she wouldn't answer. That was the moment when I knew for sure she was not on my side. She was not my protector after all, she was becoming one of them. He was hurting me so much more than that damn dog. "Why wouldn't she do anything? You shot our dog, why can't you shoot him?" I yelled at her in my head. I would stare at her and be screaming with the fury of a category 5 hurricane inside my head. I knew screaming at her wouldn't change anything. I saw my sisters yell at her, it did nothing to change anything. I was so angry with her. He was molesting all of us, why was she only mad at me? It wasn't my choice to be his favorite child to molest. It wasn't my choice to have any of them molest me. She had the choice, I didn't. My anger for her grew daily from that point. I wanted to be anywhere except where she was. The more I was around her the more I wanted to hurt her back. I struggled with it daily but I still loved her because she was my mother. Deep inside I still wanted to hurt her, I wanted to hurt her bad, like I was hurt. I started staying away from home as much as possible to avoid Dan. It was on one of those trips away from home on that 4th of July weekend that it all changed. They were arrested and we were no longer around them. It changed things between us kids and the twins. But it didn't change anything between me and mom. That day mom said she didn't want to be in the same house when they got out of jail. Well I didn't want to be in the same house with her at all.

Mom and us kids were all walking just west of downtown Oklahoma City in the shadow of the tall buildings still. Straight ahead, down Arizona Street, not quite to the McDonalds, was an old brown 2-story building. The front of it was flat with big garage doors and a regular door in the middle of the building with windows along the top floor. Mom opened the door in the middle; there was a dark skinny stairway to the top floor of the apartments. It looked really old. The walls were dingy and had longed for new paint job for many years. It looked like an old woman's closet and smelled like one too. The door at the top opened before we made it up and there stood a large man with a full beard. He looked like Santa at an earlier age before the gray hit. "Welcome to our Apartments!" he said loudly. We all walked past him into a larger hallway. The hallway went in a square through the building with apartments on the inside and outside of the hall. It reminded me of the hallways of that hotel in the movie The Shining where they seemed to go on forever. The man walked us all the way to the back to a one-bedroom apartment. "This is it". We walked in for the short tour of the apartment. Pretty much two rooms with a bathroom, the living and kitchen were open to each other and the bedroom was to the side. "This will work" I heard my mom say. She gave him some money, and that was the next place we landed. My older sister and brother got an apartment around the corner of the hall from us with Amanda's welfare check she got from the two children she had. It only took a few days to meet most of the inhabitants, there were young and old, almost crazy and way past crazy, the manager of course who lived in the apartments with us, and then there was TT.

TT was a white woman in her mid 30's, she didn't have any kids. She was overweight woman with skinny legs and a large top and middle. She was tall to me then, but then again I was short, everyone was tall to me. She had blonde stringy hair and was semi sloppy with her appearance but she was nice and funny sometimes. I met her the first day we moved in, out on the fire escape, she was out there smoking and I was waiting for my boyfriend to pick me up because I was trying to do anything but be in the house with mom. TT and I talked for a little bit about who was who in the building then his truck came rumbling down the alley. "Zoro" my first real boyfriend, he was my neighbor at the last house we just moved from on Reno. His real name was Jones, he was Hispanic, around 22yrs old, tall and thin. He was pretty nice lookin if you ask me. With a job and a truck. And of course, I dreamed that he was going to be my husband. I think about the age difference now, 13 vs. 22, and cringe remembering how I felt back then. Looking for anyone to take me out of the situation I was in. Anything had to be better than what I had going on was what I was thinking at that time. That day we went to his house, cooked dinner, watched TV and then he brought me back home. We got to the alley behind the apartment and someone had raised the ladder on the fire escape. I jumped over in the bed of the truck and used it to get to the fire escape. I climbed up and by the time I got to the top TT was coming down the hall to go out to smoke. "What's up Kid?" she said. "Not much" I replied. We sat there on the escape again talking for a while, she was easy to open up to because she seemed like she cared. I told her that mom Just wasn't capable of caring for us all and I needed some where stable so I could finish school, but I didn't want to tell her about the molestation yet because I was embarrassed and didn't think she would accept me. I told her about my neighborhood friends, our gang and the trouble we would all get in to and cause, all in an effort to seem grown and "Bad Assed". By the end of that conversation I was spending the night with TT. The nights I didn't stay with her I Just wandered around downtown, basically homeless. I couldn't stay at moms because I didn't know who she would bring in. I hated that my two little sisters had to stay with her but there wasn't a whole lot I could do about that situation. Within days my step father's twin brother had moved into the building and was trying to have a relationship with my oldest sister and the two kids they had together. I knew my step father wouldn't be too far behind. After being abused by adults mentally, physically, and sexually I knew I Just couldn't stay at home any longer. If she couldn't protect me, I had to do it myself. That was the summer of 1984 I was 13.

~Chapter 2~

The Old Coat

T didn't work and bills had to be paid, it didn't take long before I knew what was paying the bills and doing my part to keep them paid as well. TT's apartment was one of the apartments in the middle of the building. It was a two room open plan and the living room and bedroom were all one room. She had an old couch and chair to the right by the front door and a 70's style dingy yellow queen size bedroom set to the left. The kitchen /dining /bathroom area was separated by a wall with a wide-open arch so you could see most everywhere just standing by the front door. Of course with both of us being home most of the time there was a lot of time for talking. She asked one day, "Are you a virgin?" I stopped in my tracks and almost lost my breath. What was I going to say? How would she react if I told her everything? What if I don't and she finds out? And more importantly, was I a virgin? I didn't count that they had raped me, I had always believed that you lost your virginity to a person you loved, a person who loved you back. So under those circumstances, to me, I was still a virgin. I hadn't made love, I was molested. But I wasn't ready to tell her about the molestation and didn't want to seem like a little girl so I said "No!" She asked who and I put it all on a friend of mine. We had actually tried once before and it didn't work out as planned, but she didn't have to know that. The more questions I answered the more she trusted me and I was starting to trust her too. I told her about how mean my step father was but I still couldn't tell her everything. We trusted each other more and more every day and I thought I would finish growing up there and that one day I could tell her everything and she would take care of me. She proved her protective side from the beginning. There were some visitors at TT's who were "not as nice as she was" she said. When someone came that she didn't want knowing about me, I had to hide in the closet till they left cuz she said "they wouldn't take kindly to her having a kid around." I took offense to the word "Kid" of course. TT was already giving me lessons on some of the things that would make others believe I wasn't a kid anymore. Number one, I could curse all I wanted, except at her, but I was doing that already. Number two, I could keep some of my profits to have money in my pocket to look grown, I had no issues with that and Number 3 when everyone else is using drugs...I had to use. That one scared me to death. I had never used drugs before and was scared of what it might do to me. I had read so many bad stories about using drugs. But I didn't feel like I had a choice in the matter. It was do what TT said or back on the streets or even worse, back home with mom. We left the apartment and as I walked with TT to the store she explained to me how to buy, separate and sell marijuana. We talked all the way to the store. We got our groceries and were walking to the front down the pet isle. I remembered a friend in middle school acting like he had weed but it was what's called catnip, it's used for cats, not sure why. I looked and they had some so I asked TT to buy some, when she seen it she was skeptical but got it for me. I took the catnip we bought and laid it next to the weed. It looked almost the same. TT laughed, called me a genius and mixed it half-and-half with the marijuana and doubled her amount. TT said if I help her out she would let me stay, feed me and most of all protect me. My little sisters would come over and she didn't care if they were there or not, she would operate as if things were normal. She started talking to them about making and selling crank. I didn't want to do this and certainly didn't want my sisters to do this. I told TT that if she would leave my sisters alone I would do all the work for her, whatever she wanted. Just leave them out of it. That next day, I went to school with a Kool filter king cigarette box full of joints. I sold out by lunch and from there we moved to other things. Of course, this didn't sit well with the principal at school, neither did the ditching. I had been ditching school for several reasons. Number one, I had just gotten to the age where you need deodorant and no one explained it to me and I was homeless half the time and the people I did stay with didn't always want to supply deodorant or sometimes a shower. So if I couldn't mask the smell I would ditch. One of my teachers, actually my history teacher, called me out and embarrassed me several times in class. Number two, it was not easy to keep up with high school when I'm on the loop with TT all hours of the night selling and using drugs. And three, nobody around me cared if I went or not and I was starting not to care whether I went or not.

Within the first several days she had quite a few visitors. We had just gotten back from the loop and I heard a knock at the door; I headed for the closet as usual and heard her let a man in. I had heard his voice before, this was her brother Bruce. They had some small talk then I heard Bruce "Where is the girl you were talking about?" TT walked over to the closet and opened the curtain door. I always hid behind some things hanging in the closet because of the curtain. I fit perfectly behind this big old coat. I felt like it protected me when I was in there. "Where are you?" she laughed. "Right here" I said in a quiet voice as I peeked through the sleeve of the big old coat. "Come out, my brother wants to meet you" I stepped out of the closet, I was nervous as all get out. When I stepped out I looked up to see a giant in the room. He towered over me like the Empire State Building. Bruce was a big biker dude. About 6 foot - forever" and in total biker gear with long hair, bandana, leather, chains and all. "This little kid?" he asked in a higher pitched voice. "Yes, that kid, she's the one making all the money" she said. Bruce smiled, "So you're bringin in all the fuckin money?" "Ummm, me?" I said. He laughed and grabbed me up for a hug. He said, "Welcome to the family" after he put me down we all just started talking about the current stash TT had. Bruce did his best to make me not feel so intimidated, but it didn't work much. Bruce would come by every few days, it depended on whether we had a drop or not. One night when Bruce was over we sat at the table in the kitchen and BS'd with each other for a while. Then he pulled a piece of paper from his pocket that was folded in different directions like a little envelope. "Do you wanna make even more money?" Bruce said. "Of course" I said quickly, tryin to act older. "This right here is easier to sell and makes more money. Have you tried this?" "No! She hasn't!" TT said in a firm voice from across the table. "Get a glass of orange Juice" He said to TT while still looking at me. I instantly got scared. I'd never heard her sound like that toward him and it was obvious by his look that he meant business. She gave him the small glass of orange Juice but she looked upset and that made me even more frightened. At this point my body was freezing up on me out of fear. I wanted to run, I wanted to scream, but nothing was happening. He opened the folded paper and started to sprinkle the white powder in it into the orange Juice and then the rest slipped in quickly and the paper pouch was empty. "That's too much!" TT said loudly. "She'll be fine, she's young" Bruce said. He stirred the Juice with his finger and handed it to me. "Drink girl" with a face that said "DRINK GIRL" I drank it as quickly as I could I didn't know if the powder he put in was going to make the Juice nasty. The second I got over the taste the "what is this going to do to me" set in. It wasn't long before the effect of the powder set in and I couldn't stay still for nothin. I couldn't stop talkin, walkin, movin, cleanin, fidgetin. It was funny for a while, then it became exhausting. Bruce had enough and left, I was driving TT crazy. She tried to calm me by telling me that what Bruce had given me was crank, Bathtub crank was what she called it, and methamphetamine was what it was. Knowing that didn't make me feel any better. Imagine the normal ramblings and fidgety nature of a 13-year-old girl but then give her some meth. Yea, TT had a lot on her hands. That evening we went back to the loop...the fruit loop we called it. The fruit loop was a block in the downtown OKC area where the bus station was. There was also a gay club on the corner and that's how it got the name fruit loop. There was a strip of buildings caddy corner from the bus station where the peacock restaurant was, there was a hotel and some other offices and apartments. The area was right down the street from the police station so the presence of police was certainly there but they didn't mess with you unless you messed with somebody else. TT tried to take me out to "walk off" the effects of the drug especially since I had school the next day. We were on the loop all night long. I couldn't stop talking or walking or Jumping up on things. TT was so mad at me and Bruce. She kept saying she's going to end up going to jail over this; I kept assuring her she wouldn't. I never went to sleep that night and for two more nights after that. I still made it to school but couldn't stay seated or pay attention so I had to go home by lunch.... but I didn't fall asleep that was for sure. Days later when I had come down my jaws hurt so bad from all the talking I didn't want to talk for a couple more days. TT made me promise that if I used crank again that I wouldn't do it around her and make her crazy. I agreed and thought to myself, I don't want to do that again at all.

I didn't even like saying the word crank, especially bathtub crank, it just sounded dirty to me. Plus watching her make it, I didn't want anything to do with it. But to sell it, I had to know what it would do. At least that's what TT said. She taught me how to fold the wax paper to make the little pouch. We would do 10 pouches and put a rubber band around it and we would usually make 10-20 sets of 10. We had just finished folding up some "baby powder", that's what I called it, and put all the little pouch sets in a baggie and she put it under the mattress where she kept her stash. She sat down and started rolling a joint and I was playing with our turtle named Dog. It had D on the shell painted with finger nail polish. We were playing with it and laughing about its shell when we heard the steps come into the building, that was one of the advantages of the bottom of the building being empty, you could hear as soon as anyone walked into the building or out of their apartment. It sounded like a few people and big people cuz the steps were heavy. TT motioned me to the closet and so I scurried over to hide. I could still see everything from the closet if I stood just right behind that big old coat. There was a bang on the door, hard, not the normal knock. TT was already at the door looking out the peephole. She opened it quickly "Don't break my door fucker!" she yelled jokingly as she opened the door. There was a big guy coming through the door, he was about Bruce's size and he was laughing at TT. As they came in, I could easily tell they were from a gang like Bruce, they had on the whole getup of leather, chains, and bandanas with an emblem on their jacket like his. They said their hellos and he introduced the two other guys by their biker names of course. Then he told her that Bruce was caught up in a situation and had sent them "to pick up the goodies". TT bucked up, put her chest out a bit, the big guy said, "Bruce told me I have store credit". "Well, I ain't got no fuckin goodies for yah so y'all can get the fuck out!" TT yelled. TT and Bruce did have a code but it wasn't "goodies" it was "groceries" When he would come to do a pick up if he had someone with him he would tell her he was here to get some "groceries" and he would always have the money with him to replenish. My body started to stiffen and I held my breath as she started ushering them to the door, I was getting scared, and I could feel the bad vibes coming off them. As she directed them the big one quickly turned and grabbed her by her head and one of her arms, she started screaming but he hurried and put his hand over her mouth. The other two grabbed her legs and they took her down to the floor quick. While they were taking her down, they were all screaming, "Where is the shit?" "Where is the shit?" The big guy stood up as the other two were holding her down, he pulled a big gun from his side and pointed it right at TT's face. It was easy to see TT was scared and so was I. I still don't think I had taken a breath by this point. This was the first time I had actually seen anyone pull a gun like that and especially so close. I had only seen it on TV. I tried so hard not to move and not to breath, I knew I would be dead if I did, I was frightened. The two guys let her go but she stayed where she was because the gun was on her. They started tearing through the living room; the big guy had started kicking her every time he'd say, "Where is it?" which he kept repeating. They had torn up the living room and were headed over to the bedroom side where I was. TT yelped. "It's there!" she pointed to the mattress. "It's there!" she screamed. The big guy took a step over and with one arm flipped the mattress up and it landed off center. There it was... the powder we had just put together and all of TT's money. They grabbed it and walked out the apartment as quickly as they came in. TT got up and ran behind them yelling she was going to tell Bruce. I stayed put until she came back; I thought she was trying to get shot yelling after them like that. TT walked back in closed and locked the door and called for me to come out. I was scared to death crying uncontrollably and she had to literally pull me out of the closet. As I come out of the closet she wrapped her arms around me and hugged me tight. "I'm so sorry, I'm so sorry." She repeated over and over. All the while she was hugging me. It felt odd but good at the same time. I had seen others hugged like that but I had not experienced anything like that since I was very small, too small to remember. Her body was pressed up against mine and I could hear her heart beating in her chest. It was beating hard and fast. And she was breathing heavy but she was still saying "I'm so sorry, I'm so sorry." I started to release the tension that was holding my body in a stiffened position and relaxed into her chest. This was what I was searching for, what I needed. She cared about me, her actions said she cared about me. And I cared about her too, I believed that she would protect me and take care of me and I wanted to do the same for her. I wanted to make sure the men who robbed us would get in trouble for what they did. In my mind, I'm seriously thinking the police should be there any minute to get the bad guys and save us so they can't come back again. Nope, No police called, not a drop of help in site. What would you say? Yes officer, I Just got robbed of all the drugs I Just cooked up? Can't do that, I learned about street law from that, and part of that is knowing when you just shut your mouth. TT told me to get dressed to go downtown so I did. We walked downtown and she spoke with a few people about the robbery. We stopped by the pay phone and she left a message for Bruce to stop by and we walked back to the apartment. I wanted to stay up and wait for Bruce with her but she wouldn't let me so I curled up on the couch watching M.A.S.H. and passed out. I tiptoed across the room when I woke up, it was still early for TT, and she was not a morning person. I got ready for school and headed out the door, out the back of the building and down the alley. It was starting to get colder in the mornings, fall was coming. My teeth were chattering before I got to the end of the alley and I had almost 2 miles to go. I hated walking to school alone. I always had my sister with me before and we usually had some friends there as well. But not anymore, those days were over, I was on my own now. Every fourteen steps I was looking around everywhere. This wasn't the greatest of neighborhoods and I had nothing to protect myself with. I was worried that I would somehow run into the guys who robbed TT and they would know that I saw everything. Somehow they would know that I had drugs on me that I sold at school and they were going to rob me too. I clutched the pack of cigarettes filled with joints that I had in my pocket. When I got to school the robbery was all I could think about. I couldn't tell anyone what happened I had no one to confide in. The first few classes were a blur, lunch had finally arrived. This was my favorite part of the day. I was on the free lunch program and sometimes this was the best food of the day, sometimes it was the only food of the day. That was also my business hour, I sold the majority of the drugs I brought at lunch time. I had to keep my eye out for the principal, she knew I was doing something but couldn't quite figure out what it was. After I would grab my food I would go to the corner of the school and sit on the opposite side of the street so that I could sell my drugs but not have it on school grounds, Bruce said it was against his rules to sell on school grounds but that I could sell to the students if they asked me for it. I didn't sell to just anybody, I made a couple of connections and I would sell them a hand full for a reduced price and they would sell the individuals Bruce said this was the best way to avoid bringing too much attention to yourself. Lunch was over and it was class time again. School was a refuge for me for the last several years, it was one place where I could feel normal for a little while. I could do teenage things for a little while. But then the day always ended. I always had to go back to where I came from, but at least it was better than it had been in a while. Hard to imagine that, but it was. In the evenings we would watch movies and sometimes we would cook dinner together. It was a family, not the greatest, not what you see on TV, but it was a family.

My little sister used to come over to our apartment after school sometimes. She was a little bitty blonde thing with super-fast legs that earned her the nickname "Bird Legs". I was always cautious when she was over, TT had taken a liking to her and I was afraid of what that could mean. When Bird would eat with us TT would say things like "that food cost money you know". It was a difficult position to be in. I knew mom was feeding my two little sisters from the homeless shelter and they didn't have much more than bread. I also knew that if she ate with us too many times that TT would ask for something in return like she did me. I wanted to protect her from what I was feeling, I didn't want her to grow up at all. This growing up thing was not at all what they showed on TV. There was no way to explain that to Bird. She wouldn't have understood and I didn't want to even mention drugs around her. I didn't want anything to happen to her that was happening to me. I wanted to take care of her and I wanted to protect our ability to be together. Bird was the closest sister to me out of the 6 of us and she wanted to be everywhere I was, and as long as she was with me I knew I would do everything I could to make sure she was safe. Even when that meant I had to send her back to mom's apartment. The best thing about my new living arrangements was that I was still there with my sisters. We would still get together in the halls or in the alley and play together. Those were the best moments of my day. I wanted to have back what we had before, us 4 girls, constantly together, constantly being there for one another. I'd grown up in a house full of kids and although living as the only child in the house wasn't the worst thing in the world, it did become lonely sometimes. TT would leave for hours on end, sometimes she wouldn't even come home until after midnight. But I never knew when she was going to walk in the door so I always made sure that the place stayed clean and that I stayed alert because you never knew what was going to go down. One afternoon I heard a couple arguing in the halls, they were going in and out of the apartment yelling at one another. After a while I heard one of them marching around to the manager's office and start banging on the door. After a minute or two the marching footsteps were headed in my direction. Bam! Bam! Bam! "TT, open the door" she yelled. "I want this asshole out of my house!" TT had gone somewhere and I was afraid to open the door so I Just yelled through the door "She's not here!" The lady got upset and kicked the screen door hard enough that the door on the other side moved. I heard her march back around to her apartment yelling for him to "Get out!" Those were the kinds of things that happened on a regular basis in that building. If that building could tell stories, I bet it would take years to explain all the characters that walked those halls.

~Chapter 3~

"Easy" way out

Occasionally making food was a task bigger than I was able to handle. My mom, dad and big sister did most of the cooking when I lived at home. TT wasn't the greatest cook and we were attempting to make some noodles for lunch, we were on our second try. The first ones weren't cooked enough, there was still a hard part in the middle. This time we let it cook too long and the noodles were soggy. We were laughing because neither of us could boil noodles. We mixed the sauce in and sat down for lunch anyway. I thought to myself that she could be my mother, my new mother, one that would love me and teach me things. We would talk about all kinds of things. She would tell me stories about her and her family. I loved listening to her stories, her family seemed so different, they seemed happy. We were talking and I heard someone's steps start coming down the hallway. It wasn't any steps I've heard before. It sounded kind of like a small horse parading, and not the normal kind, those dancing horses. It sounded like boots, and they made a very distinct sound, like a fancy march. I could feel the hairs on my arms stand up and my body started to tingle in fear and anticipation, after our last loud stepping visitor, I didn't know what to expect. I turned my head toward the door with a worried look, TT said "Don't worry...It's my man, go to your spot." I ran to the closet and got behind the big coat where I could see. Then there was a knock at the door, I took a deep breath and held it in. TT walked over...unlocked and opened the door. It was a man right about 6ft, very muscular build; long hair in a jerry curl which was the "In" style at the time. He was sporting a hat and wearing jeans, a white undershirt, and Snake Skin boots. That's what was making the parading sound. His boots were fancy boots. They had shiny tips on the front and were nice and expensive looking. She called him "Easy". They talked for a minute but it got heated pretty quickly. Just as I was about to cry thinking about a repeat of the other day they walked out-side. They were fighting because he had come to get some money from her and she had none because we had just been robbed. You could hear them up and down the halls arguing. Eventually he left and she came back in the apartment. We talked about their fight and I did my best to reassure her that he would be ok with her by the next day to keep her in a good mood. I didn't even know him but what I did know was I needed her to stay in a good mood. We finished our food, watched a couple of movies and went to bed.

The next evening I was on the fire escape looking for TT to come back when I started to hear that parading horse step. It was him coming down the alley. I looked down his direction and I could see him raise his arm over his eye to block the sun to see who was on the fire escape. I ran back inside to TT's apartment and locked the door. TT was gone; I didn't know where she was or when she would be back. I was running through a million things in my head, hoping he would just walk right by the building. Then I heard him, he was coming down the hallway and straight to her door. He knocked a couple of times then he started talking in a singsongy kind of voice "I know you're in therrreee, open the doooorrr" "TT sent me to tell you something". I had my nose against the door peering out of the peep hole at him. After he said it a few times and started knocking harder I eventually opened the door but left the screen door locked. "What did she say to tell me" I said quickly. "Well if you will open the door I will tell you, she said for no-one else to hear" I was nervous but TT had just said he was nothing to worry about so I opened the door and he came in and closed and locked the doors behind him. As he sat down he said "Was that you on the fire escape?" "Yea, what did TT say to tell me?" I said again. I was nervous and wanted to get him out as soon as possible. He was nice but I was still scared. I was trying to be grown and fit in my grown situation so I could stay here so I tried to act like I wasn't scared but I was. "I saw you run back inside" he said in a playful voice with a huge smile on his face. "So" I replied. He went on to say "I could barely see you, you were glowing so bright I thought I was looking at an Angel, I was blinded" he said in an exaggerated voice as he mimicked the moment and put his hand up over his face. "But I couldn't stop looking at you I had to see who it was" I giggled, cause it Just sounded silly but I was totally cool with him mistaking me for an Angel. "I'm going to call you Angel!" he said, I giggled again, "Well I have a name, my name is Sarah" He said "I know, TT told me, but I want to call you Angel" "Angel is your real name!" He exclaimed. I thought it was kind of cool, him and everyone around me had a nickname and now I did too. I called him Easy and he called me Angel. We talked for a little while, he asked how I ended up with TT and I told him some of it. While we were talking he moved from the chair to the couch where I was. He was listening to me and started giving me a hug, my body froze and I didn't know what to do so I Just stayed there waiting for him to let go and he didn't let go. All of the sudden, he started kissing me…in the mouth. My brain started going 9000 mph. "What is going on here? Why is he kissing me? Why can't I move?" Easy stood me up and my body was like a walking statue I was so scared. I wanted to run but to where, and to who? Clearly TT sent him here, he already knew my name. He was telling me how much "loved me at first sight" and that "I was his Angel" Finally my voice box cooperated "What are you doing?" I screeched out. "Be quiet" he said, as he put one hand over my mouth. "TT told me to come here" he said. My eyes started watering up, I thought this part of my life was over. Just as he was coming closer to me we heard the screen door pull and not open because it was locked. Easy quickly tightened his grip on my face "Don't say nothing about this, you hear" I shook my head yes not wanting whatever the consequences could be. TT knocked and yelled "Open the door!" We jumped and I ran to the bathroom. Easy went for the door. I was so grateful that she showed up when she did but also scared to death about what was going to happen when she walks in that door. Meanwhile TT was knocking and yelling louder. She was about to rip the screen door off when he finally opened the door. "What the fuck are y'all doin in here?" she yelled as she barged in. "Nothing, Nothing!" he yelled back. "Where the fuck is she?" "I'm in the bathroom" I yelled, trying to seem normal and hide my fear at the same time. I could hear her footsteps coming toward the kitchen then to the bathroom door hard and fast. She ripped the door open leaned in on me in the tiny bathroom. She had sweat beads on her forehead and her face was all twisted up in anger. Easy had followed her and was standing in front of the kitchen sink. She started yelling at Easy while she was still staring at me. "Did you fuck her? Did you fuck her?" "NO!" he yelled back "NO no no no" he started laughing as if what she was saying was ridiculous. She quickly stomped over to where he was and yelled in his face again "Did you fuck her?" she asked again louder and slower. After they went back and forth for the third time with the same question and answer he began unbuttoning his jeans "Here, smell me, smell me, I haven't touched her, girl you are tripping, that's why I'm not coming over here anymore!" TT stomped over and grabbed her gun that was on the table. She pointed it at me still yelling at him "Did you fuck her? Tell me! I swear I'll shoot her if you did!" "Smell me" he kept yelling. I didn't speak or move I stayed right there on the toilet with my pants at my knees. I was petrified, I wanted to cry but nothing was coming out or happening. TT leaned down in front of him and back up again. "I told you, I told you!" He started yelling and jumping around like he had won something. It looked like she believed him and I started to cry. She was still pointing the gun at me until he turned the tables and started yelling back at her. "How the fuck could you accuse me of that? She's a kid? What the fuck is wrong with you?" She dropped her hand and Easy took the gun from her hand. He didn't point it at her but he kept it in his hand as he was yelling at her about her not trusting him and her thinking she's the man, that she isn't, and that he wasn't coming over here anymore. She begged him not to leave but he started heading for the door. She forgot about me and chased after him. As they went out the door, I got off the toilet and went and sat at the table. TT came back just a few minutes later, she was sad about what she had accused us of and was upset about losing him. Only problem in all that is that she was right the whole time. She knew what she walked in on but I couldn't tell her she was right because I thought she would have killed me! I consoled her, and told her I would do anything I could to help get him back for her. She asked if I would talk to him for her since I was able to calm her down and talk reason to her, she wanted me to do the same with him. I told her I would try if he ever came back, hoping he would never return. TT started listing off all the things I should say to him or ask him. I didn't want anything to do with it and prayed I wouldn't have to ever speak to him.

Days later Easy came back to the apartment. I could hear him walking up to the door. My heart sank, there he was and instantly TT told me to answer the door and go talk to him. When I answered the door, I told him I was coming to the fire escape to talk and for him to wait for me there. I went back inside got my soda and quickly went back over the plan with TT and then I walked around to the fire escape. I was sick to my stomach I was so nervous. I had no idea how I was going to say what I was supposed to say or what he was going to say. We sat there and started talking, I told him about how much she cared for him and wanted to be with him and he was telling me how much he wanted to be with me and not her. I was so confused and didn't know what to do or say anymore. Every time I would talk about her he would talk about me, and he kept calling me Angel. "Easy? What kind of name is Easy?" I said. He leaned and twisted over to the side and showed me the back of his belt. It was a western style belt that said "Easy life". "A friend gave me that name and people just started calling me Easy, Easy life" He smiled. His smile was intoxicating and beautiful. "I bet you got away with a lot of stuff as a little boy with that smile" I said. "Not as much as I wanted to though" he replied with a giggle and smile. We talked for a little longer and finally came to an agreement, if you can call it that. He wasn't giving in and I needed to get back inside before TT got upset. So if he would patch things up with her and make her happy so I have a place to live then I would consider being his girlfriend... in the future since he was 10yrs older than me. I walked him to TT's door, and I went back outside to walk around the neighborhood for a while. When I got back Easy was gone, TT was happy, and I had a place to stay. Easy was at the apartment several hours a day now. We would all watch movies, clean the house and cook dinner together, he was a better cook than both of us. It was almost like a family. A week or so had passed by, I was just sitting on the couch watching TV and TT had just come back in from going somewhere. She was only sitting for about a minute when she asked, "Do you like Easy?" "Yea, he's a nice guy for you" I said. "No, I mean LIKE, like him?" she asked. "No, No, not like that I don't" I said worried about what was about to go down. "I see how you look at him, and he likes you too, I can tell" I said nothing; I didn't know what to say, I was scared. "Well here's the deal Aaannngel" she said all drawn out and dramatic and the first time I heard her use that name so it scared me even more, how did she even know about that name? "Easy wants you." She said, as she thumped me pretty hard on the bridge of my nose. "So when he gets here in a little bit I want you to take him to Apt 9, as she hands me the key, and you do what he asks you to do. He has a test for you, I owe him and you owe me so this will help us all out!" I didn't say anything back. She was talking to me in that "I'm gonna cut your throat" tone and I believed that she would. She stared at me for a minute with those beady eyes and her stringy blonde hair. Then she leaned over me, even when we were sitting; she was more than twice my size, literally! She put her hand on my shoulder next to my neck, I thought she was about to choke me, I cringed backwards and in that moment she began to rise up from her seat. I was scared, petrified, nervous and forty-two other words all at the same time. I was so confused about what was going on. Yes, I did like him but I didn't want to be with him, I Just needed someone to feed me and protect me. I was more concerned with keeping a place to sleep and food to eat than a boyfriend, much less TT's boyfriend. Their relationship was more of a friends with benefits kind of thing but they were still, from what I saw, a couple none the less. Why is she doing this? Where had she been? Did they arrange this? How did she know he called me Angel? Is this just what adults do? And if so what does that mean? If I go with him, will he take care of me? Was he lying about the girlfriend part and just wants to hurt me like the others? Is he going to kill me if I don't do what he asks? He was frightening to see when he was mad at TT. I had so much going through my head all I could do was sit there frozen with that key in my hand. TT Just walked away when she got up. She went to her nightstand and got the gun that Bruce had given her after the robbery and she left the apartment but I could hear her outside talking to the apartment manager. It was only about ten minutes later that I heard the sound, his sound, the parading horse. It seemed to take forever and go so fast at the same time. Things started to move in slow motion I was so scared. I thought my heart was going to explode the closer he got. I jumped up off the couch when he knocked on the door. I just wanted to get "it" over with as soon as possible, whatever "it" was going to be. I opened the door quickly and almost hit him with it. "Follow" is all I could get out of my mouth. I walked quickly around the square hallway to the other side where the empty apartment was, TT walked to the other side of the hallway too but on the opposite side of the square. Number 9, it was the first apartment around the corner and was backed up against TT's apartment, same efficiency plan. I had handed him the key as we were walking down the hall. He opened the door, looked down at me and said "Did you talk to TT?" I said, "Why do you think we are here?

Yes, she told me. She said to do what you tell me do to, so what do I have to do?" I asked as we walked in the apartment. "Here, sit down over here" he pointed to the bed. I sat on the bed and he did too. He asked me what did TT tell me and I replayed the conversation for him. He told me that I shouldn't be talked to like that because I was an Angel of God. An Angel of God? I thought to myself. Not me, not this little girl he's got me confused with someone else. I'm not living the life of an Angel here. I remember them from going to church and this isn't what happens to God's Angels. He continued saying that if I was his not only that he wouldn't talk to me like that but that he would make sure no one else did either. He kept calling me Angel and stroking my hair and my face. I can't remember anyone else ever saying they would not only treat me well, but make others treat me well also. "Stand up" he said. He stared at me for a minute, looking me up and down. I was so nervous I was shaking and he could tell I was afraid. He got up and walked around me looking at me like I was a new car or something. All he kept saying was "Oh my God, my Angel, Oh my God, my Angel" I stood there for what seemed to be a very long awkward hour but I'm sure was just a moment. I was trying not to look at him. He was tall, muscular and had a tattoo of a rose on his chest. His body was the kind you see in magazines on models. Nothing like the old sloppy fat white men I had unfortunately gotten used to seeing. I could hardly look; I was still very confused about the situation. My eyes couldn't see all that was going on. I looked down at the floor most of the time, but my other senses were going crazy. I could feel every hair on my entire body move as he moved. He continued telling me how much he wanted me to be his and how he would take care of me if I was his. That he would protect me and make sure no one ever hurt me again and the more he talked the more I believed him. No one had ever told me they "wanted" to take care of me and "protect" me. I needed to be wanted, I needed to be protected, and I needed him. I felt like I had some say in it somehow, even though I knew I didn't. I still believed in what he said to me, I believed that he cared about me and wanted to take care of me and that did make it different to me. The things he said to me and promised me made me believe in him, was making me fall in love with his words and with him. He was saying all the things they say in the movies. Finally I was the girl in the movies chosen by her Prince Charming. It was just like TV, love at first sight. No one had ever cared like he said he did, I was so ready to be saved.

Knock, knock, knock, we both jumped, not expecting the knock at the door, it was TT signaling that we had taken enough time. We got up and he looked me in the eyes and said "I love you." When we left he walked me back to TT's apartment and left me at the door. It was unlocked so I went in and TT was sitting at the table. You could feel the thickness of anger in the room. I didn't know what to say or whether saying something would get me killed. I didn't know if she saw or heard any of what happened. The walls there were pretty thin. What if she heard the things he said to me? What if she asked me to tell her what he said, or what we did together? Did she already know? I walked into the kitchen where she was, she didn't speak, and I didn't know what to say so I was silent. I looked around to see if I could see where her gun was. She is totally capable and willing to shoot me right at this moment. I thought to myself that if this is how God planned it, then let it be. But I couldn't, let it be, I was scared to death. I finally walked to the bathroom and took a shower. I needed to get away for a minute to think. I was so confused, scared, and worried all at the same time but mostly worried, worried about my life, my sister's lives. I climbed into the shower and let the water rain down on me and used the privacy to break down in tears. I stood there in the water alone, sobbing like a 2yr old. I wished that I was a 2yr old, I wish I could go back to the beginning and not let any of this happen. I was trying to figure out what was going on and what was going to happen next. Why had she given me to him if it was going to make her mad? Why would she when she was his girlfriend? Why is she acting like she's upset at me now and I'm doing what I'm told? All the same things I wondered about my own mother and now her. What is wrong with me? Why was I made the way I was? What did I do? What did I say? Why was I constantly chosen for abuse? My brain interrupted my breakdown with a reminder, where is her gun? And where am I going to sleep tonight if she kicks me out? Or worse, will she shoot me now like she said before? I tried to just think about the water running over my body, I tried to send my mind off to another place to escape the barrage of questions flying through my mind. It didn't work, nothing worked. I stayed until the hot water ran out. When I got out of the shower TT was sitting in the living room on the couch watching TV. I picked up a blanket and curled up in the chair, we didn't speak. My mind continued to race wondering and worrying what would be next. I fell asleep in the chair and stayed there all night.

The next day, she acted normal, so I acted normal. She had new plans for the new situation that I bet she had been thinking about all night long, I was a kid, and the only plan I had was try not to sleep outside no more cause it was starting to get really cold at night. Later that evening TT brought this man back with her from downtown. She introduced us and told me to come with them. We walked around to #9, as she unlocked the door she looked at me and said, "You know what to do." "Is he renting this?" I asked. "Uh, no...he's renting you" she said in that mean voice as she leaned over me. She shoved me inside the apartment and started smacking me around and yelling for me to do what I'm told, the old guy followed. When she left, he took her lead and started shoving me, yelling at me, calling me names and getting all worked up which eventually lead to him hitting me, then the crazy stuff started. I was on the ground being kicked and then he flipped around and started acting like I was a little girl he had found somewhere injured. Asking who did this to me and if I was ok, like he wasn't the one who had just done this. I was so confused and scared he was like one of those crazy people you see on TV. He was holding me in his arms as if I were a baby. I wanted to want my mom, I wanted someone to help me. I had no one, I thought about Easy but he hadn't been there today. Once again, I had to save myself in the only way I knew how. When I was younger I learned that if you close your eyes and think hard you can go to another place, you could even

30

become another person in that place. I would leave my body behind for him to do what he wanted but I left, mentally I left. In the next few days, she sold me many times. A few days into it I told her I didn't want to do it anymore, it was hurting. TT's face turned red immediately. She started screaming "You will do what I say when I say it" and "You owe me for feeding you and taking you and your sisters in my house" She slapped my face and it throbbed immediately. It was still sore from the last time. She began punching my stomach and sides while she was screaming as I curled up my body went down. When she got me on the ground and started to come over me I instinctively kicked back at her. I froze instantly. I couldn't believe my leg did what it did. It kicked her! I didn't kick her my leg kicked her. Now my own body was turning against me and going to cause me more consequences. I looked up at her as her face was changing and I could see the decision for the next move had been made. To my surprise she let herself fall right on top of me, dead weight, it instantly knocked the breath out of me. I tried to suck air back in my lungs but the weight on top of me wouldn't allow it. She was crushing my chest, I was trying to scream but I couldn't get any breath out to scream with. I couldn't move anything but my hands and feet. My chest was burning and I thought I could hear my ribs begin to crack, she was 4 times my size. When I was almost out of breath she rolled over. I rolled the other direction and started to head for the door. TT Jumped up, grabbed me by the hair and quickly pulled me to the ground. One punch in the face later and I was knocked out. When I woke a few minutes later, TT was wrapping a belt around my arm. She had her body leaned over mine so I couldn't move and she stretched out my arm and stuck a needle in my vein. "What are you doing?" I yelled. "Helping you calm down, now shut the fuck up" Within seconds everything changed. I felt like I was floating right through her body on a cloud that was drifting upwards in the sky. Nothing mattered, nothing but floating on that cloud. TT walked me around to Apt 9 and just left me there. I laid on the bed and floated, there was a man there and he was doing things I didn't want him to do but I couldn't stop him from doing it. Everything seemed to move in slow motion and

31

nothing I did was effective, nothing made him stop and nothing gave me any power to make him stop. I didn't know then what was in that needle but I can almost remember the feeling.

When I woke the next day everything was as if nothing had happened. TT was in a great mood. When she wasn't abusing me she acted like everything was normal, the way it always was and she was actually cool most of the time. It was starting to feel more like where I was before, living with someone who was abusing you and then acting like nothing was happening. Just a regular day for everyone. Well it wasn't a regular day and something was happening. All in that apartment, apartment number 9. It became a disgusting place to me. One of those guys in #9 was the guy who managed the apartments. He had come over to the apartment and they were in the kitchen talking for a while real low. I was trying to hear what they were saying but I couldn't make anything out that made any sense. I wanted to get up and turn the TV down but I knew that would be obvious. I was in the chair leaning over as far as I could. I heard TT take a step toward the living room and I about fell out of the chair. I was breathing all heavy from holding my breath trying to hear them. She looked at me funny "What's wrong with you?" she asked. "Nothing" I said quickly and turned back to the TV. "Well after you finish your show you need to get the key" she said. I knew what "get the key" meant, that meant I'm going to number 9. I saw the manager smile when he looked at her. "I'm going with him?" I asked. "You're doing what the fuck I say" TT said as she raised her hand to slap me. The burn of her slaps were becoming unbearable, all I could do is put my head down, hold my breath and try to leave my body until the burning and throbbing stopped. "Your mom is behind on her rent and you're going to take care of it." He said as he giggled at TT. I had nothing to prove that mom had that conversation with them but I also didn't have anything to disprove it either. It was an awkward situation, I think the worst part was that I had to see him almost daily after that. When he smiled, it made me physically sick. I want to throw up right where I was.

TT had sent me downtown a day or so later to run a package for her when I ran into Easy. We walked around for a while and then he walked me back to the apartments. When we came around the corner to the alley, we could see that TT was standing at the top of the fire escape. She walked back inside before we got to the escape. We walked up the stairs and headed down the hallway to her apartment. Before we made the corner, I heard her screen door open and shut and she came around the corner. She had a trash bag in her hand and handed it to me. "Here! Here is your shit, Bitch!" She was pissed. "What did I?" before I could finish she started yelling in my face from about a quarter of an inch away. I had already started crying. "You mutha fuckers have been fuckin! I should have killed you the last time you little fucking whore. Take this bitch out of my building before I throw her off the top. And if she's going with you that means we are even" she said "Yea, were even" he yelled back at her. She turned around and walked away. I looked at Easy and he was just shaking his head. "Come on Angel" he said. I thought we were going to his place but no we stopped at my mom's apartment and he knocked on the door. I didn't wait for her to answer it, I opened the door and walked in. Mom was still in her room, I sat down on the couch and Easy stood over me for a minute or two. I was still crying, not because of TT anymore but because he was going to leave me there. He knew why I was crying as well. "I can't take you to my place yet because I've got some things going on. I need you to stay here at your mom's then I'll be back to get you." He said "Imma go talk to her, I'll be back", he didn't come back that night so I left the apartments, walked around for a while and then slept downtown. I came back the next morning to see if he had come back. I went out running around and came back later in the afternoon. I did this for a few days, one day when I came around the corner of the alley I seen Zoro's truck, I raced up the stairs wondering what he was doing here. I was excited to see him because it had been over a month since he had stopped by. Mom lived in the apartment right by the fire escape so it was quick to get to the door. I opened the living room door and nothing, I went to mom's door opened it and WOW ...something! That something, yea, that was my mom and Jones, my Zoro, in her bed! I didn't know what to say, or what there was to say. But there they were, on top of her mattress pile. I just closed the bedroom door, got my trash bag of stuff and walked back down the fire escape. Betrayed again, I wondered what it was that I did as a child to make her not love me to that degree. I had spent the last few years wondering what I did and what I could do to change how she felt but nothing mattered. Thinking about that stuff wasn't going to get me fed so I Just kept on moving. I hadn't eaten yet so I was on the hunt for some food. There was a snack company down the street that made the sandwiches and stuff that went into the self-serve machines, like at the hospital. They had several big trash bins in the back, which made for a good hiding place, protection from the wind and the boogieman at night. Even when I would sleep in the dumpster I would act like I was in my own bed. I would always make sure that none of my limbs were hanging off of my makeshift bed. It was a very important defense strategy from back in the day. In the small town in Arkansas where I grew up there was only one gas station, it was by the highway. The old man that ran the gas station had a fake arm. The kind that had the metal pinchers at the end. All of us kids were afraid of him and somehow I got the idea that what happened was a monster came at night and cut off all kids limbs that were falling off the bed. And that he must have been one of those kids. So I made sure that when I slept I kept my limbs close to me so they wouldn't get cut off. It wasn't that bad to sleep on, two mushy bread filled bags, way better than the ground. They also threw it out every day so that was my main source of food while I was homeless. I felt I was actually eating better homeless than I was at moms or TT's. I was getting to eat those special sandwiches every day. It didn't seem that bad that it was from the trash. But sleeping there at night was still scary. I would hear every little sound from blocks around. I would wake up every hour or so which would leave me tired on the loop the next day. But regardless of condition, I was there on the loop daily. I met another girl on the fruit loop who said she had been homeless but just had enough to rent a room for the week. She said I could stay there with her for a few days if I would "work" with her. I wasn't sure what "work" she wanted me to do but I needed somewhere to stay so I went with her to the upstairs apartment. It was tiny and old but it had a mattress on the floor for a bed so it was ok to me. We had been there maybe 15 minute when she said she was going to get high. I thought she was going to light a joint and the next thing I know she's putting her belt around her arm with a needle ready. I'm sure my eyes bulged out because that was what TT did to me and I couldn't believe she was about to do that to herself. She seen me looking, "I only have one hit sis" she said. "Oh, I'm ok." I shook my head no at her as I raised my hand at her. She put the needle in her arm just like TT had done with me then basically zombie out. I got to see from the outside what that shot TT gave me did and I was mortified. She laid there with her eyes rolled back and she was slowly moving side to side. She had a small moan that was just enough to hear and she seemed to pass in and out. She was only out for a few minutes when the door opened and this skinny crazy looking white guy came in. "Who the fuck are you" he asked. "I just met her" I told him while he was trying to wake her up. "She shot up some dope!" I said. "That Bitch!" he yelled, "You shot my shit? You shot my shit?" he was yelling as he started grabbing at her. He raised up and started kicking, then back down hitting and kept yelling at her. She was not responding because she was high but she was moaning and stuff. I was so scared, while he was on top of her in the corner I grabbed my bag and ran out the door, down the stairs and back to the street again. I walked around till it got dark thinking about what she looked like and how she wasn't able to respond even though he was beating her. Then I wondered about what else had happened to me while I was passed out on that stuff. I remember thanking God that I woke up from it when she would give it to me. I heard about people overdosing and I was all of 90lbs. After seeing how unresponsive she was I knew that was a state that anyone could do anything to you in. I tried to think about something else, I didn't want to think about what they might have been doing to me. It was bad enough to know when you're awake, I Just didn't want to think about it. That was my one and only coping skill at the time...

don't think about it. I walked over to the sandwich company to go hide my bag and hopefully secure my spot for the night. It was my 14th birthday and it was bad enough that I was alone with no family and no one who cares, I didn't need any other problems. On my way, I heard a familiar sound behind me. I turned and looked and it was Easy. He was walking about a half a block behind me. I stood and waited for him to catch up. "Where are you going?" "To my spot" I said. "Why haven't you been at your mom's?" he asked. I told him what had happened. "Well you belong to me anyway, let's go" and that day he took me home with him, it was the best birthday present ever! He lived in the bottom apartment of a fourplex. What's a fourplex? Yea, I wondered that too. It's a big house that has four apartments 2 on bottom and 2 on top. It was a pretty nice place. The living and bedroom was separated by a set of French doors and the kitchen was in the back with a small room off the backside. Easy had a small bed in the back room for guest. There was a porch on the back of the house where you could see, oddly enough, directly to the police station. We talked all night long and he didn't even ask me for sex. I felt secure somewhere for once.

I started staying at Easy's house when he didn't have other stuff going on. He was with me again and it felt like what they show in the movies, it was magical. He would say such wonderful things to me. I wanted to stay with him all day but I had things to take care of. I was trying to stay in school and keep watch on my sisters so I would go back and forth. It had been raining, Easy wasn't home and I didn't have anywhere else to be so I left a note for him and went back to the apartments to check on my sisters. I went to a neighbor's apartment, he was there but was getting ready to leave. I stayed there a while till he was ready to go, then reluctantly went around to mom's apartment. I knocked on the door, she answered and I walked in. To my surprise Jones was in there with her again. I laughed because the other alternative was to cry and I wasn't doing that in front of her, she had taken enough of my tears. He was mad "You took my ID bitch, and where is my sweater?" I could barely understand what he was saying because he was talking with his teeth together. He had been in a fight weeks earlier and had his jaw wired shut. "What, I can't understand you, you talk like an idiot!" I yelled back. "My sweater he yelled through his teeth." "What sweater, I ain't got yo sweater! You makin up shit now! You just mad cause I know you fuckin my momma, y'all's dirty ass deserve one another!" "Bitch, I'll slap she shit out of you if you don't give me my stuff!" he said as he raised his hand in the air. "I don't have your stuff! I don't have your stuff!" I wasn't sure of all that he was saying through the wired jaw and when he was mad his accent was really bad. Plus, I really wasn't trying to hear what he was saying, I Just wanted away from him and Mom. He just kept screaming at me and backing me out of the apartment. We argued into the hallway and only seconds later, I heard Easy's boots coming up the fire escape fast. He came around the corner just in time. He saw Jones towering over me and immediately jumped into the situation. He started yelling back at Jones in his face backing him all the way back into the apartment and into mom's room. I remember him screaming at Jones "I'll follow you to the ends of the world if you put your hands on my Angel!" He must have said that 20 times while he was beating and kicking the shit out of Jones. Easy didn't care at all that his jaw was wired shut or that he was still healing from a fracture. The only thing that mattered was that he was attacking me. FINALLY!! FINALLY! Someone actually stuck up for me! Someone finally said it WASN'T OK to abuse me. Easy cussed out my mom too for her inability to stand up and protect me. She didn't say a word; she didn't even look up. From that moment, he was my full-fledged Savior. Easy walked me around to TT's apartment and asked if I could stay there for the night. TT said it would be ok and that she needed to talk to me anyway. I had no idea what she had in mind but I knew I was scared of it. I wanted to go with Easy but he said I had to stay there with her so I went inside. I was worried about what she wanted to talk to me about. What if she asked about me and Easy? Did she know that I was spending nights at his house and my clothes are there? Did she know how much he cared about me? My mind was racing with questions. After Easy left I told her all about what had happened with Jones. We had been talking for a while when TT started asking me weird questions about my private area. She asked me if I had any sores or if it was burning when I went to the rest room. I hadn't experienced any of that so I said no. I asked why. She said one of the filthy men she sold me to had tested positive for syphilis. "Syphilis? What's Syphilis? What does that have to do with me?" TT explained that it was a disease and that she was going to take me to the clinic to be tested. Here I was, scared again, seems like that had become a permanent state for me. The next morning we got up and drove to the county clinic. We waited in line and when it was to my turn the lady at the counter said, I couldn't be seen at my age unless my mom was with me. As much as I didn't want to call her my mom, I needed these tests. I ran over and got TT and she went to the window and pretended to be my mom to approve my visit. We waited for what seemed to be an eternity, and then I heard my name. I followed the lady back to this little bitty office with a funny looking table. I sat in the chair and she started asking me questions about my sexual partners. I didn't know how to answer without having the police called and that was the last thing I wanted. So I Just told her that the one man I had been with tested positive for syphilis. She asked me to pee in a cup and she took some blood from me. Then she handed me a hospital gown and told me to get undressed from the waist down. From the waist down, I wondered why, but I did what she said, she was a doctor after all. It was only a few minutes when there was a knock on the door and the doctor walked in with another lady. We began one of the more uncomfortable moments of the visit. I had never had a "female" exam and had no clue what to expect. It was uncomfortable to say the least but it was quick. He handed the nurse some swabs, she poked me on the inside of my vagina and we were done. They gave me a card with some info and their number and told me to call in a few days. She handed me a pamphlet on syphilis, after reading it I was sick to my stomach for the entire 3 days I had to wait. They had a lot of pamphlets on sexually transmitted diseases. I took one of everything. I had never even heard of these kinds of diseases. TT told me a bunch of horrible STD stories about people loosing body parts, women not being able to have children anymore and the gruesome sores that would accompany some of the STD's. I started yelling to myself, THEN WHY WOULD YOU MAKE ME DO THAT? I didn't understand why she was cool one minute, then the next she's beating and or selling me. She was mostly cool so it weighed out. I was used to it after living with my step dad for years. He was so mean, for no reason. I remember when I was around 10 or so, we had all gone to the arcade that had the race track in the back. Dan and Ron would take all 6 of us kids with them but we only got one quarter each to play with. While they played with a whole role minus 3 each. So for the rest of the time you either watched people ride the go-carts or you watched people play video games. I was standing next to Dan watching him play a game and he lost. He turned and pushed me down yelling "Stay the fuck back! You made me lose and I'm taking that quarter in trade!" I wasn't touching him and I wasn't touching the game. I didn't know what I did to make him lose. But I knew what he meant when he said "in trade". That meant I was going to have to do a favor later to repay what I'd done wrong. He never forgot either. Sometimes he would wait for days to tell you it was time to "pay him back". I didn't think TT was that much different than my stepdad, except she was nice for longer periods of time. TT was trading me, just with others instead of herself. I thought I was doing better even though it was getting worse. So even though I was angry about the things she was doing to me, I wanted that strong mother figure that she was. And I knew from my stepdad, don't disobey because you don't get to guess the size of the punishment.

TT told me not to tell Easy about our visit to the clinic and actually she didn't even have to say that. I wasn't about to tell anyone that I was there let alone why and what happened. I started thinking about all the men how nasty some of them were and how they smelled. I wondered about all of the different STD's and started matching up faces with who I thought could have had what STD. I was driving myself crazy. Easy had stopped by but didn't take me with him, I wanted to be with him. I was afraid of being back at TT's. Even though she was acting like nothing had ever happened she was capable of switching to a monster in seconds. Finally day three came and first thing in the morning I was ready to call. I was up by 6:30am staring at the clock and the paper with the phone number on it. TT was still in the bed and I daydreamed about attacking her the way she attacked me. An hour and a half, 8:00am was when the phones would be answered. I sat on the couch watching the second hand roll around the clock slowly counting the minutes down while reliving every nasty moment I had been thinking about over the last few days. Finally, it was 8:00am, I dialed the number and it was busy. I almost started to cry, TT was sitting in her chair waiting with me. "Give it a second and call again". She said. When I did the phone rang, a lady answered and I gave her my number and the date on the paper, "Your results are ready" the lady said it like it was nothing, like my life hadn't been hanging on the edge of the cliff. Finally she said it…. "Negative". I had not gotten any diseases. At first I wasn't sure what she meant by negative, negative what. "What does that mean?" I asked. "You do not have any STD's, you do not have syphilis" she said. I hung up the phone and was so happy I wasn't infected but disgusted about what I had just gone through. A few hours later she left for a few hours. When she came back she started talking about all the food I had eaten and the bus fare going to the clinic. I knew exactly where she was headed. The day I got the negative, she wanted me to make some more money. I didn't want to take any chances on getting a disease. That fear actually scared some power into me so I actually said NO. TT walked over and told me in that "Imma cut your throat voice" that I would never tell her No, again. She grabbed me by my hair and shoved me to the ground. Still holding my hair, she drug me out of the door of the apartment and started dragging me around to #9. About half way over she let me get to my feet but didn't let go of my hair. I was screaming and crying but no one came out of their doors. We went right by my mom's apartment. I could hear her TV on but she didn't come out either. "Don't you know your own daughters cry? Why won't you save me, why won't you protect me?" I was thinking to myself. When we got to #9, she slapped me over and over and over, screaming at me to never tell her No. I truly think she slapped me more than 30 times the last hand full of times I couldn't even feel because my face was stinging as much as it could already. She left me there in the apartment. I laid on the bed crying and holding my face. I wondered as I had before if this is just how adults treated children. But it couldn't be all children, it wasn't happening to everyone else around me, it wasn't happening to my sisters this way. And if only some children what was the reason behind me being the one. What did I do, what signal did I send? Will this be my life? I wondered about the diseases the papers from the clinic talked about. TT came in right after. She took me back to the apartment and my face must have looked pretty bad because she got me a bag of ice for it. I sat there on the couch with the ice on my face and fell asleep. It was in the middle of the night when I woke up to Easy screaming. "What did you do to her?" he was asking. I didn't know right away but he was talking about me. My face was bruised on the side that she kept slapping and he seen it when he came in the door. She told him "She had to have some "training" and that's what happened to her face". Easy said that he was going to take me with him but TT wasn't having it this time. She said I was her moneymaker, I owed her for staying there and that he wasn't taking me anywhere. And if he did, she was calling her brother Bruce and Easy didn't want any of that. I remember there was an incident between them days earlier. I don't know what the issue was but what I do remember is Bruce standing in the hallway with a small derringer gun pointed at Easy. He had his hands up in the air and was trying to convince Bruce that he didn't do whatever it was Bruce was upset about. So after she mentioned him, he started talking about buying me from her again. At first, she said that she wouldn't sell me but then when he said that he was going to make a call to child welfare over her beating me they finally settled on a price and she sold me to him. They finished talking in the kitchen so I didn't know what the agreement was but I left with Easy that night and brought my things to his place for the last time.

~Chapter 4~

Driving Lessons

I was living at Easy's house now and I was happy about it. It was Just like what I thought a real relationship was supposed to be like, I felt protected and loved. He actually cared about me, he said there were rules if I was gonna be with him. #1 I had to get back in school and stay there and I did. #2 I couldn't use drugs or drink alcohol which I was just fine with me. #3 I had to take care of him, cook, clean, and be is lady. I had no problem doing any of that!! That evening I cooked for him, we were listening to the music and I was in awe that I was even there. I wasn't spending the night anymore. My clothes were in a drawer for good, never in a trash bag again, and he said for me to call it home. It was quiet, clean and felt safe for the first time ever. It was different than spending the night with him. This was permanent this would be my home forever. I don't remember ever being in an environment like that but I was very grateful that I was there and was willing to do just about anything to stay there. That next morning Easy was gone for a while and I passed the time cleaning his apartment, I figured it was the least I could do for what he had done for me. When Easy came in he was pleased. "And I didn't even have to ask" he said with a smile. We Jumped back in the bed for a little while and then got up and took a bath. Easy ran a bubble bath, I had never had anyone help me like that. Spending time just on me and catering to me. "Hey Angel, let's go shopping" Easy said with a huge grin on his face. Shopping, that sounded like we were going to a real store. I had always been so poor that I hadn't had new clothes since I was 9 when the house burned to the ground in Arkansas. And even those clothes were from K-mart. That was the one and only time I can remember getting new clothes from the store in my life. All of my clothes had either come from my mom sewing them, hand me downs from my older sister or cousins, and occasionally we went to the Salvation Army to get clothes. Getting to buy new clothes, I seriously thought I had arrived in heaven. We finished our baths, I cleaned the bathroom, and we headed out to go shopping. We walked around to the payphone and Easy called a cab for us. We walked back to the house and waited on the porch for the cab to arrive. When it did Easy told the driver to take us to the Soul Boutique. "Soul Boutique?" I screamed to myself. I knew exactly where it was on the corner of 23rd Street. I had seen the store many times with the big gold trim around the building and the latest fashions hanging in the window. That was one of the stores I only dreamed about being able to shop in. Now before you get all excited this wasn't like Niemen Marcus but it was still way above what I could ever afford. I had been inside the store a couple of times Just to look around when I had been walking in the area. I would go in and admire the clothes but I always felt uncomfortable because I knew and they knew I didn't have any money and therefore didn't have any business in that store. Moreover this was the fashion stop for the Black community and I was not a part of that community so I was out of place. Well not today folks! Today I was there with my boyfriend who was a part of the black community and he had money. Happy just didn't cover it. Not only were we going to be in the store with money but I was going to get new clothes that I didn't have to share with no one and no one else had ever worn them. We got out of the cab and walked into the store and Easy immediately walked over to the women's section. I was doing my best to contain my excitement and act like this wasn't one of the first times I had gotten new clothes but it was difficult. Easy started picking things up "do you like this? What about this one?" Whatever he picked up I liked. He gave me a handful of outfits and we went over to the dressing room. Oddly enough, that was somewhere I had not been either, a dressing room in a store with new clothes. It was all nice and clean. There were mirrors on the walls and a pin cushion on the wall with pins in it. Back then I wondered what it was there for, took me a minute but eventually learned that was for tailoring the clothes. I tried on all the clothes and came out with each outfit on. The first outfit was ok but not the one, same thing with the second outfit. The third outfit was an electric blue pair of parachute pants with zippers and 42 pockets and they were very form fitted. The shirt Easy picked out was a blue and black patterned shirt with a little bit of sequence on it. I looked and felt like a million bucks…with the exception of my shoes. I still had my old ratty shoes I had been wearing for over a year. Easy said I could have two of the outfits, one was the blue parachute pants and the other was a little black skirt and shirt that I felt made me look much older, and I was good with that and so was he. Easy took the items up to the checkout pulled out a wad of cash and paid for them all and they put them in one of those fancy Soul Boutique bags. To me the bag was almost as important as the clothes were. When we walked out of the store I was on cloud 9, shoot I would have been on cloud 99 if there was one. I held on to him like we were glued together, I was so in love. Finally I found my savior, there was nothing more that I could ask. He took care of me in every way possible. I would be honored to have this be the rest of my life. I wanted to someday be his wife for life. Before we headed back to the apartment we walked down 23rd street to the shoe store and Easy bought me 2 pair of shoes there. He got me a pair of tennis shoes and a pair of black heels to go with my black skirt. I couldn't have been happier. We went back to the apartment and Easy told me to wait for him there. While he was gone I cooked dinner and cleaned up.

It had gotten pretty late, and he hadn't been home long when there was a knock at the door. Easy went to answer the door and I could hear he was talking to a girl. I was sitting on the bed and I could tell by the conversation, even though I couldn't hear every word, that nobody was happy. As the voices got a little louder, I could hear him as they approach the door "I got someone I'd like you to meet". In through the door walked, what was to me, an older lady. She was probably in her mid to late 20's and that was older to me at 14. She was a little taller than me, long dark hair, and a little worn but still pretty. "Paula, this is Angel. Angel, this is Paula." I smiled nervously and said hello, she said hello back, but no smile. They walked through to the kitchen. As they continue the conversation in the kitchen, I was able to gather what it was about. Apparently, she had gone to the truck stop two days prior to make some money. It didn't take me very long after the fact to find out that she was prostituting herself at the truck stop, she was what I heard called a lot lizard. Easy wanted to know why she had been gone for two days. Paula was explaining that she had hitched a ride with a trucker to Tulsa to make better money. Easy was telling her how worried he was and how she could have let him know. Paula was hungry so she ate some of the chicken I had cooked for Easy and we spent the rest of the evening talking and getting to know each other. But of course, we were both guarding our real selves and not letting much of that out. I learned that she had come with Easy from Ardmore. Of course, with Easy life right there, I'm sure she couldn't say all the things or ask all the questions she wanted and neither could I. Later on, I went to bed with tons of questions for Easy. He assured me that they were Just friends and he was helping her out. That's why they came here together, their families know each other and Easy was like a big brother to her, at least that's what he said. I slept in the bed with Easy and she slept in the little bedroom in the back so that kind of confirmed for me what he was saying about them just being friends. The next morning after we woke I cooked breakfast and Paula said she was going out to work. She asked to borrow some of the clothes that Easy had just bought me. I didn't want anyone to wear my new electric blue parachute pants. I didn't even want to take them off to wash but after Easy had said, he would get me more if she didn't take care of them. I gave them to her; she got dressed and went out the door by noon. Easy and I spent most of the day in the bed and listening to music. We did dinner and eventually fell asleep. The next morning there was still no Paula. She was supposed to be back last night. Easy was not in a great mood and had gone down to the payphone to make some calls. I could see him from the back porch. He didn't stay long on the phone so I didn't think the news was good. I got dressed for school and headed out, I ditched after lunch and we spent the rest of the day the same way we did the day before. Later that evening there was a knock at the door. It was Paula! They started arguing about her being gone for so long and him not knowing where she was or if she was ok again. They continued to argue for a while and it had moved into the kitchen, which was open to the bedroom where I was. I didn't want to be in there so I went to the living room and started listening to music on the stereo. I could still hear them arguing. I couldn't hear every word but when it got loud, I could hear those. I heard him tell her to "take Angel's clothes off". They argued for a while longer and I think he called her every name in the book. Then I heard footsteps heading for the living room. It wasn't Easy's boots…it was Paula. She marched right through the living room with a suitcase in her hand and out the front door. Absolutely butt naked! I was shocked, I was sitting there thinking, why did she leave naked? Easy was right behind her but he just shut the door. He didn't even try to stop her. I said, "Why did she leave with no clothes?" "Cause she's a stupid Bitch" he yelled still very agitated. He started yelling and stomping around the house "That bitch never listens!! She don't understand nothing but an ass whopping! If you wasn't here Angel, I don't know what would have happened!" He started hugging me "I don't ever wanna fight like that with you Angel, but you gotta listen, you gotta listen to me, I'm here to keep you safe and if you don't listen to me you won't be safe. I've proven that to you before, Right? I shook my head yes. "Here Angel take the car and drive to your momma's house" he gave the keys to me.

I didn't say anything; I Just got up and walked outside. After listening to them fight and hearing how angry he was I didn't want to give any talkback. Easy had a 1964 valiant; it was an old beat up white car. It looked like a rectangle but not real long, kind of short and plain, nothing special to it. The door squeaked as I opened it clearly crying out for some WD40, I think everyone in the neighborhood heard me open that door. I sat in the old worn out seat and looked at the dash board which was dead ahead cause I'm so short. There were two circles with dials, one had small numbers, below 10 and the other started at 10 and went up to 100 by the tens. I've spent most of my life looking from the back seat. It looked to me like it was simple back then, didn't look so simple now. I'd not even been in the front seat that many times, let alone drove a car. But my choices were to drive away or go back in there. I looked under the dash and reminded myself which I thought was the gas and which was the break. I started the car and slowly began to drive away. This wasn't as hard as I thought it was I started thinking to myself. The house was only two houses from the stop sign. I went to hit the break and I Just about threw myself through the front windshield. I didn't screech the tires or anything but I did stop quickly. I sat there for a second Just breathing, I couldn't believe I was driving a car. I wasn't even old enough for a permit let alone driving a car all by myself. I looked for the turn signal and couldn't determine where it was but I remember my dad sticking his hand out the window when he wanted to turn so I rolled down the window and stuck my arm out. Who knows if I was actually pointing in the right direction but I did what I thought you were supposed to do. My mom was only about 8 streets down and two streets over. 10 blocks, I can do this! I had to arch myself up to see over the dash but I was able to see pretty well, I thought. What I seen when I made that turn going south down Shartel was not good. There were a hand full of police cars right around the corner from the house. I drove by trying to look like there was nothing going on but I was scared to death. I'm sure I had that "please don't look this way" look on my face. I could see Paula out of the corner of my eye standing there with a blanket around her and several officers talking to her. As I drove by I seen her lift her arm and point in my direction. I just kept it going, hoping I would make it to mom's house somehow. I made it all the way down to Main and turned, I was almost there. As I turned, I saw that a police car had come up behind me, he turned on the lights and my stomach immediately leapt up into my throat and the frantic thoughts began. I started pulling over and was thinking, what am I going to say? I just turned 14; since when does a 14yr old have a license? This isn't my car; will he take me to jail? Right then the police officer knocks on the window with his flashlight. I began rolling down the window. I was fighting myself the whole way; one half of me knew I'd better roll down that window, the other half of me seriously wanted to roll it back in the other direction. I just knew I was going to go to jail. I had never seen a real jail. I saw it on TV and I've heard people talk about it but I never thought I would end up in a real jail. I got the window down and the officer shined his light throughout the car and asked. "Do you have a license young lady?" "No, officer." "I kind of figured that, Where are you coming from?" "From a friend's house". "Would that friend be Chris Sharp?" I hadn't heard his full name before but I was pretty sure he was talking about Easy so I said yes. The officer asked "Um do you know what happened with Paula and why she was walking naked down the road? You're driving her car." "No officer, I don't. She just walked out naked." "Where were you trying to go?" "To my mom's house" I pointed to the building we lived in, we were Just a block away and could see the back of the apartment building. "What's your name?" "Angel, I mean Sarah" "Well, Angel-Sarah, step out of the car please." I opened the squeaky door and got out of the car. The officer asked me to get in the back of his car and I did. He drove us back to Easy's house.

When we pulled up all the police that had been around the corner were in front of Easy's apartment. I could see that Paula was sitting in the back of one of the cars. The front door was open and you could see about four officers standing with Easy talking. I was so scared I was shaking and had a lump in my throat the size of the car I was just driving. The officer that had driven me over walked into the house spoke briefly with one of the officers and they both came back to the car. The other officer opened the back door of the car and asked me what happened in there earlier. "They were arguing because she had been gone overnight and didn't tell him and he was worried about her" "Why did she leave naked?" "Easy had told her to take off the clothes that she had borrowed from me but that he didn't tell her not to put other clothes back on." "Did you see or hear him hit her or pull a weapon on her?" I had not so I said, "No, they were just arguing." He closed the door and walked back up to the porch of the house, as he was walking up they were coming out. He said something to Easy and all of the sudden Easy started yelling. He was yelling at Paula who was sitting in the police car. "I love you" "I'm sorry Paula, I love you I'm sorry, I love you Paula" He Just kept yelling that over and over as they arrested him, walked him through the yard and put him in the back of the police car. Even after he was in the car he was still yelling. When they drove away with him, you could see him turned around in the car looking back still yelling. "I love you, I'm sorry Paula, I love you!" I started thinking, why is he yelling for her like that? I thought they were like brother and sister? Then I started rationalizing what was going on. It's ok to love your sister. My brother and I didn't have the greatest relationship as teens but I did love him. And then the realization started setting in. What if he stays in jail, where will I sleep? What about my things at his house? I didn't have much but it was mine. And what about my protector, who was going to protect me now? The officer that picked me up at in Easy's car got back in and drove away. He drove us back to the old beat up white car, there was a tow truck there picking it up. He pointed to the apartment building and said, "That's where your mother lives?" I said yes. He drove me there and we walked up the long dingy stairs together. My mom lived in the back of the building near the fire escape so we had to walk all the way around the square hallway to reach her apartment. He knocked on the door, you could hear mom's footsteps coming toward the door and then mom opened it. Normally you would think a kid would be nervous about what their parent was going to do, I wasn't, and I had gotten used to her doing nothing. Absolutely nothing, and I figured this would be no different. The officer explained that he had picked me up driving a car without a license and that I had come from a 22yr olds apartment that went to jail tonight. He told her to keep me away from him and at home. I went inside, they talked a few more minutes, and she closed the door. She walked by me and into her bedroom, didn't say a word to me. I didn't like even going in there after the Jones thing but I can still remember exactly what her room looked like, because of that event. Her bed was a few mattresses stacked on a fold out bed frame with old blankets and pillows covering them. There was a small dresser with a 13" TV on it and stacks of clothes along the wall. I followed her to the room and stood in the door. I watched her climb back on the bed, and fix her eyes on the TV. "I'm going to TT's apartment." I said it hoping she would say no, No you can't go over there because she hurt you. I was hoping she would step in at some point and say something but she didn't. She didn't respond and so I left, as usual.

I left the building and walked around for a while trying to figure out where else to go. There was nowhere to go. I walked back to the apartments, went around the corner of the hallway to TT's apartment and knocked on the door. I could hear some sounds and then footsteps to the door. She opened the door but didn't unlock the screen door. "What tha fuck do you want? She was pissy; I was hoping she would let me in and help me instead of hurting me again. My face had just fully healed up. I didn't know where else to go for help anyways. I said quickly "Easy is in jail!" "For what?" she asked with a surprised look on her face. "Let me in and I'll explain." She opened the door and I went in. I was nervous stepping back into her house. I was afraid of her but I wanted to be around her because when she wasn't being mean, she was being nice. And coming from receiving nothing, nice was great and mean was acceptable. I explained the situation and she laughed. I didn't think it was funny, the one and only person who had ever cared about me was in jail. It didn't matter to me what had happened, it only mattered that my savior was gone. TT said there was nothing we could do tonight and for me to sleep on the couch and we would handle it in the morning. I didn't sleep at all, I was afraid if I slept that she would drug me or start beating me up. I wasn't sure what I would do if she tried but I damn sure didn't want to be caught in my sleep. I was up before her of course waiting to go help the only person who ever helped me. TT took her sweet time as she got dressed and we went to the jail. As we walked toward the jail, we talked about our prior "situation." She didn't exactly apologize but she said I was mature for my age but still not mature enough for what I was dealing with. I couldn't agree more but didn't feel like I had any choice in the situation either. "Is this what happens to other kids? Or is it just me?" I asked. "No, no, no, you're not the only one, this happens all the time. People just don't talk much about it." Not that it was the greatest thing to hear but it was strangely comforting to know that there were others and I wasn't the only one. We got to the jail and she pointed to these big glass doors on the side of building. Go in there and tell the cop at the desk that you want to know how to get your friend out. And give them his name. His name? Easy life? I didn't know his name. Wait the officer had said his name. I said hesitantly "Chris?" TT followed up with "Sharp, yes" she said. Chris Sharp, I said it to myself a few times as I walked to the building. The steps leading up to the building were super long, it was one of those awkward set of stairs. I walked in the building and the ceiling seemed to be three stories up, there was a big set of stairs to the right that went up to the second floor and there was a big desk to the left. It was tall and in a semi-circle shape, wooden with a rim around it that was Just about as tall as me. In the middle sat a cop, just like she said. I walked over "Excuse me sir" "yes" he said. "My friend was arrested last night and I want to see how to get him out?" "Name" he said with a steel face, he seemed more like an annoyed robot than a helpful front desk person. "Chris Sharp" I said. "Date of Birth" he asked. "Um, I don't know sir." With the same face and tone, he said "It's ok, I see him here. He's upstairs. Who are you?" "I'm a friend of his" "What's your name" "Sarah I said quickly, Sarah." "You go sit over there; we'll be right with you." He pointed to some benches

51

to the side. I went and took my seat. After a while a detective came out and asked me to go with him to a room in the back. He started asking me about what happened and I was telling him and then he brought in this other guy and asked me to tell him too. The detective that had come to get me from the lobby was starting to get upset. They wanted me to say that Easy had hit Paula, pulled a knife on her and forced her to leave naked. Well, for what I heard and saw that wasn't what happened and I couldn't say that it was. They threatened to arrest me and take me to jail for lying if I didn't tell the truth. I insisted over and over, "I'm not lying. I never seen or heard him hit her and she left naked on her own. I didn't hear him tell her to leave and she did have clothes there to put on, she just didn't" He brought in more men and I told them all the same story. After being there for about 3 hours, they said I could leave. I walked back to TT's house and told her about what happened at the jail. I was thoroughly depressed and didn't know what was going to happen to me now. He had come to save me and now he's in jail. I've got three choices, going back to moms and be molested some more, asking TT to let me back in and dealing with that again, or going on the streets where anything could happen. #1 was absolutely out of the question. #2 wasn't going to happen plus it meant being sold and more drug use, which I wasn't ok with. I sat there on the couch silent…Just thinking, what now and what next. I had been there several hours talking with TT and I heard it! The first step in and I knew exactly who it was. I didn't wait. I jumped off the couch and almost tore the screen door off trying to get out the door. TT yelled at me "Don't break my shit girl!" I didn't even stop. I ran down that long hallway. I bet I was going at least 15mph. I went for the lift off when I felt I was close enough and the landing was beautiful. Right in his arms, we hugged for what seemed like 20 minutes and finally he started walking, still holding me like a toddler and hugging me tight. We went all the way back down the stairs before he put me down. On the way back to his apartment we talked about my first driving lesson, "I know there's a normal way for this" I said. "Yes, there is. I'll be teaching you soon. My Angel will be driving all over the city." He pulled me closer to him as we walked. "What are we going to do about the police?" "Fuck the police, they can kiss my ass! Angel you made me proud tonight. You are much more mature than I thought. You're a grown ass woman doin grown ass shit. That's why you will always be my Angel, you will always be my number one." He made me feel so good, he was the only one that recognized that I wasn't a kid. That was taken from me years earlier, I was a woman and he confirmed it. I had found my prince and he will treat me like a princess. We were almost to the apartment when I asked "Why were you screaming that you loved her? Was she your girlfriend?" "No she wasn't my girlfriend. You are. I told you before, she was a girl from Ardmore that I went to school with. She asked to ride up here with me and she was supposed to get her own place after a while. I was saying I love her because I was supposed to take care of her for her mom. She knew I was trying to take care of her. Angel you know I didn't do anything to that girl." "I know, they said you hit her but I didn't see or hear anything, she made that up." We were almost to the apartment, he reached down and picked me up to kiss him. He carried me the rest of the way to the apartment and straight to the bed. He got up and cooked for the both of us in the middle of the night. We ate and watched a movie on the late channel and I fell asleep in his arms.

~Chapter 5~

How To Trick John

There were four apartments in the four-plex we lived in. Me and Easy in the downstairs west side, Fred was on the east side. Linda was right above us and there was an old man who never came out above Fred. I met Fred first; Fred was an older black man probably around his late 40's early 50's. He was always looking at me and telling Easy how cute I was and how lucky Easy was to have me. Fred was overweight with a big ole belly in the front. He looked like he had already eaten a girl about my size and he creeped me out so I stayed away from him. One afternoon while Easy was gone, Fred came over banging on the door frantic saying he needed some help. I went over to his apartment. He had filled the pot too full with water so when it got to a rapid boil it was boiling all over the stove and the burner knob so he couldn't turn it off. I quickly grabbed a towel and pulled the pot off the burner. Luckily, it was just water so he didn't have much of a mess to clean up. From then on Fred was always coming up with reasons for me to come over. He would pay me sometimes to clean his house or do his laundry and he always set it up with Easy so I couldn't say no. I didn't like doing things at his house because he was always looking at me funny, seriously like he wanted to eat me for lunch or something. It was a while after staying there that I met Linda. She was the woman upstairs. She was a black woman, skinny and tall. She didn't have any kids but she would have some little boy over there from time to time. Easy would leave me with Linda to babysit me while he would be out and about. Linda was quite the character, she could make you laugh your guts out! And had a great heart, she took a liking to me real quick. She used several different drugs and I would sneak and smoke weed with her every once in a while. She also smoked what we called "wet". That's where they take a cigarette and dip it in embalming fluid or other chemicals and let it dry. When she would smoke that…. boy, she would get crazy. After I saw her high on that one time… I didn't want anything to do with that. She was scratching on the wall trying to make her own doorway right next to the actual doorway. That taught me not to do that stuff, I was scared of drugs like that. One of the other things that Linda taught me was how to rob johns. Who is John you ask…well it's not a "who" it's a "what". A john is name for a guy who is looking to buy a prostitute, also known on the streets as a trick. I don't know who decided to call them all johns or tricks but that's what we called them. She told me that she was going to get a john and that after I heard her come in to give it exactly 3 minutes and then come out of the bathroom. She said that when I come out of the bathroom to act shocked like neither one of them are supposed to be here, like they don't live here. After she had been gone about 10 minutes, she pulled back up with a corny looking white man in his mid to late 40's. They got out of the truck and headed for the stairs. I ran to the bathroom and closed the door. I heard them come in and start talking. I was so nervous I was shaking and couldn't stop myself. What if this guy trips out on us? I waited my 3 minutes and came out of the bathroom. Linda was on the bed and he was standing over her pulling down his pants. I yelled, "Hey what are y'all doing in here?" Linda Jumped up and ran out of the door, the john looked scared to death and was trying to get his pants back up and I started yelling at him "I'm calling the police, HELP" as I ran for the phone. He ran out the back door still pulling his pants up. I ran behind him yelling at him till he drove away. I turned and ran back into Linda's apartment, ran to the bathroom and hid to wait for her. I hid because I wasn't sure the guy wouldn't come running back in the house. After all I was alone, all of 97lbs soaking wet. I was out of breath and my heart was about to beat right out of my chest. I thought for sure when I was chasing him that any minute this grown man would turn and grab me, but he didn't. I sat there against the bathroom wall thinking about what we had done. Then the "what if" game started in my head. My little sister Lillian used to do the "what if" thing at bedtime. "What if the walls come alive and fall on us?" "Nothing, shut up." "What if the fridge comes alive and eats us for food?" "Then we're food, Shut UP!" "What if the mattress opens up and swallows us and we can't get back out?" "UGH! Enough! What if I glued your mouth shut and you could never talk again?" In a mumbled voice she said, "Then I would have to talk like this." It used to drive me crazy. Seriously though, we could have been killed and it could have gone wrong. She came back a few minutes later. "Where you at girl" Linda said when she came back in. "We did it!" I yelled as I came out of the bathroom. Linda started mocking the John fumbling with his pants "His face was so funny, he was scared" I said. So was I but I couldn't let Linda know that, I had to keep my cool. "I bet he'll never pick up another chick at the park" I said. "Naw, he'll be back, John's always come back" Linda kept it real. She broke the system down for me. Explaining who was who and what responsibilities lay where and what could happen if you disobeyed and most importantly what to not do in the presence of another pimp. Never ever look another pimp in the eye that simple gesture can get you taken. Only speak when spoken to and never question what your pimp is doing. And most of all, be grateful for his protection and show it to him by taking care of his needs. She was the first one to call Easy a pimp. The more she told me the more confused I was. Pimp? I thought to myself, why is she calling my boyfriend a pimp? He was helping Paula out, he wasn't pimping her. How can you pimp someone who is your sister? Plus he was so upset and worried about her being out so late. It didn't make sense to me that he was the one doing this to her. I thought she was the one who decided to do it and he was upset because she was like his sister. None of that stuff was as important as me staying in a safe place with food, shelter, and the ability to stay in school. Buying me things and taking me to restaurants wasn't bad either so I wasn't able to see the full picture because my concern for survival was a greater need than the stories she was telling. Linda was trying to give me some inside information because I'm sure she recognized that I was brand new to the game. And playing that game was like monopoly. There were players, you spent your time on the streets acquiring as much cash as you can and you try to do it better than everyone else in your area. If you succeed at that then you can start charging others for using your territory. She told me what being his number one was and it didn't seem that bad compared to where I came from. It was certainly better than what I had going on before, but I was still far from where I should be and I didn't see him the same as she did. She didn't have a clue what all he brought me out of, he saved me, from old men molesting me, from drugs, from beatings, from the streets, she didn't know him like I did. She didn't know how big his heart was. Later on when Easy had come back and we were talking, I was cooking dinner and he asked "What did y'all do today?" I froze for a second because I didn't know if Linda had told him what we did. I remembered what she said about loyalty to your pimp and telling the truth even if it gets your ass kicked it will be better than the ass whoppin you would get for being caught in a lie. So I started crying and telling him what Linda had set up for us to do. He was upset but it wasn't at me. I told him about her telling me about the rules and stuff and about working on the streets. "What did she tell you?" I started telling him everything she said. "Pimps don't always work their girls, sometimes they too special to work the streets. Like you Angel, you're special, you don't have to worry about doing that with me. Even if other girls do it around us, that won't be you, that won't be my Angel." He said as he kissed my cheek. "We are in this together and there are a few things that would be important for you to know." He called them the "Easy rules to remember." "No one, not even family comes before us, we are family." He went on to say. "What goes on in our house stays in our house. We don't discuss our business with anyone but us, OK? Not even your momma." He said, "You reap what you sow" "you can choose to disobey, but you are also choosing the consequences". I didn't want anything to do with any consequences. I wanted to stay on his good side and not suffer any consequences. But what I wanted most of all at this point was to be his number one" – He said if I did all these things that I would continue to be his number one. If I didn't I would not enjoy the punishment. As his number one I would not have to work as much as the others but I did still have to "do my part" he said. When we went to bed I started thinking about what Linda had said and what Easy said and wondered how this was going to play out. I came to the conclusion that compared to where I had come from and the things that were happening to me there, this would be better, plus he bought me new clothes and food and exactly where else would I go? My emotions were so mixed up. I was frightened to be where I was and frightened to be anywhere else. When I woke the next morning Easy was already gone. He stayed out all day and I Just cleaned and lounged around the house and by the time he got home I was asleep. There were days where it was just me and him all day and there were days where it was just me but at least I was safe, fed and by this time had a full wardrobe from shopping trips with Easy. I still didn't like it much when he would leave me there all day. One day it was almost midnight by the time he came in. Of course, he was on his own schedule and didn't allow any questions about it. When he came in, I could hear that he had someone with him. They came into the bedroom and he had a girl with him that wasn't much older than me. She was kind of tall and thin, her clothes looked like they hadn't been washed in weeks. I knew right away that she was homeless like I was. I hopped off the bed, "Hi, I'm Angel" "This is Star" Easy said as he gave her a hug. "She's been on the streets for a while so I told her she could come here with us." I smiled because I felt any other response wouldn't be rewarding. Easy showed her where the bathroom was and told her to take a bath. When he came out, he asked me to get some clothes and a towel for her so I did. While she bathed, Easy told me that he found her on the fruit loop and that she had run away from an abusive home in Texas. He told me that she was going to make some money for us because the rent was coming due. I just listened and shook my head yes, I saw with Paula and Zoro, crossing Easy did not have good consequences. I had only seen him in action a few times and that was enough for me. After Starla got out of the bath, I gave her a towel and the clothes. I showed her the bedroom off the kitchen and she put her clothes on the floor by the bed. "We'll wash those in the morning, OK?" I said as I smiled at her. "OK" she said back in a soft voice. You could tell she was happy to be off the streets but not quite sure where she was or if it would be safe. It was late so we all went to bed. When we got in the bed I was laying stiff as a board. I was so unsure about what was going on. I started thinking about what Linda had said but I quickly dismissed it telling myself this wasn't what I was seeing. Chris rolled over in the bed and tugged at my waist pulling me over to him. He felt the stiffness in my body. "What's wrong Angel?" I was scared to respond so I didn't I just shook my head no like nothing was going on. Like my mind wasn't racing 90 miles an hour, playing the stupid "what if" game. What if he starts liking her more than me? What if she starts sleeping in the bed with him instead of me? What if she can buy him gifts and things with her money and I can't? Easy interrupted the game playing in my head. "Angel, no one can ever take your place, there is only one Angel God sent to me, and that is you. Even if I let other girls help us out, as long as you are taken care of that's all that matters, right?" "Right" I replied.

That morning I got up and fixed some breakfast. Starla woke up as I was cooking. "Is there something I can do to help?" she asked. "Nah, I got it, I'm pretty much done now." I gave easy his plate, handed Starla her plate and then made my own. While we sat at the table Starla told us her story. She said that her mother was an alcoholic and that she never knew her dad. One of her step dads had molested her and the current one had beaten her for trying to save her mother from him his beatings. She tried to get her mother to leave with her and go to a shelter but she wouldn't so Starla left by her-self. She took a bus to Oklahoma City because her mother always told her that's where her dad was. She didn't have any information except his name David. I told her that we would help her but I had no idea how we were going to make that happen. Later that evening Easy took Starla with him and went downtown. I assumed he was going to show her how to make money but I had no clue, and wasn't going to ask. Several hours had passed and finally I heard the door and went to the living room to make sure it was easy. When the door opened, Easy pushed Starla in the door and she fell on the floor. He started kicking her and yelling at her. "You're a stupid bitch, you won't cross me but once, dizzy bitch!" She was crying hard. I didn't know what had happened but I knew he was seriously pissed and she was getting beat. I was too scared to step into it; I walked back into the bedroom and sat on the bed praying he wouldn't come after me next. I wanted to run but I was frozen. The door wasn't locked, I was. I couldn't do anything but sit there. I was so afraid of what he would do if I ran. I wished that I could have removed my ears so I wouldn't hear him hitting her and yelling at her. "That's why your parents didn't want you, you don't know how to listen, dizzy bitch!" he screamed. I didn't hear him hit Paula but I heard him hitting Starla. I would Jump every time I heard him hit her, I knew what it felt like from my stepdad, and I didn't want it to be happening to her or me. She was crying and pleading for him to stop. "Get up, you dizzy bitch!" he yelled, "Angel!" I Jumped up and ran in the living room where they were. Starla was bleeding. "Get this bitch cleaned up" He said. I helped her up, got her to the bathroom and helped her get in the tub. I was freaking out on the inside. What had just happened here, what was this? I'm not a nurse! The closest thing I have to any experience is watching that Army show on late night TV with the medics. You could tell her body was hurting because she could barely move. The knots were coming up on her legs and arms where Easy had kicked her with his boots. I was trying to console her and make it better somehow because I didn't know what else to do. I wanted to run, I wanted to get up and start running with her and run forever. What if I ran right now? Where would I run to? I can't go back to TT's that's too dangerous. I can't go back to mom's house. Mom and my sisters were eating at the homeless shelter. Plus the question really didn't matter, I was only fooling myself. The lock was on my body, not the door. I was not capable of saving myself let alone both of us. Easy came back into the bathroom "You ain't finished yet?" "No, I'm trying to let her calm down" I said. Easy reached and grabbed my face like my mom used to when I was in trouble but he did it much harder and it hurt. He leaned in close, almost touching noses. "Get it done now or that's your ass, can you do that?" I tried to shake my head yes while he still had a hold to it but it barely moved. When he let go of my face it was more like he threw it out of his hands. I surely didn't want to get what Starla had gotten so I did my best to hurry. Easy had calmed down a lot and was actually starting to worry about how she was doing. Since he was being concerned, I asked if he could get some Tylenol or something. Easy left and came right back with Tylenol and I gave it to her. After that she went to sleep. I was so scared that she wouldn't wake up. I saw on TV how sleeping after getting your head hit was bad. I kept going to check on her, outside of that I just did my best to act normal so he wouldn't go off on me. When we were laying in the bed Easy told me that he was proud of the way I handled things and that he knew he had made the right decision to make me his number one. I was still frightened by what had taken place. I didn't know how to react to it, so I didn't. Not reacting was a safer choice for me. He promised me that he would never beat me. I did everything I could to make sure that he was happy and wouldn't want to beat me the way he did Star. After about two days, Easy left the house and I was finally alone with Star. I was able to find out what happened that night. Starla said that Easy had taken her downtown but it was covered in cops so then he took her to the park where the Johns are at. He told her to sell herself but didn't fully explain the order of what she was supposed to do. She said that he told her to wait for a car and when they ask for sex to tell them $20.00 and bring the money to him, he was waiting in the breezeway of the community center. She waited for a car and when she got in to talk to him about the money he pulled away. When they got down the street, she gave him what he wanted and then kicked her out of the car without giving her any money. When she got back to Easy and told him, he slapped her to the ground and drug her through the park by her hair then they walked home. The rest I already knew. I spent the next few days telling her what I had learned from Linda and TT to keep her as safe as possible in the situation she was in. She asked if I would help her run away from him. I was scared and had to tell her no because I knew she couldn't take care of us both. She was only a couple of years older than me and we were both still barely teenagers. I had nowhere to go and didn't want to get beaten by Easy or anyone else for that matter.

Starla was there for almost a week before he took her out again. You could still see some faint bruises but she knew what to do this time. Over the last two days, Easy had her and I practice her talking to a John so she could make some money for him. She was cooperative now. They were gone for about 3 hours and came back with $100.00. We went to the store and got some groceries. Easy gave the rest to the landlord on the rent. That evening Starla and I had a chance to talk more when Easy went over to Fred's house. She told me that when she was with the fourth john she told him that she needed $40 instead of $20 so she wouldn't have to do another one. I thought that was pretty smart of her. He was reluctant so she told him that Easy would beat her again. He gave her the $40 and she went back to Easy with it. That was her last trick of the night and then they went home. I praised her on the good job even though it seemed odd to praise something like that. I was praising her staying safe and doing what needed to be done to not get beat. Easy took her out every day for about a week. She had gotten pretty good at working the streets and was starting to build some confidence. So much confidence that she eventually ran away. The last day that Easy took her out she got in the car with a John, drove off and we never seen her again. I just figured she had him drive her somewhere away from Easy. Later I realize the possibility that Starla was abducted by that John and possibly killed. I prayed that it was not the latter. The next few days Easy was gone a lot, one night he didn't even come home until the next morning at 4am. A few days later, I found out why.

~Chapter 6~

It's My Turn

Easy came home and had some money on him and said we were going to the store so I put my shoes on to go to the store with him. I noticed when he came in that he had some keys but didn't say anything. We walked outside and there was a burnt orange Cadillac De Ville sitting in front of the house. I was surprised and excited all at once. I wanted to ask where it come from. We went to the store and after we got back, he left again. That week he was gone a lot and didn't come home several nights. Then one afternoon when he stopped by the house, I got to see where the car had come from. There was an older woman in the car with him. He came in and changed his clothes, handed me some money to put up, kissed me and left again. While Easy was gone, the landlord came by for the rent again. I never answered the door to the landlord. I would just read the notes after she left. Easy had the money to pay the rent, I don't know why he didn't. After a few days, Easy came back and said that, we were moving and for me to gather our things so I did. He took me to a big white house around the corner from where we were, it was another 4 plex. The apartment was on top and we took the back stairs to get in. I could tell when we walked in that someone else already lived here. We walked through the kitchen and bedroom to the living room. I saw a picture in the bedroom of an older woman with long hair with a little boy. It was that lady from the car, this was her apartment. The apartment was big and spacious except the kitchen. The kitchen was thin with a walkway. On one side was the sink, stove, and counter. And the fridge and table on the other side. The bedroom was big and open, so was the living room. In the living room, there was a fold out couch and an end table. On the main wall was a bookcase with a mantel all the way across and a false fireplace in the middle. There was an old timey gas heater that had fire, it was hooked up where the logs would be. Easy said he would be back and left me there, I put all our stuff in the closet in the living room. There was no TV so I Just sat on the couch and waited for Easy to come back. I was nervous hoping that the lady I saw wouldn't come back before he did. And if she did what would I say? What had he already told her? Would she call the police? After several hours of wondering, I heard someone at the back door. It was Easy…and the lady… and a little boy. He ran past them into the living room. When he came into the room and seen me he stopped in his tracks. "Hey who are you?" he said in a super cute little boy voice. Easy came in right behind him. "That's Angel." The woman stepped from around him. She was a little taller than me, older but not old like my mom, somewhere in her late 20's. She had a small figure masked by a t-shirt and jeans. She had long, brunette hair parted down the middle, kind of hippy looking. Her face was thin with little eyes, a thin nose and pretty lips that were tensing up by the second. She looked up at Easy like she was not happy. It was clear that he had not had any discussions with her about me or the fact that I was part of the package. She turned like she was going to storm off and Easy grabbed her arm. "Come here." He said as he walked her back into the bedroom. "Watch the boy Angel" he said as he closed the door. My first thought was Star. I prayed that he wouldn't do the same thing especially since the little boy was there. "What's your name?"

I asked. "Samuel" he said in a quiet voice. I could tell that he knew also that his mom was in trouble somehow. "How old are you?" He held up four fingers. "You're four? One, two, three, four." I kept asking him questions to try to distract him but he kept looking over at the bedroom door. After a few minutes, Easy opened the door and the woman came to the door with him. "Angel this is April" "Hi" I said. She said hi back. "Come here" Easy said, so I got up and went to the bedroom with them. April sat on the side of the bed and I sat at the end. Easy started talking, He said that he had explained to April who I was and told me that I was going to watch Samuel while she worked and that I would take him to the park when needed. He said that he didn't want to see any bullshit from either of us and that if he did "Somebody is going to get their ass kicked." He sent me back to the living room with Samuel. Although I wasn't in the room, I was pretty sure that he was sleeping with her to make her feel better about the situation. I was jealous but couldn't show it. I had to suck it up and be grateful someone was taking care of me. After a while, Easy came out and started playing with Samuel. Samuel was comfortable with Easy. Two plus two hit me, this is where is has been the whole time. I had so many questions, but no one to ask or get answers from. But I did know one thing. Not being able to talk much left you a lot of room for thinking. I didn't want to be homeless again and I was in love with Easy. He took better care of me than all of the other adults I had been around. He protected me and he told me he loved me all the time. He would whisper or mouth it to me when others were around if he couldn't say it out loud, it made me feel special. He had a way of always doing little things to make sure I knew that he was always thinking about me, even when he was with them he was thinking about me. It's kind of crazy now that I think back on it. I was scared of him but in love with him at the same time. In love as a lover and a father, I did whatever he asked of me, out of love, out of gratefulness and out of fear.

Easy rolled off the floor where he was with Samuel onto the couch where I was. "We're going to stay here till I get enough money to get us an apartment. I just need you to stay in your place" he said. "Your place" I thought to myself. My place is number one and I thought I knew what that was. Time was proving that I didn't know as much as I thought and this wasn't going to be as simple as I thought. But with no one else to turn to, I was going to stay where the food and shelter was and do my best to "stay in my place" to not upset him and to keep me safe. April walked in the room and handed Easy a plate of food. She called Samuel to follow her as she walked back to the kitchen. Easy gave me his plate and then got up to get another one. "Where is the plate I made for you" I heard April say from the kitchen. I could tell that she was not happy about him giving me the plate that she made for him. I heard him talking to her but couldn't tell what he said but it was with his, "I'll kick your ass" tone through his teeth. She didn't say anything else. I continued to eat and Easy came in a couple of minutes later and sat next to me with his other plate. We finished dinner then he told me to go help her clean the kitchen. It was obvious that she didn't like me. I wanted her to like me but she didn't. She was a mom and I wanted one of those, no matter how dysfunctional it was I wanted one and so I wanted to show her that I could be like a daughter to her. I started doing the dishes and she was wiping down the counters. Man, if there was any bacteria on that counter it wasn't afterwards. It was easy to tell she was taking her frustrations out on the counter, scrubbing the crap out of it. I just kept doing what I was supposed to do. I trusted that Easy would take care of me no matter what so I tried not to worry too much about it. After we finished the kitchen, she laid in her bed with Samuel and Easy opened the fold out couch in the living room. I started to get an uneasy feeling a jealous feeling. I didn't know if he was going to sleep with me or in the room with her. I didn't care much about him having sex with her but I wanted him to sleep with me. I hated sleeping alone. I grew up sleeping with my sisters, usually the only time I had to sleep alone was if I was sleeping in a dumpster or an alleyway. I couldn't ask what he was going to do so I Just waited to see what happened. To my surprise, he stayed with me. We had only been in bed for a few minutes when Easy started rubbing on my body. Normally I didn't think of it as a bad thing but this time my body tightened up and I almost stopped breathing. I knew what he wanted and I was nervous wondering what she was thinking and how she felt and what retaliation she would take against me. I was used to retaliation. My mother retaliated against me, TT retaliated against me, but at least with TT, I could say that she was a stranger, she wasn't bound to protect me. My mom was bound by birth to protect me and she didn't, so why would anyone else? I wasn't used to anyone helping me out of any situation. I also knew this would reduce my chances of her ever thinking of me as a daughter. I wanted that so bad, I wanted a mother to take care of me. Yes, Easy took care of me but it wasn't the same, I wanted a mom. Easy could see the nervous look on my face "what's wrong" he asked. I glanced over toward her room and back at him real quick. "You're my Angel and I do what I want, when I want with my Angel. Is she my number one?" "No" I said shaking my head back and forth. "I'm the only one you ever need to be nervous about. I will protect you to the ends of the earth Angel, Do you hear me?" I shook my head yes and Easy began kissing me. Easy made me feel safe but I was still scared at the same time. I knew where else I would be without him. If I made him mad, I would be back on the streets, or worse, beaten to death or home with mom for more molestation. I believed that I would finish growing up with him and that he would help me along the way. I believed that he cared and wanted to make sure I was taken care of, not just thrown away.

The next morning I got up and was nervous about what kind of mood April would be in. I went to the kitchen and she was in the bathroom with Samuel. When she came out, I went in bathed. I got dressed in a hurry and took our clothes to the laundry room at the old apartment right around the corner. Fred still lived there and he said he would tell them it was his laundry. After I got back from dropping off the laundry Easy said for me to watch Samuel for a while and that he and April were going out. Samuel and I played together, I played school with him like I had done with my sisters when we were younger. I missed that, being with my sisters. We used to have a lot of fun together. Then things started tearing us apart. There was no more "us four girls". When they got back I went to get the laundry from Fred's. For a while it was the same routine as the day before. Her working, her cooking, us cleaning, her mad, Easy sleeping in the living room with me. I often wondered how she felt and what he told her to make that ok. She was quiet most of the time, just like me. We would watch Easy and Samuel play together and we would listen to his stories. After we had been there almost two weeks we all went to the flea market together. I had never been and it was huge so I stuck close to Easy. We got a decorative license plate for the Cadillac. It was the same color as the car with "Sharp" on it with a rose very similar to the one on Easy's chest. After he placed his order there we walked around some more. We looked at several jewelry shops. We were at one when he started looking at gold for the both of us. He had us try on a few things but we didn't buy anything. We picked up the plate for the car and Easy put it on in the parking lot. On the ride home the tension from April was obvious. I was pretty sure it was from us trying on the gold. She knew that she was the only one brining in money and I'm sure she didn't want her money spent on me, especially not for gold. That evening after April had cooked dinner we all sat down in the living room to eat. Easy was going over how much money we had and what had to be spent and how much more we needed. He was saying that he may need to bring in another girl unless we knew something else to make more money. April said something, I couldn't quite make out much but my name. She said it low but still loud enough for Easy to hear. "...Angel should..." He jumped up off the couch so fast his plate went flying and food went everywhere. He leaped across and practically fell on her while trying to grab her by the neck. He got a hold of her and started choking her screaming "You don't ask the fucking questions, I do, this is my motherfucking shit do you understand that, Dizzy Bitch!" Samuel started crying so I reached over and pulled him closer to me to try and protect him, like I could do something about what was going on. I wished I could have stopped what was happening and I felt especially bad that he was attacking her. I felt like it was because of me, why was he attacking her? Why wasn't he attacking me? He threw her around some more still screaming about not asking him questions. He calmed down after a couple of minutes and turned to see his food was everywhere. I could see in his face it was about to begin again. I had learned from my stepdad that the quickest way to calm the situation down was to be submissive, in a hurry. I quickly held my plate up over my head to offer it to him. He said "No, this Dizzy Bitch is going to make some more." Easy sat on the couch and called for Samuel to come to him. He didn't want to at first so I nudged him to go, when Easy asked again Samuel got up and went over. Easy apologized to Samuel for what "his momma" had done. He was going on and on about how stupid she was and how simple she is, screaming at the top of his lungs. April had gotten up and was cleaning. I leaned forward to start helping pick up the mess. "Sit your ass back and eat Angel" Easy said as he pushed me back by my head, almost making me drop my plate. "You didn't make this mess, let her clean it!" Besides Easy still talking about her, we were quiet, except for our breath, not another sound was made. April continued to clean then went back in the kitchen to make him more food. I sat on the couch trying to finish my food. I was shaking and trying hard not show it, I wondered what I would say that would get me beat like her. I didn't want to eat; my food felt like it was rocks stuck in my throat. I still wanted to see if she was ok but I couldn't. I wanted to tell her that I was scared too. I wanted her to know that I didn't agree with what he did to her. I didn't go back to the kitchen to clean until I seen April coming out with his food. I felt if I went sooner he would question it. You could tell she was hurt, more emotionally than physically. She let her long dark hair hang in front of her face and kept her head down as she moved through the room. Her walk was more of a slow slide across the floor. She kept her face down as he took the plate from her. "Go close that door" he said to her. She closed the door to the living room and I began doing my chores in the kitchen. I couldn't think about anything except what had just happened. I kept replaying it in my head wondering if there was some way I could have stopped him. Wondering if I had said something to interrupt would it cause him to stop or would it cause him to hit me too. I didn't know what to do so I did nothing. I wanted so bad to say that I was sorry, I didn't know what I was sorry for but I felt sorry. I knew she wouldn't accept it, she despised me now. He hit her in front of me and I did nothing. I didn't help her. I thought about this woman being my mother and I didn't help her, I couldn't help her. I don't even like who I am, I'm not surprised that she doesn't either.

April went out every day and while she was gone me and Samuel would go to the playground at the school because his mom would be at the park sometimes, Easy forgot that part when he told me where to take him. I had to take him out of the house or we had to stay quite in the bedroom because April used the living room for turning tricks. I hated the days that we had to be there. Samuel would hear her come in the front door and want to go to her but I knew coming in the front door meant that she had a john with her so I couldn't let him go. After sometime I think Samuel knew it too. That was everyday life for a while. One day while I was watching Samuel I got a knock at the front door. This was unusual because we always used the back door. I started freaking out, I was panicking wondering who would be at the door. My first thought was that one of the Johns had come back to the apartment. I went to the window looked outside and saw a police car, my stomach Jumped into my throat. My body started getting hot with fear. I was worried about what they wanted or what they were going to say. About that time, they knocked again and said "Police officer" I went to the door with my heart racing. I opened the door but didn't unlock the chain so the door didn't open all the way. "Is this your apartment?" the officer said. "No, it's my friend April's apartment." I said. "Do you know where her son is?" "Yes, he's right here" "Can I see him?" he asked. I showed them Samuel. "Can you open the door, we need to make sure he's ok" I thought for sure my heart was going to pound right out of my chest. Easy was nowhere around and I didn't know what to do but I knew I had to do something, they weren't going to stay outside the door forever. I opened the door and the officer stepped in and knelt down to Samuel "How are you doing buddy?" "Do you know what her name is?" as he pointed to me. "That's Angel" Samuel said. The officer asked me "Are you staying here with April, Angel?" "Yea" "Well April was just picked up. Can we talk to you out here for a minute?" I thought it was a ploy to get me outside of the apartment and Easy told me never to step outside of the apartment for anybody, even the police so I told Samuel to go to the bedroom. "We can talk right here." I said. "Fine, your roommate April has been arrested for prostitution. How old are you?" I said 16 because that's what Easy said to say if anyone asked. If I said I had just turned 14 surely they would arrest me too, then what would happen to Samuel, what would Easy do? "Well, Angel, I need you to pack a few things for Samuel because we need to take him with us, you aren't old enough to keep him." "Where is Easy?" "Who?" I acted like I didn't know who they were talking about. "Well since this isn't your apartment you're going to have to leave so we can secure the property." I grabbed some things for Samuel and they left with him and locked up the apartment. I just walked around the neighborhood until I seen Easy driving back up. I ran up to the car yelling "April is in jail, they took Samuel. The police took Samuel! I started to cry. "What the fuck are you talking about?" he said as he opened the car door. "She's in jail and they took the boy, they took Samuel and made me leave the house!" "What the fuck did you tell them?" "I didn't tell them anything, they said I couldn't keep my cause I'm not an adult and they left with him." "I'll find out what the hell is going on." Easy let me into the house and then went out for a while and confirmed she was arrested for prostitution. When he came in and told me that, I thought for sure we were going to the police department to get her like I did Easy when he got arrested. But we didn't. Instead, Easy told me to pack a change of clothes and come on. I did what he said but I couldn't stop thinking about April and the fact that she was in jail. And that Samuel was taken by the police, where did they take him? How will she get him back? I seemed to be the only one worried about what was going on. Easy carried our bag to the car, we got in and drove away. He drove to the carwash first and washed April's Cadillac, then we hit the highway.

I didn't know where we were going and didn't ask. Finally, after we were in the middle of nowhere Easy said we were going to Ardmore to visit his mother. I was hoping my eyes only bulged out in my mind, I was scared to death. What would she think of me? What would I think of her? A million questions started moving in my head. "What if she asks how old I am?" a question fell out. As soon as I said it I braced myself. He answered "Just tell her you are almost 18." "Okay" I said. I was thinking to myself, I barely pass for 14, I'm not about to pass for 18 but ok. I already seen the results of not doing what you're told. We drove for what seemed to be forever as the questions kept racing through my head. Would she like me? Does she know about Easy and the girls? Does she know about what happened to Paula? Will she know that I'm lying about my age? Will she care that I'm white? Will she ask me about my mom? Will she know that we've been sleeping together? The questions went on and on. I stared out the window looking at the scenery and listening to the music Easy was playing. The ride was great though…until this one town. They have a paper mill and when you pass it…oh; my goodness the smell is atrocious!! I always knew from that point on that once we hit that smelly plant Ardmore wasn't much further. When we got there, Easy went straight to the carwash again and washed the car, he kept that car super clean. He washed the outside while I Armor all'd the inside. It was getting late and he was trying to get to his mom's before sundown. We made a couple of turns into the neighborhood and I thought we were going to a house but we pulled up to an apartment complex. When we pulled in you could see that there were some people outside and there was something going on, the police were there. Easy told me to stay in the car, so I did but you didn't have to tell me to stay put when the police were near, that was an automatic response. He got out and walked up to the couple that looked to be the ones arguing. He gave the woman a big hug and shook hands with the guy. He knew them? How did he know them? Is this his family? What's going on? I sat and watched as they all talked the police left and finally Easy came back to the car. I was preparing to get out and he started the car back up again. "My momma wants something to eat; we're going to go get her some fish." I just smiled back, that was always the safest response. We went just down the road and got some fish and brought it back to the apartment. Easy never said what had been going on and I wasn't about to ask so I Just waited. I helped him carry things up the stairs and when I walked in the door, I knew I was in a different kind of place. The living room was packed wall to wall with expensive furniture and cabinets with china and knick-knacks in them. There was just barely enough room to walk around the furniture. All of the furniture was covered in custom fitted plastic. ALL of it! All of the wood surfaces had glass pieces cut to size and laid on each shelf and every area was covered. The floors had plastic runners from the front door around the table in the middle of the room into the dining room down the hallway and into every room. It was like a museum. It made me nervous on top of already being nervous. When we went into the dining room, there was a dining table and China hutch full of China squeezed in together in the small space. Each place had a full place setting already there with fancy napkins and everything. The kitchen was Just on the left of the dining room. That's where his mother was. She was short like me and had beautiful hair. She was pretty and very classy, she reminded me of Patty LaBelle. "Momma, this is Angel" "Well, hello Angel, how are you" "I'm fine, nice to meet you" I said. I sat down at the table while Easy and his mom unloaded the food. I was so nervous I was sweating like I Just played basketball. I asked Easy where the bathroom was and made my way. I opened the door, stepped in, and quickly closed the door behind me. I was completely freaking out on the inside and I had to have somewhere to let it out. I am in his mother's house, a beautiful one at that, and I am about to start stinking I'm sweating so much. What am I going to do? What if I start stinking? What will they think of me? She's going to think I'm dirty. And the spiral of questions and anxiety began. It took a couple of seconds to realize where I was again. I was in his mother's bathroom and it was just as done up as everything else. Fancy curtains in front of the tub and fuzzy mats on the floor and toilet and every surface had some kind of product sitting there. It looked like a pharmacy counter, I knew there had to be some deodorant somewhere. I went through everything, and then had to start reading stuff because nothing had that familiar shape to it. I finally found it and um yea, it was some weird liquid something. I thought I was going to die. I needed deodorant bad and all I was coming up with was stuff I knew nothing about, I hoped it would work anyways. I read the directions and did what it said praying it would help me out. I stared at myself in the mirror for a bit trying to calm myself down so I wouldn't look a frantic mess when I walked out of the bathroom. When I came out Easy had made me a plate. I was just sitting down at the table when I heard someone else come through the door. Around the corner came a tall, thin woman with a very striking face, gorgeous lips, and long natural hair, she was beautiful. "Angel, this is my baby sister Channell" I raised my hand up, smiled and said Hi. I was even more nervous to meet her. This was the lady that was arguing outside with the light-skinned guy and the police. "Where are you from Angel, are you from the city?" I instantly fell in love with her voice. It had Just the right amount of country twang and was more southern than Oklahoman. "Yes, I am" Even though I wanted to hear more of her voice, I hoped her questions would end there, they didn't. "So, you're my brother's girlfriend?" "Alright, Channell, leave her alone." I was so grateful he stepped in. "Now, how in the hell did you get such a pretty girl Ris?" He just gave her that big smile and she started laughing at him. "So what's up with you and your boy?" he asked her. "He's Crazy, that's what happened!" Channell went on to tell him what happened. I listened to them talk and apparently something upset her and in the process she pulled a gun on him. That's why the police were called. They were all laughing and having a great time with it while Channell was yelling about her husband. Shortly after there was a knock on the door his mom looked out the kitchen window which overlooked the front door and said "It's your man" to Channell.

She stood up with a mean look on her face and was about to head for the door. Easy got up, held his hand out and told her to have a seat and he went to the door. Lewis had their kids and was bringing them over. Channell got up and hurried over to the window. The closer she got to the window the tighter my chest got, I thought she was going to Jump right through it. "You crazy bastard! Give me my kids!" Channell yelled. Patty grabbed her and led her back over to the table to sit down. Channell was still yelling about him being crazy. Patty gave her a plate of food and told her to "eat and not worry about that man." She was that kind of woman, the kind that could calm anything down. Her house was beautiful, her children were beautiful and she was beautiful. Easy was taking too long so Patty went to the door and came back with the children, they were just as beautiful as their mom. I was watching Channell and the care she took with her children while feeding them her food. I had hardly touched mine because of nervousness and too worried about all the excitement. We sat around the table for a few hours and I listened to them talk about family stories. I found myself staring at Patty even when she wasn't talking. I admired her and thought about her being my mother-in-law and how great I thought it was. She went on to bed and I was starting to wonder when or where we were going to sleep. We stayed up for a while longer then Easy opened the door that was across from the bathroom and motioned for me to come in. The room was beautiful, there was a full bedroom set made of cherry wood. I had only see stuff like that in the stores. We never had furniture like that when I was growing up. In fact I can't recall anything new. "Can I take a shower first?" "Go ahead Angel, the towels are in the cabinet" I grabbed the bag and drug it to the bathroom. I ran the water Just a little hot and tried to move fast. I didn't want to use all the hot water Just in case he wanted to shower too. I finished up and wrapped a towel around me. I peeped out the door to see if I could run across. I didn't see anyone so I darted to the room. Easy pulled back the covers and told me to get in the bed, I was so nervous. I wondered, did she know now after spending time with me that I'm only 14? Did she know that we were going to sleep together in her guest bedroom? I laid on his side and was trying to relax but I was stiff as a board. I tried taking some deep breaths to calm myself down. Easy started laughing at me. He knew what was up. I started giggling with him which helped relax me some. His arm tightened up and pulled me closer up on him. "So what do you think?" he asked. "I love it here. Y'all have a great family." "I can tell my mom likes you." "You think so? I like her too, she's nice and very pretty." He finally went to sleep and I stared at the ceiling for a while with my mind going a million miles. I was thinking about him, his mom, his sister, the police, April in jail, Samuel with the police, and everything else under the sun. I wore my own self out interrogating myself and eventually passed out.

When we woke I went straight to the shower. I started smelling the food before I even finished washing. I got dressed and walked out to one of the best breakfast I have ever had. She made scrambled eggs just like Easy liked them. We had breakfast chops, skillet fried potatoes and toast. The toast wasn't regular toast, it was made with potato bread. I had never had bread like that. I couldn't get enough of it. We left after breakfast to go visit family members around town. We stopped by his grandfather's home, I was nervous all over again. The house was an old wooden house with a porch on the front. When we walked in it was dark inside. The curtains were all pulled and the lights were out. Easy said hello and hugged a few people as we made our way through the house. His grandfather was in the bed in his room. I was immediately able to see he had a missing leg. The only person I had ever seen like that was the old guy who ran the gas station in my home town. I don't know how he lost his arm but he had one of those metal artificial limbs with the clamp on the end. That was scary when I was younger and it was scary now. I didn't quite understand how a person could be missing a limb and still be alive. I didn't talk because I was afraid of what to say. I just stuck by Easy's side and didn't leave it. He enjoyed the clingy attention and being quiet kept me safe. When I was asked a question, I would just look up at him and he would usually answer for me and say I was shy. We left there and went by his cousin's house. His house was beautiful and he was pretty cool. They laughed together for a couple of hours. We walked out to the car, Easy handed me the keys and told me to start the car and roll the windows down. I did what he asked and waited. The music was playing so it made waiting for him easy. They were saying goodbye and hugging so I started to get out of the car. Easy put his hand on the door and said "you drive", as he shut the door. My hand started to shake on the wheel. Easy got in the passenger seat and kissed me on the cheek. I had been watching him drive for a while, and had driven that one time before, but that was it. I pressed on the brake and put the car in reverse. It wasn't bad enough that Easy was in the car with me but his cousin was still standing in the driveway. I began rolling slowly as I began lifting my foot from the pedal. I turned the wheel and the car eased out on the street. I got it far enough out and started pressing on the gas, meanwhile my other foot in still on the brake. I didn't want to be far from either. I rolled down the street and to the stop sign. I slowed down but I didn't stop, I went around the corner at a slow cruise. Easy started laughing "Pull it over Angel". "You did good baby! You can drive more, later". When we met in the middle he wrapped his arms around me and kissed me on my cheeks. I felt special, I felt like I was loved, someone wanted me. Being introduced to his whole family made it even more official. This would be my husband one day. I knew under any circumstances he would take care of me. I wasn't the trash anymore like I had been to everyone in the past. He made me feel like I was on the top of the world. I didn't want to do anything but be with him. We got some food in the drive thru and ate in the parking lot. Then rolled back to his Mom's to get our things. He wanted to leave with some daylight still shining. Easy grabbed our bag and we said our goodbyes. Patty hugged me tight when we were saying bye and told me to come back sometime. I certainly wanted to and hoped that it was going to happen in the near future.

We drove back to Oklahoma City that evening. On the way back Easy told me several times how proud he was of "His

Angel" and how I always knew how to stay in my place and what to do. The more he talked, the more I believed in him, the more I was in love with him. He would go on and on about how he was going to build an empire and I was the Angel at his throne. The other girls are the workers to support us. Easy said he was the Alpha and the Omega and that I was his one and only. After that weekend, I worshiped him even more. I knew beyond a shadow of a doubt that this adult wouldn't fail me like the rest. He was going to take care of me and protect me. When we got to Aprils apartment there was no one there. I headed for the living room but Easy laid in her bed in the room. "Angel, come here". I went into the room and he held his arm out for me. We slept in her room that night, I took every moment as confirmation that I was his number one and no one could take my place. We awoke the next morning to the door being unlocked. Easy Jumped up out of the bed and headed to the back door. It was April, she had gotten out, and I Jumped up out of the bed and ran to the bathroom. I didn't know what else to do. I didn't have any clothes, they were on the floor by her bed. By the time I figured that out and turned to go back out, she was in the room. "You're fucking her in my bed while I'm in jail?" She started yelling at him. "Where is my son?" "Where is my son?" "The police took him when you went to jail" Easy yelled. "What? She looked around like she didn't believe him. What?" April started crying; she fell on the floor and was lumped over sobbing. There was a card that the officer left when they took Samuel so I ran and grabbed it off the dresser and handed it to her. "Here they said to call these people." April snatched the card from my hand and got off the floor. She wiped her face and then left to go to the payphone down the street. Easy threw on his jeans and followed behind her. While they were gone, I cleaned up the bedroom and put new sheets on the bed. I waited for them to get back, which was several hours. When they did Easy had a new plan.

~Chapter 7~

A New Job

Samuel had come back home and things were getting back to normal, but we were running out of money. April was a red target on the streets. If they see her talking to anyone they are going to pick her up immediately. We were sitting in the living room listening to Easy talk about what we had and what we needed again. "That's bullshit you can't even call in your regulars." April said, "What about having Angel call them and they can stop by?" "Nah then the police will have a reason to knock on the door. If they pull one of them over and they break, they'll be at this door." So if April is out, this didn't leave anyone else but me. I started panicking on the inside, I knew what he was going to say before he even said it. "You're going to have to pull some tricks Angel. We need to have money. I've been taking care of you, now it's your turn to take care of me." "Can I do like Linda taught me?" I asked quickly. "We can try that if we find the right trick". I was trying to think of any other way to get money. Sitting on the couch I could feel my throat getting tense. My eyes began to water up, I didn't want Easy to see. I was afraid that he would get mad at me for being a cry baby. But I am a baby, I'm not even barely a teenager. Ok, Angel you've gotta toughen up, you don't have time to cry about this, I said to myself. I quickly wiped the tears away and put my head back up. April could tell I had been crying she warmed up to me some now that she knew I was going to have to work. April and Easy started sharing information with me about how the streets work, the cops, and what not to say when I'm out there. "Don't ever tell them how much, make them tell you. If you tell them a price for it then your ass is in trouble." "Then what do I say, will they Just know, what if they don't want to give me all the money?" I had a hundred questions. "Wear a backpack, then you look like a student. And don't ever wave at the cars, let them stop you." April Jumped in "Don't make it easy for them. The one's that want some ass, they will keep after you. A cop will usually stop after a couple of tries." Easy was sitting next to me with his hand in my lap, he kept rubbing my leg and I kept seeing April look at his hand when she was talking to me. She was not ok with it but, just like me, she couldn't do anything about it. "Give them three minutes, if they don't finish, the job is over. You are on a clock and the more tricks you can turn while the cops aren't patrolling the better." "What do I say to them if they don't finish?" "You just start getting up, and make sure that you get the money before you do anything." She went over a few more things then asked me to repeat it back to her so I did. She got up and started walking away. I think this was the most I heard her ever talk. She wasn't mean this time but she wasn't nice either. I put on the skirt and shirt Easy had bought me at Soul Boutique and the heels that went with it. Easy and I walked down to the car, as he was driving he went by the hotel around the corner. "This is where you take them, have the first one buy the room. I'm going to drop you off on 10th and I want you to walk down Shartel toward the house. If you have any trouble I'll be riding around the neighborhood." We got to 10th street and he pulled to the light. He pulled me over to him for a long kiss then I got out of the car. My first step out of the car was a very wobbly one. What was I going to do out here? What if the first person that picks me up tries to kill me? The "what if?" game

81

began and I'm sure my face looked scared the whole time. To my surprise no one tried to pull me over. I walked all the way down to 6th street and no one tried to stop me. Cars whizzed by left and right but no one attempted to stop let alone talk to me. Easy rode by a few times, when I got to the end he told me to walk back up the other way. I had just started to breathe because I thought it was over, but here I go again. I walked back the other direction to 10th and again, no one attempted anything. Easy pulled up next to me at 10th street "Get in." I opened the car door and gratefully got in the car. "What was you doing?" "I was walking, just like you told me to." "You wasn't doing something right, they be stopping April all the time." I sat there quietly, being quite was the only defense I had. I wasn't able to say "Maybe they thought I was too young!" like I wanted to. I sat quietly and listened to him come up with various reasons why it was my fault that no one stopped. We got back to the house and he walked in ahead of me. I went to the couch in the living room and sat there. Easy asked April "What about your regulars?" April had a few old guys that only came to see her; she had their phone numbers and would call them on certain days. "Call them and ask if they want a young girl" Easy said. Now all the sudden it was ok for them to come to the apartment. They went down to the phone together and when they came back, I had a 3pm appointment. April said that he would come to the apartment and I would let him into the living room. "What about the police?" I asked. "We will be gone, they will think he's going to the other apartment. You need to be worried about making some money, fuck worrying about the police." "What does he look like?" I asked. April said that he was an old overweight white man. I got sick to my stomach instantly remembering all the other old men. It was several hours till he got there but it seemed to fly by fast. Easy and April left the house and took Samuel with them.

I was all alone, waiting. It was almost 3 and I heard the door at the bottom open. I was super scared at this point. I could hear each step he took up those stairs, and it took him forever because he was overweight. The whole time he was climbing the stairs I started with the "what if" game. What if he is a cop? What if he is a killer? What if he hits me? Finally the knock at the door. I got up and opened it and there was exactly what she said. An old overweight bald white man slightly leaned over toward the front. Probably from belly weight. "Are you Angel?" he smiled. "Yes, come in" I said. "I'll pull the bed out" I said. I think I was hoping he would say...oh never mind, we don't have to do this.... Well that didn't happen. He took his clothes off and it was just as horrible for me as you could imagine it would be for a little girl. He laid on the bed on his back with a huge mountain of belly sticking up. There was no way he could see what was going on the other side of his belly. I opened the rubber but when I was trying to position myself while holding him he started making noises like I was already doing it. So I Just kept moving around and holding on. It was only about a minute and a half when he did what he came to do. I jumped off and he sat up. "Little Lady, that was worth leaving the office early" I can still hear the way he said that. He reminded me of Boss Hogg from the Dukes of Hazard, size and everything. When he was sitting on the side of the bed, he picked up his pants and got his wallet. I saw when he opened it he had lots of money. He pulled a twenty out and handed it toward me. In a quick second I said "its $50, cuz I'm young" He hesitated for a minute, I'm sure thinking about consequences then gave the extra money. He put his clothes back on and left. I was worried whether he ever knew that we weren't having sex and if he would tell on me to April. I went to the bathroom and started to run the water. It was only about a minute before they came through the back door. Easy came in and hugged me and asked if I was ok. I felt like my skin needed to be peeled off but I said I was ok. "I just need a bath" I said. "Money" he said as he rubbed his fingers together. "It's on the mantel" Easy walked over, picked it up and counted it. "How did you get 50 he said?" "I just asked for it" I said as I walked into the bedroom. Easy ran over and picked me up and kissed me. "That's how you do it Angel, That's how you do it! See April, That's how you do it, just ask!" He put me down and came into the bathroom with me. I ran my bath and he asked me to tell him what all happened and how I did it. When I told him that I had tricked the old man and not actually had sex with him he was even more excited. April was cooking dinner and we ate then went to bed a while later. The next morning I got up and got dressed for the day. I knew I was going to have to make the money and I wasn't sure how many more "tricks" I could pull. I walked around the neighborhood for a while and turned down a few johns because they were too young. Finally, I was approached by the right age, I took him back to the apartment and did the same thing, and it worked again. So this became my M.O. when I could find the right old man and I actually had repeat customers. The more money I made the more Easy showed his love to me. He was constantly telling me that he loved me, kissing on me, holding me in his arms. And most importantly sleeping in the bed with me at night. After a couple of weeks April started working the streets again with me. We were bringing Easy twice the money he was used to having. We had the cabinets and refrigerator so full of food. We could eat for weeks and not run out, and it wasn't even food stamp time. April got a check and food stamps on the 1st of the month and we were used to eating good then, but not half way through the month. Things were looking pretty good. We would work the day and ride around at night listening to great music. Samuel always loved it when we made trips to the east side for Burger King, he would always play with the toy first and then eat his food. We went on for a while like that then there was a new situation.

April came home and said she was pulled over by vice and they were asking her where I was. They knew she knew me from before when they took Samuel. The word that a young girl was working the strip didn't take long to hit the vice cops and they were trying to find me to arrest me. After April told Easy that they were looking for me, he told me to pack up a bag that he was going to have to move me for a minute. I put some things together and was wondering where he was going to take me to. I was kind of hoping it would be to his uncle's house on the east side. I didn't ask but it also didn't take long to figure out that he was taking me to my mom's house. I hated being back there; he would come get me during the day on most days so I Just had to sleep there. We would ride around in April's Cadillac. Easy had Samuel with him every day so I knew April was out working. I was starting to feel some jealousy about April working and giving him money and me not having the ability to. He was sleeping with her at her house and I was sleeping without him. When we would stop by her house or pick her up, he would always hug and kiss on her and call her his baby. He seemed to do it more than usual and I wondered if it was because she was making money and I wasn't. I wanted to be the only one he kissed and hugged on. I wanted to be the one giving to him and receiving from him, but what I wanted didn't matter much. Mom had moved for the umpteenth time and was living on the south side now. I would try not to wake up too early so I didn't have to deal with her much. After a few days, he moved me back to April's apartment and would have her go get the tricks for me to turn and make the money. This was when my "tricks" stopped working and things got really real. April knew what I was doing and didn't want me to have any advantages so she was bringing whoever when Easy wasn't around to watch. The younger men, oh they know, I did my best to act like I couldn't make it happen and some gave up but there were others that didn't. I started telling Easy about those and I would cry when I told him. He told me that I wouldn't have to do it much longer that he was working on something new. Easy told April to stop bringing me johns and for her to continue getting her own work and that he would be the one to get my johns. We were getting ready for bed one evening and they were talking in her room. I couldn't hear everything that was said but I knew it was about me. All the sudden I heard someone getting hit and then landing on the bed pretty hard. Easy came through the door with anger all over his face and his arms bowed out like he was ready to fight. "Don't ask me no more questions dizzy bitch!" he yelled to her from the living room. Easy pulled out the bed in the living room and got in. I slowly got on the bed with him and laid there. One of them usually shuts the door between the rooms when we sleep but tonight the door just stood open. Easy climbed on top of me as usual and did his thing, he didn't make any attempts at being quiet. I was embarrassed, for me and for her. I didn't want to be a part of what he was trying to do to her. No one needed to give her any more reasons to hate me. I kept imagining April standing in the door way with a knife, ready to kill us both. This went on for a few days then one day when we came back from being out, April was gone. At first nothing seemed wrong. It was not uncommon to come in and she is gone to the store, the laundry mat or the pay phone. I started looking around and noticed that important things were missing. Easy pulled open the drawers and they were missing clothes but the laundry basket was still in the bathroom. She had packed some of their things and left. Easy was so upset, he began yelling and throwing what was left there around. I went to the living room and stood in the corner in case something came through the door it wouldn't hit me. "Angel!" he yelled. "Yes?" I said as I came through the door. "Put all this shit up." I leaned down and started picking up all the things he threw around. He was just pacing around the house. Every once in a while I would hear him cuss or knock something over. It took a while but he finally calmed down, but by no means was he over it. Easy stayed up for almost 2 days waiting at the back door for her to come in. He even ate there. I kept trying to get him to leave the door but he wouldn't. The only time he would leave the door was to use the bathroom. He would call me over and have me stand there while he went. On the third day, we started going about business as usual and leaving the apartment. I wondered what happened to her, where she went and why she left a lot of her stuff and her car. I can't say I wasn't a little happy that she had gone but I was still worried about where she was. It was just me and Easy again, but for how long, I didn't know.

By this time it was winter and one day, April came back in the house to get some more things. She had apparently been watching the house and coming in while we were out. While she was getting things Samuel went and stood by the heater in the living room. I'm sure she was in a hurry hoping that Easy didn't come back and catch her there. While she was grabbing things she started smelling burnt plastic. She rushed into the living room to find that Samuel's back was on fire. He was standing too close to the fire from the heater in his coat and it caught fire. April put out the fire as fast as she could but it had burned Samuel's back bad. She had to take him to the ER and he had lots of aftercare she had to do. She couldn't stay in the shelter anymore because she was worried they would call child protective services so she decided to come back home after they left the hospital. When we walked in the house to find April and Samuel back home Easy was happy. He was kissing all over her face and telling her that he was sorry and that he would make everything right. April called Samuel over and raised his shirt to reveal a large bandage covering the majority of his back. "What the fuck happened?" He asked in a loud voice. "He got burnt by the heater while I was in here trying to get some things." "That's why you should have never left, this wouldn't have happened to him." I could tell Easy felt bad about Samuel's burns, I think we all did, but he blamed it all on April. He yelled and screamed at her for what seemed to be forever. By this time Samuel was sleeping and on pain meds so hopefully he didn't hear all of it, I heard every word. I hated seeing Easy's bad side. His good side was so good and it was what you got to see most of the time but his bad side was bad, he could be very mean. After that we both worked every day and Easy kept Samuel with him to make sure April couldn't leave again. One day Easy took me over to an apartment on N.W. 16th street. We walked in the manager's office and Easy asked if we could see one of their apartments. We looked at the apartment together and I was excited. "Is this for us?" I asked. "Yes, Angel, this is for us." He said as he kissed me on the forehead. He filled out the paperwork and paid the man the first month's rent. Finally, we were in our own apartment again. It was an upstairs one bedroom. The stairs leading up were skinny and enclosed like the stairs at the Arizona apartments were I met Easy. The bathroom was right at the front door to the left then the door to the bedroom was next and on the right was the opening to the living room and to the right of that was the kitchen. It was a small kitchen with cabinets and the sink on one wall and there was the stove and a big pantry with doors on the other wall of the kitchen with a table in front of it. We went shopping around for stuff for the apartment. Easy brought April over to see the place and she brought some things over too. Over the next couple of weeks April and I both worked the streets to fill the apartment with what it needed. Easy had Just picked up a new girl and he was training her. This was good for me because I didn't have to work as much. However, she only lasted a few days and made less than 200 dollars. Right back with the old, nasty johns. Fortunately, for Easy and unfortunately for me there were lots of them. I continued with the trick I had learned earlier but when I couldn't make that happen I would close my eyes and Just pretend I was in another world, as time went by it became easier and easier to leave myself mentally with them and come back when they finished.

One evening when I was walking around the strip looking for work a nice looking new car pulled up on me. The man was probably in his late 30's or early 40's but he was a little overweight so I figured it would be within the rules. Plus he looked like he had some money so my first thought was to see if I could get a higher price out of him. He yelled at me as he was slowing down beside me as I walked. "Are you working?" he asked. "I'm walking" I said back to him. "Do you want a ride?" he asked. "Depends on where you're trying to take me" I said as I stopped walking. He put the car in park and asked me to come over. As soon as I walked over he flashed a badge. It was shining from his wallet like a silver bullet. My heart immediately began to beat like crazy drums in my chest. I'm going to jail, I'm going to jail. That's all I could think. I'm sure I lost all the color in my face. I was scared to death. "What is your name? Where are you walking to? Where is your pimp? He didn't even give me the opportunity to respond. "Vice, you're going downtown with me so I can verify your identity" he said as he was getting out of the car. He opened the back door and told me to get in the back seat. My first instinct was to run, but he was the police so I couldn't. I slowly climbed into the back seat and he shut the door behind me. He got in and started pulling off. My stomach was in knots, I felt like I was going to throw up in the back seat of the car. I started thinking about when April went to jail wondering what would happen. What Easy was going to do to me for getting caught and what I was going to do if he kicked me out? My eyes started to water up, I instantly got mad at myself. I hated crying. I hated being upset and I hated that I was in the backseat of a vice officers car. I quickly wiped my eyes, I seen him look at me in the rear view mirror. "No time for crying now. You need to stay off these streets. So I won't have to take you downtown." he said. "I'm not crying!" I said with a ton of attitude. I gave him a cold stare through the rearview mirror. We went to the police station and he pulled up in the back. He opened my door let me out and we went to the elevator. He took me to the counter and told the guy behind the window what he knew of my info. "Put her over there" he said as he pointed to a cell behind me. The vice cop walked me over to the cell and another cop was opening the door. I walked through to the cold dusty cell. There was nowhere to sit but I wasn't interested in sitting anyway. I was pissed off and scared all at the same time. Pissed off that I was taken downtown, and scared because I didn't know what Chris would do. I stood in the cell and watched cops move people around. They all had one of two looks when our eyes would meet. They either looked at me like trash, or like trash they would have sex with in a heartbeat but still, trash. They treated me like I wanted to do this, like I was making the decisions. I wanted them to see the kid that I really was. At the same time, I didn't want them to know anything about me. They weren't trying to help me, they were disgusted by me. The elevator door seemed to be constantly opening. More in, more out. I don't think it was more than an hour or so when the officer opened the door and walked me to the elevator. I assumed I was going to some other jail. I walked out of the elevator to see Mom standing there. The officer repeated to her why they had me and where I had been. Mom told him she was going to take me home and we walked away. "Easy has already been to the house looking for you" she said. "What did he say?" "He just asked if I had seen you, I told him no and he walked away." When we got to 6th and Shartel, we went separate ways. I walked the rest of the way to April's house and around to the back stairs. Chris came out of the door before I could get to the top. "What the fuck is going on Angel?" he said as he grabbed my arm and hurried me the rest of the way up the stairs. "I got picked up." "I know, April told me and I called your mom. You ain't too good at this yet but you'll get the hang of it. You just gotta do better Angel. You gotta be more careful." The next day I was right back out there. I was trying to stay in areas that weren't so open and still look for the obvious, "slowing down cause I wanna buy a girl" car. This became the new daily routine. I was glad that I was able to get more money than April because that meant I didn't have to turn as many tricks. I usually went at lunch time and at the end of the work day. That's when you find the most customers and can get things over quickly. I was out one day, had turned a few tricks and was hoping for just one more to make what I was supposed to. My quota today was just $200, it changed daily depending on what the needs were. I was walking through the park when I saw a slowing car. It was your regular white guy, he was on the low end of old but he qualified for the rules Easy had laid down. He motioned at me to walk over to him so I did. As I was walking over I was running a thousand questions through my head. This was the conversation in my head every time I walked up to a "slowing car" "Is he vice? Is he not vice? He looks ok, like a regular dude. Is he a regular dude? Is that his car? It's a four door car and those are sometimes vice cars." I was driving myself crazy, but I needed the money so I kept walking to him. By the time I got there he had gotten out of his car. "How are you today?" he said as I arrived. "I'm fine, how are you? Are you lost, why did you call me over?" "Oh, I just wanted some company. Are you up for some company?" "What do you mean company?" I asked. He smiled and said "You know, company." "What kind of company are you talking about, I don't have much time." He smiled and said "Vice, get in the car. We're going for a ride." I climbed in the backseat asking him "What did I do? I didn't do anything!" "You just solicited me for sex, I'm taking you in." "I didn't ask you for anything, you were asking me and it wasn't for sex." I sat back in the empty seat and was getting more and more upset. I just got back out here, he's going to be so pissed at me. I hope it doesn't take as long for mom to get me this time. I wasn't too worried about the trip downtown, this wasn't my first time. I mean, I was a little scared but I knew this time it would be ok. I was a minor and all they would do is release me to mom. We drove for a block or two then he pulled into the parking lot of a building and he went around the back. I thought the whole time that I was going to jail, I wasn't paying attention to where he was going. "I've been watching you for a while, I know all about you Angel" How did he know my name? I didn't tell him my name. "I know your black pimp too. What's his name?" Easy had made it very clear, if we are in contact with the police we are never to mention his name. "Take me to jail or let me go!" I said. He pulled over, got out of the car, came around the side, and opened the door. I thought he was going to just let me go or something because we weren't at the police department. He stood so close I couldn't get out around him without pushing him and I knew better than to push a vice cop. "Leave me the hell alone!" I yelled. "You wanna go downtown? He yelled back. I didn't want to be arrested and I didn't know what else to do, I wanted to run, but I couldn't. I sat there listening. He was talking the whole time calling me a n****r lover, whore, slut, bitch and all those other words. He was cursing Easy and the fact that he was black and a pimp. He started grabbing and pulling on me, I knew what was about to happen. My mind was racing, why was he doing this? Is he even a real cop, cops don't do this, do they? Is he going to kill me? I was thinking this could be the end. Why do these kinds of things happen to me? What is it about me that makes men want to hurt me or be mean to me? Why can't I be a normal girl like the rest of them? He quickly pulled me from the car. I wasn't expecting it, I lost my footing and fell to the ground. He knelt down over me and I flinched as he did because I thought he was going to hit me that was the only thing left to do. He grabbed my face and looked me up and down. "You ain't hurt, stop crying you fucking whore. Don't let me hear no radio calls about you, or we'll all finish the job, Angel." I knew before that the police weren't necessarily your friend, now I know for sure they were the enemy. Just like I had been taught. He left me there in that lot on the pavement. I laid there for a while crying. Hoping that someone would come rescue me. Hoping that Easy would drive up and save me. No one came, no one even knew I was there, and if they did, they probably wouldn't care anyway. I was a prostitute. I didn't deserve anyone's sympathy. I started walking home, as I walked I could feel the scrapes on my knees burn every time they bent. I kept running through what just happened, imagining what would have happened if I had ran in the beginning, what if I refused to get in the car? What if, what if, what if, what if I was just dead? I played the "what if" game all the way home. I watched for police cars or four door cars and would hide when I saw one. When I got home Easy was there, he was mad as hell when I walked in "Where tha fuck have you been?" he yelled as he ran up on me. "The police had me, the police had me!" I yelled quickly as I threw my arms up to protect what was coming. My face was still red from crying. My skinned up knees had streams of dried up blood running down to my shins. I told Easy the cop left me in the parking lot, and that he said he knew who I was and knew him too. "What the fuck, who the fuck! I'm going to fuck these mutha fuckers up!" Easy was furious, pacing back and forth screaming, yelling and flailing his arms around. I couldn't even understand a lot of what he was saying, just cussing a lot. "Angel, come here." He said as he motioned his hand by the bedroom door. "Come on!" he said louder as he met me half way. He walked me to the bathroom. "Take ya clothes off" he reached down and turned on the bath water. "Get in" he said as I climbed in the empty tub. "Sit there until the water gets high enough." He left the room for a minute but kept coming back and forth talking about what happened. Once the water was full I turned it off. "Stand up" He grabbed the bowl he brought in and started pouring water down my body. He grabbed the hand towel and lathered it with soap and started washing me down. He scrubbed my skin hard. He kept saying he was "washing off the fucking pig". I kept telling him he was hurting me but he wouldn't stop. My skin was red and raw. He reached over and got the rubbing alcohol and started wiping me down with it.

The first sensation was ice cold, then the cold turned to a burn, it felt like my whole body was on fire. "It burns, it burns, please stop" I wanted to dive back into the bath water but every time I started to lean downward, he would hold me up. "I'm almost done, stop crying Angel!" He wrapped his arms around me and held me tight to his body. I stood there with him until my skin was dry and most of the burning was gone but it seemed like an eternity. Finally, he picked me up and carried me to the bed. He laid there with me and promised me that I wouldn't have to work on the streets anymore and that he would figure something else out. For the next couple of days he didn't make me go out. I stayed around the house waiting for him to come home. My skin scabbed in some places where he was scrubbing; it took about a week or more for it to all go away. I looked like I had road rash from a motorcycle accident. I was putting Vaseline on it hoping it would keep me from scaring all over. During that time, Easy was not spending much time at home. He had gotten a TV from his mom for the apartment, it was a fancy floor model too. At least I had something to watch until he came home to sleep. That not having to work the streets didn't last long. Easy said we needed to have some money until he figures something out. He promised me he was working on it. I did get to work a new area though. Instead of going back to the old beat I was working the strip on 16th street by the apartment. Oddly enough it was just a couple of blocks away from the high school where I was supposed to be. I was still going to school but not as often as I used to. Mostly I was working, there was no one else working 16th street at that time so it was easy to find a trick and lots of money to be made. Almost every time I would walk over to the store someone would proposition me. I had only been working 16th street for a couple of days when I picked up a trick in a really nice car. He was the usual, older white dude in business clothes. I got in the car with him and assumed I would be doing it there like I did most. "I'd rather get a room instead." "That's cool, you can turn right here on Classen, there's one down the street." "Nah, I know where one is." He got onto 63rd street and started heading to the east side. At first I thought he was talking about one of the motels on Lincoln. He kept going past everything and further out. I was getting really scared. I was starting to think about the possibilities of him taking me out to the country to kill me. "Where the fuck are we going? I'm bout to jump out this car!" "No, no, don't worry. I'm not trying to hurt you. I just need some young tail. Were almost here, its right up here. I'm not gonna hurt you, promise!" He said as he pointed his finger ahead of us. About a minute later he pulled into this little motel place. This did not look like any motel I had ever seen. It was scary from the first touch on the driveway. It was made of dirt, tiny pebbles, and old asphalt underneath. You could hear the tires crunch through the driveway as he slowly pulled in. The drive went up to a one story brick building that looked all of 50 years old. There was an opening with a solid brick area on one side and a brick area with windows on the other. He stopped at the window and the guy on the other side of the glass held up his fingers. Two fingers on his left hand and the shape of a zero with the other. After digging in his pocket for a minute he stuffed a 20 under the slit in the glass. He pulled past the opening and I could see what we were driving into. There were rooms all the way around made in a rectangle with a dirt area in the middle where people drove. There were garages next to each of the rooms. As he pulled into the garage my body was so tense. I much preferred turning tricks in their vehicle. This way if something were to actually happen I could at least attempt to jump from the car. If fact I was thinking it while in the car on the way to this scary place. The door to the room was on my side of the car. He got out and I let him walk around and open the door to the room. Paralysis was what I was wishing for, to be frozen in his car so I didn't have to go in. Being in a room, in some creepy place, with some creepy guy was not where I wanted to be or what I wanted to be doing. Matter of fact I would gladly have tons of homework everyday then to have to keep doing this even once. But that wasn't my life anymore, that wasn't my life. This is my life, going into strange places with strange people doing strange things. My hand finally pulled on the handle of the car door. He was standing in the doorway looking at me like "are ya coming?" I walked the two feet to the door and into the tiny bedroom size motel room. It was dark and dingy. The furniture was way old. It looked like something my grandmother would have loved if it wasn't all broken down. I pulled the blankets back on the bed because you never want to lay on one a blanket in a motel. That was one of the tricks Linda taught me. She said them druggie hoes be layin on top. "Um, I need to get" "Oh right, yes, it's right here." He said as he dug in his pocket and handed me a wad of cash. I counted the money, put it in my pocket. He did his business and we got back in the car to leave. Being in the car with them before was scary. Being in the car with them after was nasty and gross. He was trying to have small talk on the way back. I guess now he thought he knew me. What he did know is that I was just a kid. Not really even a full blown teenager. I mean, I didn't get to do the things teenagers do, so. I wondered if he had a daughter, he had a wedding ring on his finger. We got back to my side of town and he dropped me off at the store where he picked me up. I walked across to the apartment and went upstairs. I was excited to see Easy, I ran up at him when I got in the door and he caught me in the air. We hugged as he took me to the bathroom to take a bath. We kissed for a while. "Come on Angel, take your bath and hurry. I wanna watch a movie with you." I took my bath and we watched movies for the rest of the evening.

Easy got up early one morning and started his showering routine. He had a very particular way of doing things. From his shaving to showering and dressing. I ironed his jeans while he was still in the shower and I was working on his shirt. He left not much more than an hour after that and within another hour I heard someone pulling up in the drive. I looked outside and he was in a brown Chrysler New Yorker not the Cadillac. I could tell someone was in it but I couldn't tell who.

~Chapter 8~

A Wedding For A Ring

Easy came into the apartment in a rush "Angel, come here, hurry!" as he ran to the kitchen. I was in the bed watching TV when he came in, didn't have on any clothes, and didn't have time to grab any. I ran to the kitchen after him. He pulled the table away from the pantry and opened the door for me to get in. I climbed into the cabinet, I was pretty small so I fit in easily. Easy closed the door behind me and everything was dark except a sliver of light where the doors met. I could hear him push the table back. I had no clue what was going on and didn't ask, I was trained not to. I sat there and listened to him go back down stairs and then back up the stairs with someone else with him. Who's with him I wondered. Is this a new girl, what does she look like, will she stay here or at Aprils? All the questions started racing in, I almost couldn't hear them for my own thoughts. I leaned my ear against the crack in the doors. It was a woman, this sounded like an older woman, not someone my age. They came in the front door "This is nice Ris" I heard her say. I started running through the voices that I knew and

I didn't recognize her voice at all. I guess this is where he has been, I thought to myself. I heard him show her around the apartment and the kitchen. I tried to look through the crack but the only thing I could see was that she had short natural black hair and that she was short, and small like me. Then I saw her turn her head toward the pantry. I jerked my head back from the crack. I was balancing on my knees and almost fell over. My heart was beating so hard I could hear it, I was hoping that she couldn't. Why is your table in front of the pantry?" She asked as she walked toward the pantry. I was pretty sure he wouldn't let her pull the table away but I still held my breath. It seemed like an eternity waiting for him to answer her. Finally, he spoke "I don't use it and the table fits there." "Oh, well the kitchen is cute." She moved on and I was able to breathe again. They only stayed long enough for the tour and then they left. I sat there for what seemed like an eternity waiting for him to come back inside. I heard the car pull off earlier, I figured he was talking to someone outside or had walked over to the corner store. I didn't even consider that he wouldn't come back and let me out. But he didn't, he didn't come back. I yelled his name a few times just to make sure I wasn't right, to check to see if he was somehow in the apartment and just forgot to open the door. Or that he was playing a game on me. He wasn't, I had to kick my way out. Lucky for me the table wasn't too hard to move and the fridge was just far enough away that it let me open the door enough to get out. I stared out the window for a while and eventually went out on the ledge to wait for him. I was so upset, not that he was with her but that he didn't let me out. That means he forgot about me. He always tells me that I'm the most important person to him and I know it's true. I just don't understand how he could forget me in there. I went inside and watched TV until I fell asleep. That next morning I woke up to the noise of him coming in the front door. Easy or "Ris" as she called him came in the room and plopped down on the bed and pulled me up to him. He started kissing me all over my face and sucking on my cheeks. "I'm sorry I left you in there Angel. I gotta work on this woman and get this money. I was trying to run back upstairs but she said she had to pick up her son, so we had to go. I won't do that to you again." He said as he continued kissing my face. I melted instantly in his arms. I was the most important person to him. We have to have money and that's one of the ways we get it. What's most important is that we work together because we were a family. Easy told me all about the lady from last night. He said that he had met her at a stop light, she had a good job, and he was going to get money out of her. And that was the only thing that mattered. We stayed in bed most of the morning making up time lost.

That afternoon after we got ready we went to Shepard Mall. There was a jewelry store there that had a ring that he wanted. It was a horseshoe shape with gold and diamonds, the band was thick and so was the top. It was $1500.00 and he wanted it, but we didn't have the money Just yet. We left the mall and went to the flea market. There were so many different kinds of shops there. I had only been to the flea market one other time. I was trying to see all the things on display but it was almost impossible, there was so much. We went by some jewelry shops and looked a couple of different things for him. "Let me see that necklace there." He said as he pointed to the ladies side. The guy behind the counter was a big country lookin dude with a big beard. He pulled the necklace out that Easy was pointing to and handed it to him. Easy opened it and put it around my neck and closed it. I was so excited. I didn't know what to do or what to say. He was buying me gold, a gold necklace, real gold. I felt like the most loved girl in the world. He was showing his love for me and I was keeping my eyes open so I wouldn't miss a second of it. We went back to the apartment and I stood in the mirror in the bathroom so long Easy came in after me. When he opened the door he saw me looking at and touching the necklace. He smiled real big and wrapped his arms around me. "It's me and you Angel, It's me and you against the world sugar." He said as he kissed on my face. I knew it too, it would be me and him, forever. The next morning I was just getting out of the shower when he came running in the bath room. "Get in the pantry, she's here, get in the pantry!" He said as he rushed me to the kitchen in Just a towel. I heard the bottom door open Just as he was closing the pantry door. Click clack click clack, I could hear her coming up the steps. Before she could even knock on the door Easy opened it. "Hello Beautiful!" he said as he let her in. I could tell by the pause they had kissed. "Who was in your shower, you're not wet?" "I had the shower on getting ready to get in and then I heard you pull up so I turned the shower off. Why you questioning me?" he said with a joking tone in his voice. "Did you come over here to be the police or to see me?" "I came to see you silly" I heard her let out a squeal "Put me down Ris, put me down." I heard them land on the bed and start laughing together. I hated being in the pantry, I started feeling like I was something he was ashamed of. I was able to meet and be around all the other girls from day one, why is she different? What if she becomes number one instead of me? Will he make me go back to the streets? And the "what if?" game began, as usual. This was Just one of the many things I did while waiting in the pantry. I never knew how long I would be in there. Sometimes it would be 15 minute while he changed and sometimes it would be hours while they watched TV or had sex. And me…in the pantry, starting to wonder… is this what life is? What about all that stuff on TV? Why can't I have a life like them? What happened to my Brady Bunch family? I wasn't like those kids on TV, I was in reality, harsh reality. I quickly dismissed my ability to have a regular family or life. But at least I had someone who was taking care of me and who protected me. I was still in our apartment and I was still his number one. I just had to adjust to what was going on around me and keep my mouth shut so I could stay safe and fed. I never questioned being in the pantry because questioning is something I had watched others get big consequences from. I did however, learn the hard way to keep something to eat and drink in the pantry just in case I had to get in unexpectedly and be stuck. There were a few times where the chair getting stuck between the table and fridge wouldn't let me open the door enough to get out and I would be stuck. I even had a blanket and pillow in there. A book too, The Outsiders, it was a book we had started reading that year in 9th grade. I read it about 12 times it seemed. Of course, the only light I had was what came through the crack of the door and only in the day time. When I was in third grade or so we had those machines that you put your book in and the bar moved down to teach you speed-reading. I just moved my book up and down in the light line to read it just like the reading machine. I was just happy to have something in there with me. Sitting with nothing to do but think, wasn't always the best thing for me to do.

One afternoon when "Ris" came home he said that I had to go stay at April's house for a couple of days. He said that Brenda wanted to spend the night so I had to pack up all of my stuff so she wouldn't see anything there. So I packed everything up and we left. We went by the boot store and Easy got another pair of snake skin boots. We dropped them off at the boot repair shop to get the tips and taps put on. We got something to eat and then he took me to April's apartment. She was living in a different place now, she knew I was coming this time but that didn't make her anymore excited about it. We walked in the door, April was in the kitchen. This apartment was much like the other one, a fireplace with a big mantel and stuff. She walked into the living room and pointed to the couch. I put my bag over by the couch, she had already put some blankets there. They went to the bedroom and after a while April came out and started cooking while Easy took a shower. After he left I Just stayed quiet in the living room watching TV. The next morning I woke to the smell of breakfast. April had cooked and it looked like there was enough made for me too. I leaned back and looked at April sitting at the table and she nodded back to me the OK to get my plate. I did the dishes after I ate and wiped everything down. April was in the living room reading to Samuel, I walked in and sat on the other couch and listened. "So how have you been?" she asked. "I've been ok, and you?" "I'm good, ready to be back home already but I'm good." Samuel was starting to color in his coloring book so I got down on the floor and started playing with him. Over the next few days I helped as much as I possibly could because I wanted to stay on April's good side. The two days he said I would be there turned into a week. She was ok with me at first but by this time, April was saying that she wanted me gone; she didn't want me there in the first place. I was so sad, I still wished and daydreamed sometimes that I could be nice enough to her that she would let me be her daughter and not what we were. She took good care of Samuel and all I wanted was a mom who would take care of me like that. April was constantly on me about money though. Every time I ate, she would talk about how much it cost. I wanted to tell Easy on her but at the same time I didn't cuz I knew the results. He hadn't been by in days and I had already went a day without eating to avoid hearing her. I didn't know what else to do so I did what I was taught. I went to the streets, turned a couple of tricks and gave the money to her. She was cool for a few more days then she wanted money again. I went back out again and it was raining so I went with the first truck that stopped. It was a new red truck but it wasn't an old guy and this was against the rules. This was a young guy around 35 or 40 with a good build. I told him I had made a mistake and that he could let me out. As he was pulling over, he grabbed my arm and said "I didn't make a mistake". He pulled out his wallet with his other hand and put it on the dash. It was raining and the windows were all fogged up so you couldn't see into the truck. We were right there on the side of the road with cars passing and no one could see anything. He finally let go of me so I Jumped out of the truck and Just started running back to April's apartment. I finally got to the apartment and went immediately to the bathroom. I was crying so hard I could barely see. I started running the water and undressing. April came in behind me "What's all the mess?" "Get out, leave me alone" I yelled. I didn't want to see her or anyone else. "Make sure you clean up your mess" she said as she closed the door. I sat in the tub until the water turned cold then I ran it out and did it again. April came to the bathroom door "You've been in long enough, get out!" I didn't want to move let alone get out of the tub. I sat there for as long as I could. I heard her footsteps leaving the living room so I got out and dried off. I put my towel on and went to the couch and got one of my three sets of clothes and put them back on. Nothing had been washed because first, I didn't expect to be there that long and second it wasn't time for April to go to the laundry mat yet, I think she was prolonging it for my sake. I fell asleep and hours later in the middle of the night; I woke up to his voice. I heard him coming in the door. I jumped off the couch and ran to him I was so excited and so ready to go home. I jumped up in his arms and hugged him. "Take me home please" I begged. April came into the living room about that time. "Yea, take her home" she said with a smart tone. "Okay get your stuff together" he said. When I went to get my stuff, he went to the bedroom with April. He was only in there for a few minutes and then we left. I couldn't have been happier. We got in the car and I was finally where I was supposed to be. Me and Easy rollin around town in the Cadillac listening to music. We jumped on the highway and rode out west on I-40. We pulled off where the truck stop was. There was a fast food joint place so we went through the drive thru and got a couple of burgers then we parked. "I been missing you Angel, I been missing you and needing you" he said. "I've been missing you terribly, I don't like being away from you!" I said as I reached over to hug him. "Angel, you're gonna work here tonight." "Here at the restaurant?" I asked. I was thinking to myself it's awfully late at night for that. "No Angel, the truck stop" I froze right where I was and my body started getting ill. I started feeling like I was going to throw up and have diarrhea at the same time. I had never worked the truck stop before and there was no one there with me to show me how. I remember talking to Paula and Linda about it a little bit but I didn't really know anything. Easy could see all over my face that I was scared to death. "I'm going to stay right here. You Just go over there and knock on the doors and someone is gonna let you in" he said in an assured voice. "Now go on girl, we don't have a lot of time. Watch out for the police, make sure you look before you go running around." There was no such thing as saying no, and after seeing what happened to others, I didn't want that to happen to me. I took a deep breath, opened the car door and got out. I looked around for a walk way but couldn't see how they all connected because it was so dark. The trucks were diagonal across from me, between us was a large dirt field. I figured to save time I'd Just walk in the direction of the big trucks. I was so scared I could barely walk. My knees were shaking and the rest of me was too. I didn't know who's door to knock on and what would I say when I get there. This is nothing like the johns on the streets. They pull up to you so you know they want to be a customer. What if I choose the wrong one? What if there are vice cops in the big rigs? What if there's a serial killer in one? I had a million questions going through my head and I'm sure I looked lost because I was. I made it across the field and come up behind the trailers of the trucks. I walked between two of the trucks and came up on the side of the cab. I looked at all the handles and different levels and tried to determine how I would get up there to even knock on the door. I decided that one was too complicated and looked to see if I could see any that appeared to be lower to the ground. I peeked out in the lane but could hardly see because the trucks across the way had their lights on. I took the chance and sprinted across the road to another truck. I climbed up the side and knocked on the door. I had no clue what I was going to say and whether I would be able to talk period since I had a huge lump in my throat. The door opened and I saw an older man that looked like he could be someone's grandpa with the long gray beard and all. "Delivery?" I said in my 'I'm trying to be sweet voice'. "No, I didn't ask for no delivery" he said. "How old are you little one?" I froze right there and probably had that "I'm caught" look on my face. He stared at me for a minute. "I bet I got grandkids your age. You need to get on out of here, this ain't no place for a little girl." I climbed back down and started snaking my way through the trucks looking for someone with the lights still on in the cab. Just as I started to round a corner I ran right into a man who was walking the isles too. I about peed my pants, I didn't expect anyone to be there let alone to bump into someone. "Come with me young lady" he said as he grabbed me by my upper arm. I started to scream and as I was opening my mouth I realized he was a police officer. I didn't know whether to be grateful that he wasn't a serial killer or upset cause he was a cop. We walked over to his car and as we were I could see Easy pulling away from the parking lot. I sat down on the curb and started to cry. The cop started asking me questions; who brought you here? What kind of car did you come in? Were you trying to prostitute? Where are your parents? How old are you? Where do you live? And a million other questions it seemed. I already knew I couldn't trust the cops so I didn't tell them anything. I answered their questions but not with the answers they were looking for. "We're taking you downtown." The officer said as he gestured for me to stand up. I stood and he led me over to the car and put me in the back.

While we were on the way back into the city he was communicating with others on the radio. He had given them my street name Angel, and they read back to him my real name and my mom's name. He asked me where she lived and I told him. He drove me over there instead of downtown. When we got there he walked to the door with me to verify that my mom lived there. He told her that he picked me up for prostitution at the truck stops. Mom nodded her head and said ok. The officer asked me to come back to the car for a second. He gave me a pep talk about how much my family loves me and wants me to be home and being a teenager. I listened and got out of the car. He had no clue who I was or what I had gone through and who my family was. My family didn't love me, especially my mom. I was the other woman to her, not a daughter at all. I walked in mom's house and said hi. "Was that you in the police car?" my sister asked. "Yes, he gave me a ride home" I responded. Mom knew it was more than that but she didn't say anything. "Where is your phone at?" I asked. "He already called" "I called him when I saw you pull up, he's on his way over" mom said. What if I was calling someone for help? What if I didn't want to go back with him? I would ask why she was selling me up the river but I already knew. She had become even more jealous of me than she was in the Dan situation. She was jealous of my relationship with Easy and the things he did for me. She didn't want the best for me at all, she wanted it for herself, and she was willing to use me to get it. I went and talked to my two little sisters until Easy showed back up. When he did, he came in long enough to say let's go and we were out the door. The sun was starting to come up and I was happy to see that we were heading to our apartment. When we got there Easy told me to get in the shower first and boy did that water feel good. It had been a long night and I was ready for sleep. I got out of the shower and climbed in the bed where he already was. "I'm not mad at you Angel but you could have done better than that. Were gonna have to go during the daytime so you can know your way around before you get yourself lost and arrested again." I laid there thinking about what I could have done better and why I was even having to do this in the first place. I wanted that fairy tale life. That life I see people have on TV. I wanted that.

That next day we went to the truck stop and he drove around a little bit pointing out landmarks. This was supposed to make it easier for me that evening. When it had been night for a few hours he came and told me to get dressed. It was almost midnight so I knew what we were doing, we were going to try the truck stop thing again. I took my time getting dressed hoping somehow he would change his mind but he didn't. We rode out to the truck stop and I did the same thing as before, knock on cab doors and ask if they wanted some company. I was about to give up because I was on truck number 10 or so. As I went to knock on the door it began to open. There was an older heavy set man in the seat of the truck, "come on in here darling" he said as he gestured me in. I climbed into his truck scared to death about what could happen. "I've been watching you go around to the trucks and I was hoping you would knock on my door" he said. "I need some cash" I said right away. "I figured as much, and I've got some of that" he replied with a cheesy grin. We did our business and he gave me the money. He got on the speaker and put out the code that I was looking for customers. He showed me the next truck to go to and that guy showed me the next one. I made my quota and made a bee line back to Easy's car in the parking lot. He had already started the car when he seen me coming, I hopped in and we got right back on the highway headed to the house. I gave Easy the money and he was much happier. "That's how you do it Angel, I knew you could do it. But next time you need to do more, this isn't enough." He was talking about how to watch for the right kind of guy, like he had ever done this. How would he know? We got home and he only stayed long enough to eat some left overs. He stayed out all night. I was so upset, I just risked myself for him and he took the money and left. Easy had been spending a lot of his time with Brenda and he needed money to show her that the financial side wasn't only on her. This was part of his "master plan" he would talk about. He talked about those credit cards of hers like she could buy the world with them and he wanted the access to them. And heck, for all I knew he could buy the world. I had never known anyone with a credit card. I'd only seen those on TV. We were rolling back and Easy got off the highway at the exit I wasn't expecting. I thought he was taking me back to our apartment but he didn't he took me back to where my mom was staying. He told me to spend the night there and find my older sister's ID. My mom had a one bedroom garage apartment. Everyone except Kathi and our brother Brian were there so of course this puts me on the floor, in the kitchen no less. After everyone went to sleep, it was easy to get what I came for. Amanda had left her purse on the table and I Just took the birth certificate and her social security card out of her purse. I put them in my pocket and went to sleep. The next morning Easy came back to get me. He didn't come in he just honked when he got outside. I ran out and got in the car, hugged and kissed him then showed him the id's I had stolen from my sister. The rewards he gave in paying attention to me and loving me were sure worth the trouble I was risking.

~Chapter 9~

Knights n' Pawns

We spent a lot of time in the car rolling around town. Easy had decided that he needed to do some upgrades to the exterior of the Cadillac. There was a shop on 10th street where he had some people he knew. When he rolled up there was a guy who came out and started talking to him. They were talking about putting a new paint job on and a new rag on the back. They agreed on a few hundred and he said we would drop the car off tomorrow. While we were out Easy was saying he was so proud of me and started telling me, how smart I was and how I was going to be able to do so much for us now. How we were going to make lots of money and get whatever we wanted. He said "Angel you are growing up more and more every day. We are going to buy you a car with some of the money we're gonna make." He had been letting me drive the Cadillac so I was much better at it now. We were headed out to do some shopping, the ride to the flea market was pretty short with all the conversation. We walked to the back to the jewelry shop and Easy got his self 2 more rings and bought me another necklace and a ring made of gold. Then we went to the mall and got some new clothes. There were parts of this that were like living a fantasy life, I never thought I would be in the position to have one gold necklace let alone two and a ring. I felt like a queen. Easy and I went back to the apartment and watched some movies. The next morning we got up and got ready for the day. It was Monday and we had important business to handle. We got to the drive thru just in time for them to switch to lunch for some burgers and then he took me downtown to get a bar card. Back then in the 80's in order to work in a club you had to have a bar card. This was an ID that you got from the authorities that certified that you could work in a club. Easy had already called ahead and knew where I should go. He dropped me off at the door and I followed the signs to the counter. I was shaking like crazy, I just knew I was going to get caught. I was looking around to make sure I didn't see any of the officers that had arrested me in the past. I snuck around corners and down hallways to the licensing area. There was a form you had to fill out so I did. I had memorized the information just in case someone asked questions. My hand was shaking as I handed her all of the information and she asked me to stand behind the red line. She took my picture and within about 10 minutes I was walking out with my bar card. It was hard for me not to run back to the car. I knew I had something I shouldn't have and I also knew that Easy was going to be happy. I was hoping that I wouldn't have to work on the street or the truck stop anymore with this new card. I got to the car and handed him the ID as I was getting in. He was as excited as I was. We drove right to a bar on 10th street. "This is a strip club" he said as he pulled in. I didn't know it was a strip club. What exactly was a strip club? I had never been inside a strip club. Was it what I thought it was? I wondered. I heard of strip poker, I knew what that was. Was this that? Easy had taken me to a nightclub on the east side one night. I got all dressed up in the clothes he bought me and we waited in the line to enter. When we got to the door guy Easy gave him his ID and told the guy "That covers both of us." I had never even seen the inside of a nightclub. I had seen inside a bar, this little hole in the wall bar, but never a nightclub. I knew I was safe with Easy but I didn't feel like I belonged there at all. I was looking at everyone around me wondering if they knew I was only 14 years old. We sat at the bar for a while and then we danced and it was cool. But naw, never a strip club. Let alone that I was going to be the stripper. I didn't know that until after I got there. I seriously thought I was going to be a waitress or something like that. When we went inside, he was talking to this tall white man like he already knew him. The white man called over a lady who was wearing lingerie. Easy told me to go with her. The club was in a long skinny building. The door was toward the back and the bar was right at the door. The pool tables were to the right and to the left at the end was a small dance floor. The dance floor was a raised semi-circle with a pole to one side. There were mirrors everywhere. The back of the stage, side, along the walls of the club, I mean everywhere; even the ceiling of the stage had mirrors. We walked past the stage and around to a little room behind the stage. It was a long skinny room with a mirror along the back wall. There were chairs along the wall and a ledge where you could put your makeup. It had a couple of lockers and she said you've got to get here early to make sure you get one. She was talking to me as if I had already done this and so I assumed Easy had told them I had. I just went along and acted like I knew what I was doing and what she was talking about. But I didn't, I was scared to death. I couldn't even breath good I was so scared. I kept looking toward the door and while she was talking, I was overwhelmed. I got up and walked back out to Easy. I grabbed a hold of him and whispered in his ear "I'm so scared." He kissed me. "Don't worry Angel, I'm not going to let nothing happen to you, I take care of you." I wanted to go home and they didn't know they were babysitting. I thought to myself, plus what is their version of "take care"? I was scared and didn't know what to expect. What was a strip club? I still didn't know all of the rules. Was it just dancing? I had a million questions going through my head and there was only one person I could talk to and I couldn't ask him. It was only about 1 o'clock in the afternoon so there were only a couple of men in the club. I walked back to the dressing room and grabbed the outfit I borrowed from the girl

I was talking to earlier. "Sorry for walking out on you, I'm just super nervous and I've danced before but not on stage like that." "Don't worry about it so much all ya gotta do is stare out over them and just keep moving and you'll be fine" she said. Great, Easy said to stare at them, she says to stare over them. I finished putting on the outfit and walked back out to Easy. He started grinning ear to ear with that intoxicating smile when he seen me coming. I was embarrassed and trying to hide myself. I wanted to cry but he was all happy so I held it in. I didn't want to be naked with a room of men staring at me. But here, that was the job, dance in front of a room of men staring at you.

Easy met me half way and we sat over on the side in one of the booths for a minute. Easy started running off the rules and what was going to happen. "You're going to stay here and dance. Watch the other girls until it's your turn, then do the same things they do. When you're up there stare back at the ones who are staring at you. Same thing goes here, no brothas and no young dudes. Don't leave this club with anyone, not for food, not for a trick, not to talk to yo people, nobody, nothing! I'm trusting you Angel and I know you don't wanna upset me. I'll be here for a while and I'll come back to pick up tha money. I don't want any of these bitches trying to steal from you. And don't be running your mouth when you sit with these fools". Sit with them?? What do you mean sit with them? I thought to myself. "Am I turning tricks here?" I asked. "Not today, tell me if anyone asks, get their phone number or something" he said. "What if the police come in?" I asked. "They won't, stop; do you need an attitude adjustment?" "No." I quickly replied and lowered my head. "Enough questions" he said through his teeth. I sat there and watched them dance for a few rounds and then he nudged me to get up there. I went over to the DJ and told him to play something recent. He suggested some stuff and I walked back to the back to wait my turn. The walk to the back was like walking in the twilight zone. I was scared, nervous, anxious and about to pass out. I could feel my fingers and toes tingling. The girl that had showed me around was back there. "You doing ok honey?" she asked. "I'm really nervous" I replied,

I wanted to yell "I shouldn't be here!" but I couldn't. "It's safer in here than it is out there honey. Plus it gets easier as you do it. Soon, you'll be bored of it" she laughed. I laughed with her to fit in but I was scared to death. That didn't help me calm down, not even a little bit. Then I heard him announce me in that creepy DJ voice. "Coming to the stage, for the first time here at Knights n' Pawns, let's give a warm welcome to Aaannggggeeeelllllll." It was about as cheesy as it could get which made it even worse for me. I wobbled out on the stage on rubber legs and acted like I was dancing by myself in my room. I had no clue what I looked like up there and didn't care. I was so frightened I was surprised my body kept moving. I looked up at the ceiling and if I looked down it was at Easy. We had to dance three dances in a row so when he played the next song I kept going and staring at Easy or the ceiling. I tried to look at the customers but I couldn't do it without feeling like I was going to cry. The second dance you take off. I turned around to take my top off because I couldn't do it looking at them. When I turned back around I stared up for a minute then I looked back down at Easy and he wasn't there. I started looking around the club and didn't see him anywhere. I started to panic but was on stage so I had to try to keep it inside. I don't know how well I was or was not doing. I was hoping no one could tell how scared I was but there was still part of me that wished they did. I wanted to leap off the stage and run for the door hoping he would still be outside. Then here came the first one. An old skinny white man had walked up to the stage and was standing there holding money. That was the signal that you were supposed to go over there and give him a personal dance for the tip that he had in his hand. Since there was only a few people in the club, I only seen one other customer get up and the girl talked to him most of the time. I sashayed my way over there and started dancing in front of him still looking around hoping Easy had gone to the bathroom. I did a few twirls and dips and then opened the side of my bottoms like I seen the other dancer do to put the money in and he did, he put the money and practically his whole hand in. I backed up real quick and danced away like it didn't scare the holy crap out of me. Then the last song was over and I walked off the stage holding my breath and holding back my urge to run. I sat down in one of the chairs in the back and started talking to myself in my head. Oh my God, Oh my God, I did it, I made it through. Ok gonna have to do it again here in a little bit. Man I wish Easy was still here. I walked out to the front and looked around everywhere. The bartender guy saw me looking and told me that Easy had left. I hurried to the bathroom before the tears started rolling. I cried in the bathroom for a while and then sucked it up. I started trying to talk myself into how safe it was compared to the streets like ole girl said and the more I talked the more reasons I found that the streets were safer. I had almost 8 hours left before he came back. What if they decided to kill me or something, I'm inside where no one can see and if I yell for help, no one would hear. Those were the advantages to being on the street that I was talking myself into.

As the night went on the club got full and more girls came in. We were all in a row on the DJ's list. When it was your turn, you would dance your three dances and when it wasn't you would stand or walk around unless a customer was interested in you. If they were interested in you they would ask you to sit with them and they would buy you a drink. This was a way for the customer to pay for time with you and pretend like it wasn't a form of prostitution. There was a menu of drinks that ranged from $12 to $500. The more expensive the drink the more time you spent sitting with the customer. And sitting with the customer was not at all, at least most of them, what I thought it would be. Within the first hour or so, I was offered a drink. The guy bought a $64 drink; this meant that I had to stay with him for a little while. I sat down in the booth with him and he asked all the typical stuff. Where are you from, what do you do when you're not at work. The majority wanted someone to complain about their wife to or about their job. But the perverted one's that I already knew would be there…didn't fail me. I had some of the nastiest proposals and one even pulled his thing out. It was more confirmation for me that I shouldn't be there. As the night went on and got busier, it didn't get any easier to cope with but I kept watching that door. I looked every time it opened. It was around 9 o'clock when I saw Easy come in the door. I was up on stage and seriously considered running off stage I was so happy to see him but I knew I couldn't do that. When I finished I ran out to him and was excited to tell him about how much money I had made. He was proud of me and told me to keep going. I worked until 2:00am instead of the 12am he told me. My feet were so very sore and I just wanted to be off of them. I wasn't used to wearing heels let alone for 13 hours and I hope I didn't look as bad walking as I felt I did. It was a long day but by the end, I had made almost $500.00 and didn't have sex with anyone. I had to deal with their nasty hands on me but it was better than before. It was a hard day but much easier and safer than working on the streets. In the end, in my world, that was a positive.

When we left the club we went to our apartment, I hadn't been there much in a while. I could tell that he had been staying there with Brenda but I couldn't say anything. I was happy to be back home. He spent the night there with me. I continued working every day for the next week and he only stayed home a couple of those nights. Then one day he told me that he and Brenda had gotten married. And he was going to bring Brenda over for us to meet. I was nervous and didn't know what to think. I was jealous about the marriage but happy that he got his plan to happen. He had married Brenda and that was how he was using her credit cards to buy me clothes and jewelry. I didn't know how much she knew or didn't know and what I would say around her. Easy could tell by my face that I had a million questions going on. He told me to calm down and do what he says, which didn't answer anything, as usual. That afternoon Easy left for a little while and then I heard a car pulling up in the driveway. I ran over to the window to look out. It was him, he was getting out of the car, that brown car he drove of Brenda's. Then I saw the passenger side open, he had come back with Brenda just like he said. I started sweating and my heart started pounding in my chest. They disappeared under the awning and I heard the door at the bottom of the stairs open. I couldn't figure out where I should be, I went to the bedroom and then to the kitchen. I was headed back to the bedroom when he opened the door. As they walked in Easy introduced us. "Brenda, this is Angel, Angel, this is Brenda. I was pretty surprised because I had never seen her close up before. She was a nice looking lady she looked like she would be a social worker or bank worker or something. We said hello to each other then Easy said for us to come in the room with him so we did. He sat up in the middle of the bed and hit the bed on either sides of him with his hands. We both got on the bed me on the right and her on the left, it was abundantly clear that we were both nervous. I battled tears almost the whole time. I already had to deal with April being in the situation and now I've got to deal with Brenda. I thought he was just going to get the ring and then leave her. I was jealous that she had a real job, not that I could get one but I knew she wouldn't be working with her body like me and April did. We laid there and watched a couple of movies then Easy asked if I would cook us all something to eat. So I got up to cook. When I went back into the room to let the water and oil heat up, Easy and Brenda were under the covers. I was shocked but couldn't respond because I didn't ever want to anger Easy. I went to the other side of the bed like nothing was strange; meanwhile inside I had a whole storm going on. A million questions were swarming again. I stared straight ahead at the TV but couldn't see a thing. I was so shocked at what I was seeing. I wanted to say something but I knew the consequences wouldn't be good. I did my best not to make any facial expression so I wouldn't give away how upset I was and get myself in trouble. I was still cooking so after a minute I got back up and went back to the kitchen. I started to cry because I was hurt. I had spent a whole day working for him and made a lot of money too. More than anyone in one day that I knew of. I knew that he was having sex with everyone but I hadn't seen him actually in bed with anyone. What kind of reward was this; I didn't understand what was going on and thought about running away. But where would I go, back to Mom's house?? She was still having contact with Dan and Ron, no thank you. Plus she would call Chris on me. On the streets again? This was still better than that, plus what if I failed and he found me, what then... I cleaned my face up and finished cooking. I made the plates and carried them to the room. I could tell that they had been having sex again, I could hear them from the kitchen and you could smell it when you walked in the room. I handed them their plates and Brenda went on and on about how good my pork chops were. Easy's mom had taught me how to make fried chops on one of the weekends when we went down to Ardmore. She was happy because she felt that she had the number one status at the moment. And, I guess she did. We ate and I cleaned up the kitchen. When I came back in the bedroom Easy told me to get in the bed. I didn't know what to think but I knew not to question. I climbed in the bed on the other side of Easy and we laid and watched TV for a while, I was fighting back the tears the whole time, trying to distract myself with what was on TV, it wasn't working. Easy looked over at me with a smile and a wink. He mouthed I love you and gave me a kiss on my cheek. I used to love the way he kissed my cheek. He would not just kiss it but he would suck on it just a bit. He actually left small hickies a couple of times. We all fell asleep and when I woke up Easy was wrapped around me and she was wrapped around him. The sun had come up and we all got up and showered and stuff. There wasn't much talking between me and Brenda. Just a few verification questions. I could tell by the questions she asked that "Ris" had told her about me shortly before we met. "How long have you known Ris?" she asked. I looked over at him and he shook his head yea so I told her for almost a year. Which of course pre dated their marriage, by a lot. She looked over at Easy and he looked at her with his "don't start shit look." This was the first I had been around her outside of hiding in the pantry so I didn't know if he had already beaten her or if she had already seen him beat others, did she even know about the others? I knew nothing about what she knew and didn't know. Brenda got up after that and said that she had to go. She said she had to go check on her son and she left. I found out while she was there that she had a teenage son and he was with her mother on the east side where she lived also. This was the house Easy had taken me to before, I thought to myself. I didn't go inside but he would stop by there and would park past the house and walk back to it so no one inside would see me in the car. Easy still had her credit cards so we went shopping again after she left.

I went to work that afternoon and it was still scary but a little easier the next day. At least I knew what to expect and what was expected of me, well most of it anyway. I still felt dirty when I would get up on stage and even worse, when I had to sit with a customer. At least on stage they weren't trying to hug on you, rub your leg, or hold your hand. I know it sounds like a simple thing but there is nothing grosser than holding hands with an old guy while he looks googly eyed at your body. What I did like was talking to the other girls it kind of made me feel like I was with my sisters. What I would do right about now to have my sisters sitting around me doing make-up instead of these chicks. I missed my sisters so much. I thought about them every day. I didn't have much of anyone to talk to in my life. April and I would talk sometimes but there was always the underlying issue preventing us from connecting. Most of the conversation ever had was teaching me about working the streets, what we had done on the streets and occasionally Easy. It was about half way through the night and I was sitting in the back talking to the girl that had helped me get started yesterday. She was telling me her story and doing her make-up. I much preferred listening to her than being out there with the men in the club. I had already made half my money because I was the new girl and the young one. One of the other girls came back and said that some guy was asking the bartender about me. I walked out to the bar and asked the bartender "Was someone looking for me?" "Yea, that guy that dropped you off." "Did he say anything?" I asked. "Naw, no message, just walked out." I hope I didn't look like all the blood rushed out of me but it did. He came looking for me and I wasn't there. I was nervous about what was going to happen. I made sure that I stayed out in the club after that and even tried to hold my pee to stay out there to wait for him. Finally, around midnight he came in, I was sitting with a customer and I knew the minute I looked at him that he was pissed. He Just stood by the back door for a minute and nodded at me when I was able to look his way to make sure I seen him. After that, he walked back out. I finished up the night and made a little more than the night before. When the club closed, I got dressed quickly and asked the bartender to look outside for Easy. He said he was out there so I went to the car and got in acting like there were no issues hoping he had settled. Boy was I wrong. He started screaming at me "Where the fuck were you at? Huh Bitch, where the fuck were you at?" I froze, I could hear him still yelling at me but everything else was in slow motion. I could see the spit flying from his mouth in individual droplets spraying out in slow motion as he yelled. That intoxicating smile of his had turned to a growling, angry, roar. I heard it several times before but not directed directly at me, not like that. I knew the possibilities of what was coming and prayed that it wouldn't be bad. "I was in the back" I cried. "Why you in the back all fuckin night, ain't no fuckin money in the back, are them bitches paying you?" I was still frozen and couldn't get the answer to come out. Easy grabbed my hair quick pulling me over to him causing me to raise out of my seat. "Answer me bitch" he screamed. "No" I cried, as I attempted to shake my head as no as well. "You're there to make my mutha fuckin money not talk to these dizzy bitches!" "You keep yo ass on that mutha fuckin floor bitch!" "Let me walk in again and see you ain't working Imma fuck you up more than you're gonna get tonight" The whole ride home was a continuous stream of the same things over and over again. He would ask a question, if I answered he would thump my head hard and tell me he wasn't asking me. But if I didn't answer, he would grab me by my hair again. When he grabbed my hair I would be even more scared. We made it to the apartment and he cursed me all the way in the apartment leading me up the stairs by my hair and kept going after the door shut. When we got inside I put my things down in the closet, I went to the bathroom and was going to take a shower to get ready for bed and wish this never happened. I was leaning in to turn the water on when Easy came in the bathroom. "What tha fuck do you think you're doing?" he said in a crappy tone. "Shower and bed" I responded in a low nervous tone. "Pick up your shit" he said. I picked up the clothes I had taken off. He reached and grabbed me again and marched me into the kitchen by my hair screaming and cussing at me. "You need a mutha fuckin lesson, dizzy bitch. I should stomp yo ass right here" he said. He threw the table away from the pantry in the wall, opened the door and literally threw me in. He shut the door and I could hear him pushing the table and other things around. He knew I pushed the table away when he would leave me there and he didn't want me to get out so he made a way to lock me in the pantry. This was the first time that I was scared to be in the pantry. It wasn't ever fun to be in the pantry but I was hiding before. Now I was trapped. I cried until I ran out of tears. I was naked and realized that I had dropped most of my clothes. I had my underwear a sock and a shoe. I still had some of my stuff in there but I hadn't restocked since I had been back so I had no food or water. I had a blanket, pillow and the Bible. What happened to The Outsiders you ask? Easy seen my book one day, he took it and gave me the bible. He said that was the only book I needed to read so I did. I remembered some of the big stories and some verses from when I was a little girl going to church but not much more. That night there was no light at the time so I laid on the pantry floor and fell asleep. I woke up to the apartment door closing and him leaving. It was complete darkness so I knew it was still dark outside but I had no clue what time it was. I laid there for a while knowing he would be back eventually and fell back asleep.

When I woke up there was broken light coming through the top of the slit of the door so it was morning finally. I didn't hear any noise in the apartment but I still banged on the door hoping that he would come and let me out but he didn't come. I had to pee pretty bad so I started pushing on the door but it didn't budge...not even a little bit. I started thinking about the things in the kitchen and what he could put there that wouldn't move. I thought I heard him put the table back but maybe not. He must have moved the fridge or something big. I laid back down and wondered when he would be back. I eventually I fell back asleep when I woke up it was still light so I had no idea what time it was. I sat back against the wall and my head started pounding. It was so tender from the night before and I had lumps all over my head. I couldn't do anything but just stay still that was the only method I had for controlling the pain. So I laid there and thought about him screaming at me and pulling my hair. I started crying again thinking about the situation I was in, the situation I came from and what my future looked like. The same questions were swarming in my head. Why can't I be one of those girls on TV? Or even one of those girls I see at the store with their mom looking so happy. I thought about leaving when he let me out but where would I go? I let the questions go on in my head for a while and then heard the door at the bottom of the stairs open and my heart started racing. I knew within two stairs that it wasn't him it was the neighbor. I slumped back down and sat there. I still had to pee pretty bad the feeling had been going and coming now it was mostly coming. I fell back asleep again and when I woke up this time, I had peed on myself in my sleep. I was so upset. I started crying again and got mad. I started kicking at the door and yelling for someone to let me out. No one came. The light was barely visible so I knew we were coming up on night again. I Just sat there thinking again about everything that was going on and what my options were and mostly weren't. In the end, I talked myself right back to Easy. Even with what was done, it could have been worse and I clung to that part that kept him from beating me. So I just sat there. Go to sleep, wake up, read, and go to sleep, wake up, read, and go to sleep. Finally light again, and this also meant I had been there more than a day. I yelled for him and of course, he didn't come, he wasn't there. Then I started thinking about how long he might leave me there. What if I die in there? He knows I don't have food or water. Is he trying to kill me? I started crying but there were no tears. I tried to push and kick the door but I was so weak it didn't mean anything. I just laid there, I read the bible for a while then I started thinking about being a little girl in Marvell. I was a real little girl then…with a real family. We played outside, we went to church, and we had birthday parties with friends over. I missed all of the things about being a little girl. I fell back asleep and woke to the door down stairs opening again. It was him coming up the stairs. I got so nervous I almost threw up. He came in the door and came straight to the kitchen. "Angel?" he called. "Yes" I called back. "You wanna sit in the back with them bitches again?" "No" I said quickly. I heard him start moving things around and then he opened the door. I guess I had gotten used to the smell of the pee but it hit him hard when he opened the door. He leaned back real quickly like it was attacking him. "Shit, you stank! Get this shit cleaned up and go get in the shower" he said. I picked up everything and took it with me to the bathroom and got in the shower. The first thing I did was drink the water coming from the shower. I washed myself but I was so weak, it felt like I was sick with the flu but I wasn't. I finished my shower, put on clothes and took the dirty stuff to the laundry in the back of the apartment. Easy followed me to do the laundry because he knew what he had put in my head keeping me in there like that. We both knew I had nowhere to go, but still, the possibility existed. We went back up to the apartment and I asked if I could have something to eat. He motioned toward the kitchen and I went quickly to the fridge. I ate 4 pieces of sliced cheese and opened the pickle slices and was dipping in there between cheese bites. There was frozen meat, stuff you had to cook and condiments in there at that time. After I ate some, I went and sat beside the bed where he was. I was afraid to get on the bed, I don't know why but I was, so I didn't. After a while, he told me to get up on the bed. He pulled me over to him. He started rubbing on my skin and holding me close to him. "I do hate this Angel, I don't like being mean to you, I love you, but you've got to listen and do what I say. We've got things to do and we need money. I need you to stay focused. I don't like to see you cry. I love seeing that smile on your face" as he started kissing my cheek. "I don't ever want to have to put my hands on you Angel, please don't put me in that position." That was the last thing he said before he went to sleep. I laid there for a while wishing I could sleep but things were swirling in my head. I didn't want to be here anymore but I didn't have anywhere else to go either. I tried to change the subject in my head and distract myself. I eventually fell asleep and the next morning life went on as usual. Life took no time to stop for me so I had to keep moving too.

I had been working at Knights n' Pawns for a little while and I had gotten much better about following the rules. I didn't want to experience anything like before so I made sure I went to work "to work" and kept the social side to a minimum. I became the quiet girl and so that pretty much left my daily conversations to tricks and johns who were paying to have that conversation with me. Sometimes it was a regular boring conversation and sometimes it was gross. Questions and comments that would definitely not be ok if these men were in the line with me at the grocery store. I tried to listen to the music instead of them. I would pay attention to their facial expressions to know when to shake my head or make a comment. I tried to find any way to give me a few seconds in the day were I could pretend I wasn't doing what I was doing.

One evening we were in the middle of a regular night and then all the sudden the club filled up with police officers. Customers tried to leave but they turned off the music and on the lights and told everyone to have a seat. The police collected the ID's of all the customers and employees, and me. They checked each one for warrants and released the ones who didn't have warrants and arrested the one's that did. All of us girls were sitting to the side. They weren't saying anything to us at first. After they cleared out the customers one of them said loudly "Can I have your attention please" All the girls and other staff looked his direction. "The purpose of the raid is because the city had passed an ordinance that requires you to wear latex, pasties, or some kind of covering over your areola when you are in the club with your top removed. If you do not comply with this ordinance you will be arrested and taken down town. They brought the product with them and watched as we each placed it on. It was humiliating. They had us all lined up half-naked and I'm sure they were getting off on watching us paint the latex on our nipples. They were checking to make sure we were putting enough so they were looking close at our breast. I wanted to kick them, freaking perverts! I was already in a room full of perverts but at least they didn't pretend to be something they aren't. I hated the police and every contact I had with them made me hate them more. They were never there when I needed them but they were certainly there to abuse me along with everyone else. I was starting to get scared that they would figure out that the bar card wasn't me somehow. One of the officers was calling off names on ID's for us girls to collect our ID. When he called me up for mine, he looked at the picture and then looked at me, then looked at the picture and looked back at me and my whole 14 years of wisdom. "You look awful young little lady, what is your birthday" I rattled my big sisters birthday off for him real quick. He looked at my ID again and then handed it to me. What is your stage name "Angel" I said. He walked away and I heard him talking to another cop about my stage name Angel and another Angel they had been looking for from the streets. The other officer looked over at me and said "the one we want is 14, not 18" and he started walking away. I was pretty sure my heart had stopped beating in those first few seconds. They had the right Angel and didn't know it. I wasn't going to tell them either. They were trying to take me to prison. I was so frightened of going to prison. I had imagined many times that I would be raped and beaten in there. I didn't see the police as protectors, I saw them as abusers. They finally left and the club was empty. The manager of the club had a meeting with all of us and we went over the rules and asked him some questions. He said he would do his best to find answers for us but to have our nipples covered tomorrow. He closed the club for the rest of the night because we were all pretty shaken up. I called Easy but he didn't answer. I called April's house, he was there so I asked him to come and pick me up. I knew he was going to her house when I was at work. Well, I didn't actually know but I figured as much. I was upset thinking about what I was going through each day and he was chillin with her or Brenda like I wasn't doing nothing. I tried to calm myself down before he got there. Attitude was not something he dealt with very well. When he got there, I told him about what happened and he wasn't happy. He was glad that I kept my cool in the situation though. The mall was still open so we went and bought some clothes. This was one of the few things that I did want to continue. We weren't able to buy new clothes when I was growing up. Now I was making enough money to buy new things, nothing second hand anymore. No hand me down clothes and all the fast food I wanted. Well, as long as Easy wanted it too. Still I felt like a queen during those moments. We went through the Church's drive through and got some chicken. When we got home I modeled the new clothes for him. It was a great ending to a horrible day. Easy had a way of making things better when I was having a hard day, even if the hard day was because of him.

Before work the next day, we went to the adult store on 10th street. I got some pasties and the latex they said we had to have. They had stripper outfits there too so Easy had me model some. Every time I came out of the dressing room he was grinning ear to ear with that beautiful smile of his. He bought the one's he liked the most. When I got to work several of the other girls had gotten pasties also. Thankfully, we had this one girl who was an older woman and she had done burlesque. She knew how to work the pasties so we had class in the dressing room. We were all standing there in our bottoms with boobs all out. I was looking around at everyone trying not to be embarrassed. I had been around 4 sisters growing up so I was used to being in the room with girls with their tops off, but not like this. Not in a boob class. She had us start painting the latex on our nipples. She said to do two layers. In order to get them to stay on you had to attach them at just the right drying point in the latex and it had to be thick enough too. And not all pasties were made to actually wear with action. Once we finally got our pasties on it was practice time. All you had to do was find the rhythm in the bounce of your breast and from there it was just a little bitty bounce. However finding that bounce was much easier said than done. We had girls flinging pasties all over the place. It took some practicing to get it but most of us got it. There were a few who couldn't get the rhythm to make them go right. It was funny watching them try to get it. The DJ started the music, which signaled for us that the doors were open so we made our way out of the dressing room. I was able to have some fun with the other girls and have a feeling that I knew someone instead of feeling alone. But for the most part the day went much the same as the last. Me being frightened every time I had to get up on the stage. Feeling like I was being molested over and over again every time I had a customer come up to the stage or buy me a drink for some time with me. I worked every day and most days I made $500 or more, one time it was almost $700 in one night. I was amazed at how much money I was able to make without having sex with anyone. I was making more money in one night than my mom was getting in a whole month for her welfare check. After about 10 days of that Easy put a limit on the night like he would with us on the street. I had to make around $500 or there would be consequences. Well one night I didn't make enough. I was so worried. I kept trying to talk myself out of it, saying he would be happy that I had still made so much money and that he would probably give me a warning or tell me to make it up the next day. But I was wrong about all of that. On the way home he didn't say a word. I tried to act normal, like there was nothing wrong. I watched the street lights flash by and avoided looking his way because I didn't want to see his mad face. My body was already tense from the moment I got in the car. I was starting to get the rocks in my throat and stomach. I waited for him to start yelling and grabbing me by the hair but he didn't, the anger was clearly there though. We pulled up to the apartment and I let him open his door before I opened mine. I didn't want to do anything before he did and make any assumptions. I followed him over to the doorway to upstairs and wished that I could just stand there all night. I didn't want to go inside because I didn't want to face the consequences that I knew were waiting for me. I was busy all night, I don't know what else I could have done to make more money. I started to wonder about doing tricks in the club to make more money. We got to the top of the stairs and Easy unlocked the door and promptly marched me right over to the pantry and locked me in. That's where I spent the night any time I didn't make $500. Of course, if he needed me for something like my duties, he would let me out for that. So if I knew I wasn't going to hit the 500 I would try to borrow from another girl to hit it. If I couldn't make the quota I would eat in the dressing room right before leaving because when he was mad and putting me in the pantry, giving me something for dinner was usually last on the list. I had confided in one of the girls about my punishment so she would help me sneak food to the back. We were not supposed to take food to the back but I was afraid he would walk in while I was eating at the bar. I didn't have permission to spend any of the money I was making. I worked every day for several weeks and finally he gave me a day off. When we woke that morning we washed up and took the car to the carwash to wash it also. We already had our bags so we hopped on the highway and headed to Ardmore to see his mother again. The drive down there was nice. Easy had a great music collection. We had almost everything to listen to, including each other. We pulled up in Ardmore in the afternoon. Miss Patty was even more accepting of me this time. After being back and forth a couple of times we were getting used to each other. She hugged me and kissed me like she honestly missed me. Like I was her child. We didn't say a whole lot to each other that morning. Mainly me answering the few questions she asked. I was still shy and didn't know what to say, sure didn't want to say the wrong thing so I waited for others to start the conversation. I thought it went well, I was starting to feel like she liked me. We rode around town and visited a few of the same family we had visited the first time we came here. It was starting to feel more like I was a part of the family. They all remembered me and they all welcomed me. I was still stuck to his side and let him do all the talking. After a while we went to the Piggly Wiggly and got some chicken for dinner. Miss Patty cooked it up and I helped her as much as I could. I watched carefully while she cooked. "The small things make the difference in a good meal" she said. The grease should bubble when a tiny bit of flour falls in, that's when you know it's ready for the meat. We ate well that night. I didn't eat much the first time but this time, I stuffed myself it was so good. We sat around the table sharing stories. Miss Patty was talking about her job, she worked at the entry gate of something. Channell had made up with Lewis and all was well there. It got late and Miss Patty went to bed. We slept in the guest bedroom again and I was just as afraid as the first time. The next day we did pretty much the same thing and rode out a little before the sun was about to go down. Easy was always so romantic on the rides back and forth to Ardmore. We would talk about our lives and how great things will be in the future. He would sing with the music to me when there was a love song on. I would get so giddy when he would sing to me. He always held my hand when we would ride and would occasionally pull it up to his lips for a soft kiss. The way he made me feel when we were together made all the other complaints disappear. I kept the hope that it was all temporary like Easy would say. We were going to make and save a ton of money and then move away to somewhere. We got home late in the night and we went to bed all wrapped up together.

~Chapter 10~

Cherries Anyone?

I got ready for work and Easy dropped me off at the club. I went in and drug my bag to the back. I sat down to do my makeup and cover my real face, the real me. They weren't interested in the real me. They wanted the fantasy, I wanted my reality to be a fantasy too but it wasn't. I caked on the makeup to bring my 14yr old face closer to an 18yr old face. Some of the girls would be dressed early, go to the bar and have a drink or two before we got started. I wanted to have a drink but Easy already said "No drugs or Alcohol." I wanted something to numb me from the guilt and shame I was feeling. I wanted something to make it a little easier to live with what was going on. I had seen Steve giving drinks to several of the other girls who were not quite 21 yet. I still remember the numbness I felt from the drugs I took with TT. I remember how it would make everything disappear and the escape door would open. Problem was my escape door would close when the drugs wore off. I started thinking about what the consequences would be and quickly decided to stick with the sprite with cherry syrup. It was my turn on stage for the beginning of the lineup and still my stomach would be in knots when I would head that away. I had been on that stage more the 50 times and it still gave me the same feelings as it did the first day. I wanted to erase what was going on and go back to the small town in Arkansas that I was supposed to be in right now, where I was born and was going to live until I moved on to college. I wasn't even supposed to be here. I got to the back and turned the corner to go up the stairs. I stopped behind the wall to wait for the music to start. I could hear my heart beating through my chest and I started sweating. It was the same routine over and over but it never got better. I took a few deep breaths, pulled myself together and danced my way onto the stage. I had developed a system, In order to make it through you had to develop ways of making the worst parts a little better. I figured out that there were a couple of places on stage where the light shined in a way that you were blinded from seeing who was beyond the row. So I would alternate between the two so I could avoid seeing most of them stare at me. The only thing I couldn't avoid was pervert row. Bet you're wondering what pervert row is. In strip clubs there is a bar around the stage where guys sit for a front row view. To them it was the best place in the bar, to me it was the worst. When the guys on pervert row wanted you to dance for them they would put a bill on the stage, usually a dollar but here and there it would be more. I would try to wait until there were several bills on the stage so that I wouldn't have to dance in front of them for as long because the others would be waiting. As soon as I would find ways to try to relax a bit there would always be something to shake up the atmosphere. After the raid the cops started coming in every few days. They didn't shut it down or anything but they would pull random girls to the side and check the latex and their ID. I made sure I had my ID with me at all times. The only girl they had arrested so far was one who didn't have her bar card. Easy decided that the Knights n' Pawns club was too hot now and he was worried that the vice police had started looking for me to be there. After working at Knights n' Pawns for a while, I was getting more used to the fact that I was a stripper and not a 14yr old. I did my best just to get through those days. So when we went down 10th street to another club, Pegs Star Bar, it was a little easier to deal with. That club was huge; it looked like it had been somewhere that pageants took place or something. It had a full stage raised up with curtains like at school but with a long runway that came out into the middle of the bar. There were bar seats around the runway, rows of tables and chairs behind that and some booths on two of the walls behind that. There was a DJ booth in the middle of the front of the building where you entered and pool tables over to the side. The bar ran along the same wall as the pool tables. The owner, Steve was a tall white guy with a regular build and curly light brown hair. He actually lived there and slept on a mattress on the stage at the club with his wife/dancer Trisha and their "slave girl" Trisha called her. I don't remember her name because we didn't get to see her much and when we did, she didn't talk much. She was a black female; she looked like she was not native to Oklahoma. She had hard features but it was hard to catch a look at her. She always kept her head down and she followed behind Steve Just the same as I did Easy. Steve was that kind of guy who had the club Just so that he could have access to lots of naked women. He was always trying to get into someone's pants. Trisha, his wife, knew it but still acted like she was his one and only. She had the bighead over being the boss so she put off this billy badass attitude but she was cool once she liked you. If she didn't, you didn't work here. I was always nice to her and laughed at her stories. I couldn't have her dislike me. Losing my job was the last thing I needed to do. I had built up a bag of stripper outfits so I didn't look like a newbie anymore. When you look young and inexperienced, you get a lot more questions. However, bigger club meant bigger money so I had to stay on my toes and do the best I could to make as much money as possible and keep my fear and identity a secret at the same time.

There were quite a few characters at this club. The DJ was a cool guy, his name is Smooth. He looked like a Smooth too. He was around 6ft and was thick, not fat, and stocky. He had black shaggy hair and facial hair to match. He looked a little like Wolf man Jack to me, that old radio DJ from the 70's, sounded a little like him too. He had codes he would use to let us know when the vice were coming in the building or when the police were coming in. "There's a cabaret of stars tonight" he would say. We knew then not to sit close to the customer and not to ask or let them ask for any drinks so we wouldn't be busted by vice. They would march in and look around. I would get nervous but had to keep it hidden so I wouldn't give myself away. They never asked too many questions or anything. I was only asked for my bar card one time and he Just glanced that it was a card and gave it back. I always thought they were trying to catch a look while at work. I had been there for about two weeks and there was finally another new girl. I was able to get that label off of me. Being the new girl wasn't all that great. She was a small girl like me but in her mid-20's with two kids. She had a narrow face with a nose that was slightly too big and orangey red wirery long hair and was quite the loud mouth. Well, she came with a surprise. Her stage name was Angel too, and since she had been there before me and had seniority, I had to change my name. And this all happened after Easy had already dropped me off at the club. I had no way to reach him. There wasn't enough time passed for him to be home and had no clue what to call myself. I couldn't use Amanda, the name on my ID. "Coomming to the SSTTAAge Aaaaamanddaa. No! I don't think so. I was standing there at the bar with Steve after he told me and he was making me a drink. "Here you go Cherry girl." That's what he called me because I always got lots of cherries in my sprite or anything else I drank. I even started bringing my own cherries when Steve tried to limit me. Cherry girl? I thought to myself. Hmmm, Cherry. Cherry it is. So from then on at work, I was Cherry instead of Angel, or Amanda, or Sarah. These names were starting to pile up. Easy came back to the club later that evening and was not happy at all about the name change thing. He went and talked to Steve about it but came back with no result and was almost bared from the club so we moved on from that. Another regular girl at the club was Barb the "Bombshell from Allen County" was how Smooth would introduce her. She was an older woman in her late 20's early 30's with dark shoulder length hair and the girl next-door look. She was like a mom at the club. She knew I wasn't very old; she used to mess with me all the time about it. "I don't care what your Cracker Jack bar card says" she used to say but she didn't push it too much. Back then there was a Jukebox that we played our music from until the DJ got there. We had to go around to the customers and get money for the Jukebox to play our music. It was just another way to make money for the club. We all hated collecting for the music. I mean, who do you, think emptied that Jukebox. If you didn't get the $3 for the three songs. Then Steve would play some old country song or some unintelligible super hard rock song. So if you didn't collect the three then you threw in the rest yourself. We had this one old man that came into the club every Tuesday afternoon shortly after we opened at 2. He looked like he was at least 85 years old and I hated going to ask him for music money. But we had to ask everyone and Steve would be watching. When we would go over to the old man to ask for $1 for the music, he would offer us a stick of juicy fruit or big red gum instead. He kept it on the table, lined up and ready for us. He always sat in the far back corner in the club and one afternoon I found out why. I walked over to do the routine and get my gum and as I got closer, it looked like he was wearing shorts because I could see his knees but then I quickly noticed that his pants were around his ankles, this was about the time I reached his table. I was totally grossed out! I tried not to totally run away but I was certainly moving fast. I was red-faced and the girls at the bar were all laughing at me. They thought it was hilarious, I thought it was horrible. I didn't matter how many times I had seen an old penis before, it was still horribly nasty to me. But still yet, he was there, every Tuesday. Why not on other days? I wondered that too.

On the weekend at Pegs Star Bar you could make a lot of money and Easy would come and sit at the bar and watch me work to make sure that I was "maximizing the money", he would say. However his rules didn't allow for maximization of anything except control of me. Just like on the streets when I got into the club I had some of the same rules. I couldn't sit with any black men and if they come up to tip me I wasn't supposed to acknowledge them much and the same went for young white men. Not that the club was just full of them but still. I had this same scenario play out a few times in the first few weeks at Pegs Star Bar. One day I get off stage and the other girls are already sitting with all the old men in the club and I've got these guy's I'm not allowed to sit with staring at me. Then I've got Easy staring at me wanting me to make a move. I have no clue what to, so I froze and start tearing up. All I could do was run to the bathroom to cry. The first time, Easy waited for me and when I came out he offered to take me home. I got my things together and we went to the car. "You've got to make a decision Angel, you can't freeze up and I can't make all of them for you." "I know but I'm afraid of making the wrong decision and making you mad at me." "Don't worry about that, if you think about the money and nothing else, you'll make the right decision. You know how to follow the money so follow the money Angel." Easy had talked many times about how to spot the money. When we would be out and about he would point things out and give the run down on it. Or at the mall he would show me the different things to look for. When I was on the streets, it was the car, the shirt and the hair cut. You didn't get that much up front information. In the strip club you could see the shoes, pants, walk everything. He said that the number one give away is shoes. Even the low key rich guy will have on good shoes. Watches were something to watch also, not necessarily the brand but if it was scratched up. If he works with his hands even if he dresses up the watch and tough knuckles will give it away. These were a few of the things he taught me to look for with men to "follow the money". After the pep talk I went back in the club and finished out the night. Easy didn't stay and I was glad, he makes me extra nervous on top of being nervous when he's there. Unfortunately that wasn't the last time froze up in fear and ran to the back. The second time, he just got upset and left. I stayed in the back for a while and Trisha was watching to see if he came back. I gathered myself and went back to work. Easy was mad at me when he picked me up. He kept the music turned up and didn't talk to me. I could feel the tension the whole ride home. To the pantry I went. The third time was a little different, me and another girl was playing pool at one of the tables. There were two guys at the table next to us and we started talking. They were offering money for us to hike our leg up over the pocket where they were going to shoot the ball. This gave them a direct view to between our legs. They would take forever to shoot the ball of course. I was flirting with him to make him give me more money and had my leg hiked up at the corner. I was telling the guy to hurry up when I saw him. It was Easy, he had come in at some point and was standing against the wall watching me. When my eyes caught his it was obvious he was pissed. I stood there for a minute frozen and then ran off to the back without even getting paid. I was just beginning to cry but I was already clearing myself up at the same time. I was starting to get better at holding it in. I had leaned down over my bag to wipe my face and felt a rush of air behind me as hands grabbed my hair. It was Easy, he had followed me to the dressing room and had grabbed me by the hair to drag me out of the club. I was instantly mortified, everyone was staring at us. He was screaming "Stupid bitch, there ain't no money in the mutha fuckin dressing room" I was not able to keep up with his pace and kept losing my balance. I fell once and he just kept going dragging me behind him. The dressing room was way in the back, it was a long way to the front door. I just started working here, if they didn't know before that I was abused, they knew now. Time seemed to go in slow motion, I kept my head down, and I didn't want to see them look at me. I climbed back on my feet as he continued marching me out of the club screaming at me. This whole time the other dancers, Steve and them, the customers, no one did anything. No one said nothing, did nothing, oh wait, they did do something, they stared, they just stared. Easy threw me in the car and I went home for more abuse and another night in the pantry.

The next day Easy opened the door to the pantry. "Come on." I started climbing out of the pantry and went right to the bathroom. "You know it hurts my feelings to have to discipline you Angel." He was standing in the door of the bathroom. "Can

I take a shower please?" "In a minute, come out here and let me talk to you. If I ever see your ass talkin like that with a young ass cracker I'm going to have to fuck you up." "I was trying to make money, it was for money!" I exclaimed. "Do it again, do it, see what happens." "There were only a few customers and they all had girls sitting with them. I was trying to make more money." "I don't give a damn if there is another girl sitting there. Start a conversation, ask about his shoes or his tie. It makes you sound intelligent like you know what is in his world. He'll choose you over the other girl, promise Angel." However, there was one big problem in this setup. It was totally against the rules to go and sit at a table that another girl is already at unless they invite you. But I couldn't say anything about that to Easy because he had already decided how it should be and he would have seen that as disrespectful and consequences would follow. I had no clue what I was going to do and I was a little preoccupied by my headache at the time. Sometimes after he would pull my hair so much I would have a lot of lumps in my scalp and I would get a bad headache. I took my shower and got ready for work. When I got there Tracey was acting all concerned and stuff but I knew she was just acting. Some of the other girls asked if I was alright and of course I said I was ok but I wasn't. I was thoroughly embarrassed and mortified over what they witnessed. No one offered to help get me out though. So back to the routine again. I got on stage for my three songs. Everyone kept saying "Eventually you'll get used to it" I hated it every time. At Knights n' Pawns the stage was low so the men were just below shoulder height, at Pegs Star Bar the stage is high so it puts them right about the middle. They would stare at you and look up at you and smile. I would do my best to look right past them. Looking at them still made me want to cry, get sick to my stomach, run off the stage or all of the above. It didn't matter who it was there were all ages, races, sizes, whatever, all the same, they all acted pretty much the same. And the girls were all the same too. There was so much drama between the girls. I tried to stay out of it, mostly because I had my own issues. But when they weren't acting consequences had to happen. There was a girl in the club who would always flirt with Easy when he came in. I hated seeing them talk. She had just left his side as she seen me coming and mouthed to me "He's my boyfriend" as she walked by me. I was furious. I couldn't say anything to Easy, I would end up in trouble. I had to think of a way to get her back and show her that I was his woman and no one else would be. When we danced the last dance we did it nude and often time's girls would step behind the curtain and take off their bottoms for the last dance. She was one of the one's who left her bottoms back stage. When she was out doing her last dance I put a whole tube of super glue in her bottoms right before her song ended. They were usually moist anyway from dancing so I guess she didn't notice the wetness of the glue when she put them on. It was a little while later that we all heard the scream from the back. She was in the dressing room trying to get her bottoms off but they were glued to her. The manager went back and there was nothing he could do. I never even went back to see. Hearing her scream was enough for me. It didn't matter that she didn't know who did that to her, I did. She left with one of the other girls to go to the emergency room. Everyone was talking about it after she left and wondering who did it. Several of them asked me but I knew not to tell them anything. There was no trust with anyone in the clubs. I didn't get along with too many of the girls. The owner Steve was a customer in the club as well. He loved the women. I was sitting at the bar talking to him and he offered me money to go to the kitchen with him. I was a trained money making machine so of course I said yes. We went back to the kitchen area. He was trying to show his affection for me, telling me he wanted me to be his lady. I just stared at the wall. I didn't have any feelings about it that I could express. Throwing up would have been one of them but I couldn't do that. A couple of days later when I got to the club Trisha was marching around the club cussing about someone trying to steal her man. I asked her what was going on. She said that their slave girl had seen Steve making out and having sex with one of the girls in the kitchen. She said it was one of the short white girls with long hair. Well that was several of us and I was the first one of us in the building. She said that she thought Tiffany did it and I agreed with her. I knew their slave girl was talking about me. We didn't have sex but it would have looked like we were making out. I agreed with her that Tiffany was probably the one. When Tiffany came in we ran and got Trisha. She ran to the dressing room and immediately attacked Tiffany. She beat the living day lights out of her. We all broke up the fight and Tiffany left the club. We didn't see her at that club anymore. I had some remorse over it because I didn't know what happened to her. I didn't have enough remorse to tell Trisha it was me. But I wasn't there to make relationships, I was there to make money. I wasn't there for the girls, I was there for the customers.

There were some who would come in on a regular basis. Some that were there enough that I started to feel like they were friends rather than customers. I was sitting with an old farmer who had come in several times before. Kind of what you're thinking but not exactly. He was a farmer with farm hands and help in the house. He had a large farm in the area and had plenty of money to spend. He didn't wear overalls or suspenders he wore new wranglers, fancy western shirts and a nice cowboy hat and boots of course. He looked like an old country singer to me. He would stay for hours and I was able to make a lot of money when he was there. It was much better than having to hop from man to man. He would buy me drinks of course and when it was my turn on stage he would tip me with $20's and $50's. It was still uncomfortable when he would stare at my body. When I sat with him I would try to keep my arms and legs crossed to cover as much as possible without looking obvious. He wasn't real pushy like some of the others. Sometimes when men would spend a lot of money on you they try to force you to do other things too so I was just waiting for it. He would talk forever, telling story after story. We would talk about the farm and the things going on with the animals and the crew. Occasionally he would talk about the government and how they were messing with the farms and how stores are getting bigger and making it harder for farmers because they want lower prices we talked about his family and all kinds of things. He would always ask questions about me but I never gave him much info or if I did it was never the whole truth. He made the comment many times that he was very aware that I was not the age I said I was. He would tell me that it was one of the reasons he would drive all the way in to see me. Sometimes when he would see me instead of saying hello he would say "how old are you today?" My answer remained the same, "Old enough!" He saw Easy several times in the club. He would make jokes about black people here and there. It wasn't hard to figure out that he was racist, so were most of the men in the clubs. I had customers stop spending money on me after they seen me with Easy. It didn't matter to me, I was better off without their tainted money. Plus there were 5 new customers for every one that disappeared. One of my other customers worked at or frequented the state capitol area. He would talk about politics mostly. At first I had no clue what he was talking about. He used names I didn't know, words I didn't know. He would ask me if I saw certain things in the news. I would try to go along with his stories but it wasn't easy. He would come in every week or so, I got to the point to where I would start looking for him to come to find out what was going on. I started to have a bit of a clue but more on a soap opera level, not an "I know what you are talking about" level. He would tell me who hated who and what kind of marriages they had, it was kind of exciting. I had this one customer that I thought was hilarious he was a mechanic and he would spend most of the time joking about what everyone else had on and who they might look like. He would tell me about crazy customers he had and of course have me cracking up laughing the whole time. It wasn't uncomfortable with him until it was time for him to leave. He would always try to get a kiss and hug good buy. The first time thought I had to and he had already paid me a good amount of money while he was there. I couldn't go through with it, I couldn't kiss him. When he leaned in for my lips I quickly leaned and turned past him to give him the cheek. He still tried every time though.

It was amazing what some of the guys would try to tell you and try to do to you. I had customers who had asked about everything. This guy was a mechanic I learned while I was sitting with him. He had come in a couple of times hinting that he wanted to "buy some time with me". I tried to ignore those kind of questions. Well this one day he had been sitting with me for a while. I could tell there was something bothering him. I asked if he was ok and he said "Cherry, how much is it going to cost me to get you under covers?" I was a little shocked, he just laid it all out right there. If you were sitting in any of the tables circling ours, you would have heard him. Plus, I learned long ago not to answer that one, you never know if it's vice. I spit out the first thing that hit my head. "I don't like covers mister, they make me itch" It was my lame attempt at distracting him with a joke. He laughed and then looked at me real serious "No Cherry, I'll give you anything you want?" "You talk to my boyfriend and if he says yes, then ok." Hoping he wouldn't want to risk talking to him. "Where's your boyfriend, I'll ask anybody" "He's not here right now but he will be here later on, I'll let you know." He was excited and we carried on with the conversation. Honestly I was hoping that Easy didn't show the rest of the night. He came in most nights but not every night. I was still stuck at the table with him. I was doing my best not to heave on the table we were sitting at. It wasn't more than an hour that Easy came in. He always played a game of pool when he came in so he could seem like a regular customer. He wasn't so regular with all his gold, nice clothes, snake skin boots with tips and taps. I pointed Easy out to my customer and he went over to play pool. It was my turn to dance so I could see them talking and laughing it up the whole time. They were thinking about business, I was thinking about running out the door. I was distracted the whole dance. After I got off stage I tried to take as long as I could to come out from the back. When I did Easy motioned for me to come over. He said that he and the guy had talked and that I was going to go to his house after the club closed. My stomach dropped to the floor, I didn't want to do this again, wasn't I making enough money to avoid this? I started thinking about the savings and how we were trying to build for our dreams. I went back to the floor trying not to think about anything. Trying to just listen to the words of the music and avoid my own mind. There wasn't that much of the night left so I did the routine until it was time to go. I went to the back and again I took as long as I could to come out. I picked up my bag then the knots started coming. As I walked out to the car I felt more and more sick. If I was smart I would have said no and never said anything, I thought to myself. Somehow I thought he would know so I helped promote my own abuse. I had gotten to the point that I would help line up the abuse. I started getting mad at myself for what I was doing. As much as I didn't want it to happen I also didn't want to miss opportunities to make more money. The more money I made the happier he was and keeping him happy was crucial to my wellbeing. When I got in the car Easy showed me several hundred dollar bills in his hand with a big smile on his face. "My Angel is makin it big time, ain't ya baby" He was happy and I was pretending to be happy. We pulled out behind him and tailed him down the street. After we followed him for a minute the realization that Easy had the money in his hand came upon him. "We ain't doing this." as he was saying that he slowed so that the guy made it through the light and we didn't. I could see that the guy had slowed down for us but he was still going. Right after the light turned green Easy jetted over in the turning lane and started going down McArthur to the highway. Now I was starting to get happy, I wasn't going to have to do this after all. When we got to Reno he turned through the backs of the restaurants and took the back way to the service road of the highway. I was still getting nervous that the guy had turned, followed and caught up with us. Easy was enjoying out smarting the guy, but then again, most everything Easy did was smarter than other guys. We got on the highway and headed to our side of town. We stopped on the way home and got some chicken. Easy kept cutting up about the guy and mimicking in a country voice what he must have been doing in his car. "Where are they, where are they, I can't find em and they gots my money." We both laughed. "What if he shows up tomorrow at the club?" "I wish he would show up, I'll be there Angel, you don't have anything to worry about."

That next morning we got up and went to the flea Market. Chris was in the mood for some more gold and I was hoping

I would get some too. He was trying on different things when he came across a nice lion ring with rubies in the eyes and a diamond in his mouth. That was it. That was the one he needed to have. After he was content, he started picking out things for me to try on. I found a cross that was similar to the one Easy had gotten and tried it out. It was on one of the new fancy design kind of gold chains. Easy let me have the necklace and a gold bangle bracelet. After a great visit to the Market we got something to eat. It was almost time for me to be at the club so we headed back to the west side. Easy was showing me off to everyone including himself as we walked in the club. I felt like a million bucks and the luckiest girl in the world. Now I have three gold chains, one ring, and a bracelet. Easy dropped me off and said he would be back, he was just running to the store. As I had feared, but couldn't mention since I can't question his plans, the guy comes back into the club and walked right up to me. I saw him coming, unfortunately I was the only one. "Where the hell is my money? What happened to y'all?" he yelled in my face. "What do you mean? What happened to you?" I said. "When you ran that light and left us at the inner section we couldn't find you after that. Why didn't you pull over?" I started blaming him so he would get off focus that I was the one to blame. I had intentionally started raising my voice because I wanted Steve to come, Easy wasn't in the building yet. Steve came over and asked what the problem was and I yelled at the guy, "Go ahead tell him, tell him what you are upset about, and tell him your crazy story. Steve, I don't even know this guy!" I gave a bit of a smile. I knew and he did too that he didn't want to tell anyone that he was trying to buy prostitutes out of the strip club. "Nothing" that's all he said as he walked back out of the club. I stayed where Steve was, I didn't want to get caught alone again. A few minutes later Easy came in and sat at the bar. Steve and I both told him about the guy being crappy with me and me having to yell at him. No sooner than we finish telling him, here comes the guy again. He must have waited until he seen Easy's car pull in. He was talking all loud trying to bring attention to his self, I think he was already drunk. I was working my way to the back of the club because I didn't know what else to do and I sure didn't want to be near a fight. So the guy lunges at Easy with both arms flailing in an attempt to attack. As the guy is lunging in Easy clocks him with a straight fist to the face knocking him to the floor. He landed on top of the guy and then starts pounding on him. I was so freaked out and scared that it seemed like everything started moving in slow motion, my heart beat completely stopped. I ran back toward them to try to stop it, like I could really do something. Easy was so powerful. I was afraid of him doing damage and us having to deal with the police. Steve and Smooth both ran over to get Easy off of the guy. As they were picking the guy up to carry him out Steve was telling him that he couldn't come into the club anymore. "I'm going to call the cops on his ass for assault!" he yelled. "And I'm going to call the cops on your ass for disturbing the peace and destruction of property!" Steve yelled back. They sent him out the door and I was hoping that would be the last we'd see of him. Steve and Easy were talking about what happened and replaying the scene. Most of the girls were swarmed around to find out what sparked everything off. The anxiety I had from watching them fight was starting to calm down. I wasn't shaking anymore and my heart wasn't beating out of my chest. I had calmed but I was still scared and didn't want to deal with anymore customers. But, this was my job and I didn't get any breaks on the drama. I had to move on, I still had a whole night ahead of me. It was not unusual to have crazy things happen on any given day. Every day was different but the same. Same routine, different challenges to navigate through to complete the routine.

The routine continued for weeks, then one evening I was faced with familiar challenge to navigate again. I had a customer that had been there for a couple of hours. He was your average white man, he said he worked in education. I figured he was a teacher and a weird one at that. He stared at me when we sat together and would always follow me to the stage when I had to dance. He came to see me every day for almost a week. I was making about $250 on him each time so I was glad to see him there again. He didn't talk much so he was an easy customer. I had gotten off stage and he had gone back to the table. As I was walking up I could see that he had ordered me another drink. This meant I would be there for a while longer. I climbed up in the booth. "I love watching you dance Cherry, your body is so beautiful. Would you be interested in being my private dancer? I tried convincing him that I already was, I knew what he was hinting about. I kept trying to avoid what I knew he was asking for. The more I avoided him the more his price rose, it went higher than I had ever made in a night. I was extremely nervous and Easy was in the house tonight. He was watching the whole time of course. He went over to the DJ booth and Smooth called me over. That's how he did it so it wasn't so obvious. I excused myself and walked over to the booth. "What is going on over there?" "This guy is asking me to be a private dancer for him, like somewhere outside of here." "Is he talking about some money?" I shook my head yes. "Tell him to come talk to me." I walked back over to the table and told my customer. He wasn't that pleased but he still got up and played a game of pool with Easy. It was late but not the end of the night, Easy told me to go cash out with Steve and that we were leaving. My stomach knotted up. I thought I was stripping to avoid being alone with men. I had hoped we were going to do it like last time, with no fights though. I told Steve I was leaving early, I got my stuff and went outside to the car. Easy and the Customer were talking by the car. I got in the car and they separated, Easy got in and the guy got in his car. We were following behind him and Easy started telling me about their conversation. "He has another guy at the hotel and he wants you to dance for both of them at the same time". I didn't believe they wanted dancing at all. If that was what he really wanted he could have gotten that at the club. I didn't like being alone with one guy now it will be two? I felt like fainting, wondering what is about to happen to me now? I couldn't say anything but it was clear to Easy I was frightened. He seen me starting to tear up as he continued telling me the things this man wanted to do. "This is money in my hands, good money Angel, you are worth a lot of money little girl. Maybe I'll stay to make sure they don't do too much to you. I don't want any damage on you. Saying these things was not making me feel better about this at all. What was he going to let them do? What did they want to do? If there are two of them is Easy going to be able to stop them I wondered. The further we went down the highway the more knotted up my body got. We started pulling off the highway way over on the south side of the city, we were almost to Moore. As we started pulling into the hotel parking lot my body started shivering and I was fighting back the vomit that was piling up in my throat. The guy slowly pulled to the back and into a parking spot and Easy pulled in beside him. I could see him smiling when he was getting out of the car. Easy got out too and told me to wait. I was glad to wait. He walked with him to the room and stepped inside but didn't shut the door. He came back to the car with money in his hands and motioned for me to get out. I didn't think my legs were going to work when they hit the ground but they did, and part of me wanted to just take off running but I couldn't. I knew I was walking too slow when Easy came over real fast and grabbed my arm to help me move faster. We got to the room and when I stepped in I could see that the other guy was older, probably 60 something. After short introductions I was told this was his father. "His Father??" I yelled in my head, "This is sickening!" Easy told me to sit on the bed then actually looked at me before walking out the door and said "Are you going to be ok?" I just stared at him, he knew I wasn't going to be ok and he gave them permission to do whatever. Easy shut the door and if I would have been standing I surely would have fell. I could feel separately every single hair on my entire body tense up and rise to attention. My body started to go numb and the humming sound started in my ears. I quietly sat there, the old man asked how old I was and the younger quickly answered 14, I guess Easy had confirmed it for him. The old man smiled and asked if it cost him all the money. "Every penny, but she's going to be worth it, her pimp says she follows instructions well" as he walked over to me. He reached and grabbed me by my hair pulling me up to stand. "So why didn't you tell me you were 14 when I asked the first time?" "Because I couldn't" as I was finishing my last word his hand landed right across my face. It burned bad and I screamed, the old man started chuckling like he had been told a joke. I'll bet that's what my step-dad will be like when he's old. That was what I was thinking. The younger guy shoved me down on the bed and climbed on top of me and started choking me. I screamed and was trying to fight him off. At first I thought he was just trying to scare me. It only took a few seconds to figure out he was really trying to choke the life out of me. I started fighting him harder and kicking harder so his dad came and grabbed my legs and was helping hold me down. He was continuing to choke me. My face started tingling and it felt like my eyes were going to pop right out of my head. Just when I was starting to black out, he let go. I gasped for air for over a minute. When I finally caught my breath, he started choking me again. He would let go for me to catch my breath and then he would do it again. This went on for what seemed to be an hour but I'm sure was a minute or two. I thought he was actually trying to kill me. I started screaming at the top of my lungs and doing my best to fight them between. There was knocking at the door and the old man went to see who it was. It was Easy he was outside the door knocking. When the old man barely opened the door Easy came busting in. "What the fuck is going on in here?" He pushed the old man down on the floor as the younger one came at him. Easy started punching him in the face and they fell back on the bed. "Don't put yo hands on my Angel, Don't put yo hands on my Angel! I'll follow you to the ends of the earth to kill you for hurting my Angel" he was screaming. I ran toward the door way and started yelling. "Let's go, let's go!" Easy looked up at me and got off the guy, kicked him again as he got up. "Don't touch my shit you sick bastards!" Easy yelled. We quickly went to the car and pulled away. I was scared to death and was still kind of out it from the choking. I was waiting for SWAT or something to start pulling into the hotel or people outside gathering around from all the yelling and stuff. But no, there was nothing, not a person in sight, especially not police. We got right back on the highway and Easy was asking "Did they hurt you baby? Did they hurt my Angel?" "What the fuck did you think they were going to do?" that's what I was thinking and wanted to say but you know the drill. He rubbed the side of my face that was still burning and my throat felt like I had a huge case of strep. It hurt to swallow and my neck was super stiff. We got back to the house and I had to do what I had deemed the "bath ritual". Early on it became the thing to do. When I would come back from working on the streets Easy would help wash my body down and then after my rinse he would rub me down with rubbing alcohol. And if you know anything about rubbing alcohol and mucus membranes, can I Just say FIRE!! There were parts of the bath that were nice to have and there were other parts that I could have lived my whole life without. After he cleaned me he carried me to the bed, my face and neck still red and tingly and bruises were starting to come up. Easy paid a lot of attention to me that night. Easy let me stay home from work the next day because of the bruises on my neck. We went around looking for the right makeup to cover them for the next day cuz it was time to go back to work, as usual. When I got to work the girls could see the bruises and I told them some of the story but left out the part about Easy being a part of the plan so they would know it wasn't him this time. The club was dark so I didn't have to worry about them seeing my neck but my neck was still so stiff I couldn't hardly turn to see them. I'll bet I looked like a robot on stage trying to look around. I continued working and had become like a little stripper robot. Doing the same routine day after day, making him money.

~Chapter 11~

Daddy's Phone Call

Easy had gotten to a point where he was making a lot of money between me, April and a couple of other girls here and there so he could afford to have different places for us. We moved to an apartment off NW Expressway. The apartments were really nice. They were like brand new. I had never lived in anything that nice. The kitchen even had a dishwasher. That was a first for me. The new place had to have new stuff too. This place was bigger than our last apartment. Just like at his Mom's house, the living room was museum quality. All the furniture was oiled, electronics wiped down and glass cleaned on all surfaces. We even had those plastic runners like his mom. And you'd better not step on nothing but those runners. If you did, he would stomp on your foot with his boot. It didn't take too many of those to stay on the plastic. The cabinets were full of food and so was the fridge. I took special care of his things and made sure everything was clean at all times. If I used a glass, I cleaned and put it away when I was done. Everything was perfect in there. The routine became normal as normal could be for me. I would sleep in with Easy. Get a shower out of the way. Watch movies or roll around town with him. Then get ready for work and be there by 2pm each day. Months went by of the same ole same ole. I started getting more and more comfortable with what I was doing. The best part was I had some friends, well I had girls at work to talk to. I had to find the good parts in all the bad to keep from completely losing myself. I had forgotten most of what a young girl like me should be doing. I was living the life of a wife. I was his lover, cook, maid, friend, and movie critic. I didn't see April all that much anymore. I know he would go over there when he wasn't at the club but at least I didn't have to see it anymore. Easy had dropped me off at the club and I was in the back with the others pulling my crap out of the bag. Steve comes walking through the door "Men coming in Ladies" he announced loudly as he walked in. and "Men" he meant. There was a parade of them, about 8 or 9 in business clothes. Then I saw police officers trailing up the back as the first man walked right up to me. "Can I see your ID young lady?" "Sure" I said as I reached in my bag for my bar card. I handed it to him with confidence and he looked at it front and back. "Where did you get this?" "Downtown, at the station" I said. "What's your name?" "Amanda" I blurted out quickly. All the girls were still standing around staring. Steve was standing right next to the guy asking me the questions. I started shrinking on the inside, this was it, and I was caught. My brain started racing, have they arrested Easy? Are they going to arrest me? Does Easy know what's going on? Will he see the police cars outside the club? Why are they asking questions and what do they really know. The officer looked up and spoke. "Are you sure your name isn't Sarah, 14 years old, born in 1970, Sarah?" I tried to stand there with confidence "No, that's my little sister, my name is Amanda" "Is this you?" as he holds up a wallet of my freshman year, high school yearbook picture in his hand. I just stared at it for a minute, then I stared at him. "Your dad called us Sarah" he said. I could hear the other girls start talking in the background but it was all kind of weird like I was in a sound booth hearing myself and the man in front of me and all the others were background noise. My dad called??? I thought to myself. Then the brain started racing even faster. I didn't even know my dad was in Oklahoma. How did he know I was stripping, how did he know where? I didn't say anything else to them. I started picking up my things. The man who was talking to me put his hand on my bag that I was filling back up "You're not going to need these Sarah." I just stopped what I was doing and walked with him. When we got out to the front they had the few customers and the rest of the dancers lined up in the seats at the front of the stage. They were handing people back their ID's and they would leave after that. The dancers had to go through more, they searched everyone's bags looking for drugs and stuff. When they got to Rochelle's bag, a transgendered dancer we had working with us, they found a prescription bottle with more than one kind of pill in it and so she was arrested too. They put cuffs on her and sat her next to me, they had an officer on each side of us. They went through everything and everyone and when only the people that worked there were left the head man gave a little speech to everyone. "This young lady here is only 14yrs old, that man you see her with is her pimp, if you see them in a bar somewhere again, call us, she can't work in these bars." Everyone was whispering to each other and looking at me with disgust. I started shrinking from the inside out, they all hated me now, I messed it all up. Steve spoke up. "I was unaware she was 14 she had a bar card, how did she get that? How am I supposed to know next time?" He was clearly upset. They were ticketing him for having a minor working in his establishment. I didn't have anyone on my side, not the girls anymore and I didn't have Steve either. They were not my friends anymore. I was losing the only friends I had. "We are going to look into how she got the bar card, it might be a fake." It's not, I was thinking to myself, I got it downtown. I looked in Rochelle's direction to smirk about him calling it fake. She turned away when I started looking her direction, she was clearly pissed at me. Rochelle was usually very talkative but she didn't say a word this time. She didn't even look my way. All my "friends" that I had built up at the club were now either mad at me, laughing at me or whispering about me. By the time they were finished it had been about an hour. When he said let's go, the officer reached under my arm to raise me up and I felt about 2 inches tall. I felt so completely different and alone. I had to go through this by myself, no Easy to help me. We walked toward the front and they opened the door to a sight I didn't expect to see. There were news cameras everywhere. Three or four of them right in my face. There I was, my 15 minutes of fame on TV. What happened to that freshman girl Sarah who doesn't come to school anymore? Well, question answered on the evening news. I've never seen the footage myself as I was in jail when it aired but I'm sure it was quite interesting to see. A little girl and a 6/2 transgendered manly looking dancer being led into the back of a police car. If I hadn't already been embarrassed enough by the fact that I was poor, homeless, molested, prostituted, and uncared for, then this would surely do it. I started thinking on the way to the police station. Is my dad going to be down there? Is he here in Oklahoma or did he call from Arkansas? Is he coming to get me? Is he going to save me from all this? Would I go live with him and where would that be? I had 50 million questions going off in my head and was actually getting a little excited as we got to the police station. I wondered if my dad would be mad at me. I began thinking about the only moment I can remember being scared of my dad when I was around 6 or 7 years old. We were living in the small town in Arkansas and we didn't have a big grocery store there. When it was time for groceries we traveled to the Grocery in Helena. It was a rare occasion that my parents took all 6 of us kids with them, but on this visit they did. We were wondering around the store while they shopped. As I was walking down one of the isles I noticed a small rubber ball the clear kind with the colorful swirls in the middle. I reached down and picked it up thinking to myself that some kid had dropped their ball. They must be mad but I was taught finders keepers, loser's weepers. I ran to my sisters and told them about the kid losing the ball and me finding it. So they wanted to see if any other kids lost their balls so we went back to that isle. We all got on the ground and looked under the shelving. Boy was it dirty under there. Sure enough there were other kids who lost their balls too. There were enough for us kids to have a few each. We gathered the balls and put them in our pockets. After mom and dad bought the groceries we went to the van and got in to head home. We started playing with the balls immediately. When dad got to the end of the parking lot and put on the breaks, several of our balls rolled to the front of the van. Dad picked up a couple and asked where they came from. Kathi piped up and said "From under the shelf in the store, some kid lost them and we found them." Dad turned the van around and headed back down the parking lot. We started looking at each other wondering what was going on. "Martha, you take these kids in the store and give those damn balls back! I don't have thieves for children!" he said as he parked. We immediately began to cry. Dad had used a cuss word and called us thieves, we knew that was a rare thing and that when he did, it was really serious. We went with mom in the store with the balls and gave them to the manager. He said we could have gone to jail for that and it was scary to hear him say that. The whole way home dad talked about how mad he was that his kids were thieves and that he was going to take a belt to our behinds. We were scared to death. He dropped us off at our house and went to take Aunt Janell home. When we got in the house we all huddled around mom and were crying, she was crying with us. She was saying "He's not going to whoop you kids, he's not going to whoop my babies!" She's started pushing the couch over in front of the door. We were so scared of a whooping, we had never had one before. Dad was the grounding kind of dad, not the whooping kind of dad. But we knew he was mad, that was for sure. When dad finally got into the house and saw how afraid we were he let us off the hook. I climbed up in his lap and laid with him in silence. I wanted him to know I was sorry. I didn't mean to mess up. In that moment I wished I was still small enough to climb into this lap. I wasn't the same little girl he saw last time in Arkansas. I started imagining how it would be when we saw each other again. Would it be like on TV where the kid and the dad run up and hug and it makes all the stuff in the past run away and disappear? Or would it be bad, will he ignore me, will he disown me? I wondered what it was going to be like but most of all I was glad that he had finally stepped in to save me.

We got to the police station and they pulled into the garage section. I didn't want to get out of the car. I wanted to stay there. I hoped that the officer would not touch his door. My hope didn't help. He got out of his door and opened mine. I climbed out and he held me by the arm. The officer walked me to the elevators and we waited for it to open. There were about 10 of us by the time it got there. We all got on and rode up a few floors. When the door opened it was clear to see I was at the jail, it was becoming a familiar place. There was a big desk straight ahead with bars on the windows and officers standing behind talking with officers and arrested people on this side. There were 3 holding cells to the right side that were about 5x7 foot each with a concrete floor and bars, no chairs or beds. That's where the officer put me, in the first cell, he took my cuffs off and said "Wait right here, someone will be here to get you" I walked in and he locked the door behind me. I walked around thinking about what I would say to my dad and how I would explain how I got into this mess and how happy I was that he was here to get me out. I wasn't even that scared of where I was, I was nervous about seeing dad again after so long. I hadn't seen him since we lived in Arkansas, matter of fact we hadn't had any contact. No phone calls, no birthday cards and no Christmas. But I was ready to make up for all that, so I waited. I wondered what it would be like, if he had gifts for me, I thought about a wooden beaded purse he had gotten me for my 8th birthday a few years earlier. Dad had gotten back into town just in time for my birthday 8th party at my aunt's house. He gave me a little purse made of round wooden beads. It had a sticker inside that said Mexico, I honestly believed he went to Mexico and got it for me. I believed he would go anywhere and do anything for me. I waited in my cell for a long time, finally this detective came and got me from my cell. He started asking me questions about Chris, my Easy. He wanted me to give him information to arrest Easy but I couldn't do it, I was too scared. I knew Easy was smarter and stronger than the police

151

and I didn't want to suffer the consequences of talking to the police. I had already seen that with a previous girl and it wasn't nice. "When did you meet? Do you live with him? Do you give him your money? Does he hit you? Do you have sex with him? Just question after question after question. Meanwhile I kept noticing him looking down at my body while he was talking to me, just like the others. I didn't answer any of his questions, I Just stared at him. He put me back in the cell and said it would probably be a while longer. "When can I see my dad?" I asked. "Your dad?" he said with a weird look on his face. "Yea, he's the one that called right, is he here?" I asked. The guy laughed a bit "no darling, he's not here. We've called your mother to come get you, your dad called the news, they called us." And he walked away. I wanted to cry but I didn't, I was too hurt to cry. I wanted to tear the concrete floor up. I slammed my hands down on the floor, it was the only thing available to hit. I was quickly going from hurt to pissed off. If he hadn't cheated on mom and left her I wouldn't be in this position. It was all their fault, I was so angry. I wished that he was there, so that I could attack him. I wasn't completely shocked that he didn't show. I was still with the "Black Man". This wasn't a rescue at all. He didn't care, he Just wanted to embarrass me and probably knew it would get me beat as well. Bottom line was, he didn't want me. As bad as I didn't want to want him either, I did. I was still hurting so much inside. I wondered why I was even here, what was the purpose in even being here if my own parents don't want me. Why did they bring me here? It's not like I was the first child and they didn't know how it happened. What am I here for? Is this it, is this my great destiny in life? The hours went buy and they all went about their business like I wasn't even there. I couldn't do anything but think. Think about my family that I was born to, think about how I got to this point, think about what's going to come next and how or if I would make it through. I was so crushed over where my life was. I know all my friends from school saw me on the news. I could never face them again. I can't go back to school ever. School is no longer an option for me. I have no one but Easy, no one else to turn to but him so I resided that's where I will be so I better make the most of it. Later an officer finally came over to my cell and said that my mom was there to get me. He opened the cell door, walked me over to the elevators and down we went. Mom was at the bottom waiting for me. We walked home and I can't remember much of what was said. It was Just small talk, I remember her telling me that she seen me on the news, oddly enough her tone almost seemed proud. "Your sisters are calling you a TV star" I looked at her wondering if she would ever be aware of the things she said. I quickly decided that wasn't ever going to change. She told me that Easy had been over and was waiting for me to get out of jail. I was supposed to call him when we got back to the motel. Mom had moved, again, and was staying in the Queen's Royal Inn motel downtown. It was one of those cheap pay by the week motels. It was like a square building with the middle cut out. There was one way in and one way out. Two levels of rooms went around the perimeter of the square and the middle was a small parking lot with room for a hand full of cars. We walked up the metal stairs and across the concrete platform to the room in the corner. When we got to the room Lillian and Tyana were in the bed asleep. Mom gave me the phone and I called Easy and told him I was there. He said that he would come get me the next day so I laid down to try to fall asleep. I still very freaked out about the events of the day and had absolutely no one to talk to. The lights were out so I Just stared at the crack in the curtains where the light was coming in. It made me think about being in the pantry at the old apartment. It wasn't a fun place to be but at least it was my home. I actually wished I was there instead of here. At least there I didn't have to be victim to all the men she put me in contact with. I eventually fell asleep. The next morning my sisters woke me up. They had seen me on TV and were asking all kinds of questions that I couldn't and didn't want to talk about, especially to them. They asked if I saw Dad they said that he was on TV too. I was immediately confused. They said he did an interview with the TV station outside of the strip club. He was there, he was there! And didn't say anything to me. I waited the whole way down to the police station to see him and didn't know I had driven away from where he was. I was crushed, this was even worse. I couldn't make up any excuses for why he didn't make it there to save me. He was there, he was right there, and did not say a word to me. I did my best to ignore their questions. I didn't want them to know what was going on. The less they knew the less chance they would end up in the middle of things.

Easy showed up that morning and knocked on the door. I was so happy to see him but so nervous as well. Usually he would have picked me up for hugs and kisses but he didn't. I had been thinking all morning. What was going to happen now? How would I make money? I didn't want to go back to the streets. Was I going to be in trouble for being arrested? My mind was racing again. What was he thinking, was I in trouble? It wasn't my fault. I put my shoes on and we walked down to the car, it was obvious that I was nervous. When we got into the car he hugged me and kissed me and was saying how worried he was about me but that he was upset as well. "You could have gotten away from them if you tried, you didn't try." "There were too many of them, I couldn't do anything. We rode out to the burger king on the east side to get cheese burgers. We ate while I finished telling him about how everything went down. He was mad at the police and my dad. Especially about him calling the news channels, he had seen the broadcast as well. "This brought a lot of heat on us Angel. You're going to have to stay with your mom for a while to let it cool down." It was too hot on the streets to be with him. If the police pull us over, that's it. He was pulled over that same day I was arrested. The police kept him on the side of the road for over 2 hours, but didn't have anything on him so they had to let him go. We rode out to our apartment so I could clean the house and get some clothes. Easy kept hugging and kissing on me all the way there, up the stairs and into the apartment. "I've been sick about this baby, I didn't know what they were doing with my Angel." He picked me up and carried me to the room. I packed a bag for about a week so we could let things settle down. He drove me back to the motel and I went up to mom's room. I walked in the door and tossed my bag to the side. "I need to stay for a couple of days and then I'll be gone"

"Fine with me" mom said. Easy came back about 20 minute later with a bucket of chicken. He did stuff like that every once in a while for my mom and sisters. He didn't have to, I think he was just trying to make sure everyone thought of him as a good person. I enjoyed having some time with my sisters but being around my mother again was incredibly difficult. My plan was to keep us away from the room as much as possible when she was home. That next morning mom went to work and we watched movies all day. It was almost time for mom to get home so I asked the girls to get dressed. Easy had given me some money to keep in my pocket so my sisters and I were going to walk to the store down the street. We were coming out of the door of the room and I looked down to see Dan and Ron down stairs working on a car. I Just froze in my tracks and stared at them hoping I was wrong about who I was seeing. When I was able to move I hurried the girls back into the room and shut the door. "Was that Dan and Ron?" "Yea, they came a few weeks ago, Mom's been talking to them again" Tyana said. I was so upset. "Have they touched you again?" I yelled. Both girls shook their heads no. I was scared but at the same time I wanted to run up to them and Just start swinging my fist. I wanted to give them every ounce of hurt they ever gave my sisters and brother. I was so angry at my mom, what was she thinking? I wanted to make them leave. I thought about telling the manager about them but then I worried that he would kick mom out too. I had battled them before and I was willing to battle again to get them away from my little sisters. I called Easy and told him that my stepdad and his twin brother was staying over here and were outside right now. He said he would come get us to take us to the store. I watched for him to pull up and when he did I told the girls to turn the TV off and come on. We walked outside the door and seen that Dan and Ron were still there working on their car. Chris had gotten out of his car, looked up at me and pointed to them. I shook my head yes and he walked right over to them. I saw him say something to Dan and immediately punch him in the face. Dan stumbled backwards and Chris was right on top of him. I pushed the girls back in the house and watched from the window. He hit him again and Dan fell to the ground. Ron was coming around the corner of the car and Chris raised up his fist to hit him. Ron took off running the opposite way, up the stairs to their room. Chris was yelling at him "Don't touch those fucking girls, I'll kill you if I find out you touched them!" Chris motioned for us to come on, we went down the stairs and he had the car right there. Easy had a big smile on his face and so did I. I felt power in that moment, finally, some power. It felt good. I was protected and my sisters were protected. It was about time someone let them know that touching little girls was not ok. I was proud that I was able to get us away from where they were, at least momentarily. We all got what we wanted from the store and Easy paid for it so I kept the money I had in my pocket. We went back to the room and Dan and Ron were nowhere to be found. Mom was there at the room when we got back. I started asking her why she was having contact with them and why she told them where we were and why did they move in. She didn't answer any of the questions I had. She walked into the bathroom, shut the door and stayed in there. Me and the girls watched TV for a while and then she finally came out. Easy said that he was going to come back for me and for me he couldn't come fast enough. I didn't want to talk to her, I didn't even want to be in the room with her. I went outside and walked around the motel for a while.

Finally I seen lights pulling in and it was Easy. I ran down to the car and jumped in "Please get me out of here." I wanted to take my sisters but one little white girl in the possession of a black man was a big enough red flag. He got on the highway and we headed to the apartment. When I got there I went to the kitchen to get a drink and he jumped in the shower. I put my bag in the room and joined him. He enjoyed being washed and so did I, we washed each other. "You are the most beautiful thing God has ever made, you're my Angel" he would say to me. I loved hearing him speak to me that way. He loved me like no one else ever has. This was real love, this was what I saw on TV and in the movies. We made love and there were fireworks and everything. I wanted to lay there with him all night but we were both paranoid about the police knocking on the door so he took me back to my mom's motel room. We went back and forth for a few days.

~Chapter 12~

Teen in my genes

One afternoon while mom was at work me and the girls were sitting in the room and heard a knock at the door. I looked out the window and it was the police. I panicked instantly. What was I going to say? Had they already arrested Easy? Was I going to have time to call him to find out? I didn't know what they wanted and I didn't want to open the door but they had already seen me open the curtain. I told them to hold on and ran to the phone. I dialed Easy's phone and they started knocking at the door louder. The phone rang and rang, I didn't have time to go past three rings so I hung the phone up. The officer started knocking on the window and talking real loud "Open the door, now!" I didn't have much choice so I opened the door. There was a black lady in regular clothes with a few police officers. "Where is your mother?" "She's at work. Why?" I asked. "Please put on some proper clothes. You're coming with us" I remember her saying that "proper clothes" I had no idea what she was talking about, I had clothes on, I Just thought she was weird. But when she told us that we were going with them, we all got upset, they cried and I started asking questions. Go where? With who and why? The lady had a long packet of paper and said that it would tell my mom what happened and what to do. I grabbed the paper and started reading it. The majority of it was gibberish to me but I could understand that it had something to do with neglect and reports given to the child welfare agency. We were all telling them that we didn't want to go and we made it pretty difficult for them as well. There were four of us because Kathi was there at that time and getting us into the back of the police car wasn't as easy as they thought it would be. Eventually they won and we were all in the car. They drove us on the highway over to the area where the children's hospital was. I thought about where they were taking us and what it may be like. Of course I thought about keeping my sisters safe most of all. I recognized the hospital buildings in the area but I didn't recognize the one they parked us in front of. It was at the very end of the buildings. On the other side of the street was houses and the drug store. When we got out I looked around and started to get nervous which made me want to protect my sisters even more. When we went inside we were met by two women who took us to a room and told us that we were in the Juvenile shelter and that we would be there until either we go back to our mom or to a foster home. How would I get back to Easy? He's going to be really pissed off when he finds out that they took me again. I had no idea what a foster home was so I wasn't sure if that would be better than my sisters being with mom or not, but as long as we were together, I was going to make sure we were ok. Kathi was the older one but she was also the tiny one. She had some issues growing and was small like Tyana and Lillian so I was the big sis by size and attitude. After they got the information from us that we could give them, they told me, Tyana, and Kathi to go with them away from Lillian. I told them no, we weren't going to be apart but there was nothing I could do about it but be upset. They took us upstairs and sat us at some tables while they took the paper work into the office that was in the middle of the big area. It had glass walls all the way around it. You could see that on the other side was a room with a TV and some couches. To one side of me was a kitchen surrounded by tall cabinets and the other side I could see hallways and doors I figured that was the bedrooms. When we were sitting there a girl came over and sat down. She said Hi and we started talking. It only took an hour or so to get a little more comfortable with where we were. We were in a place full of kids just like us. I wish I would have known about this place earlier, it wasn't so bad, I think the girls would be safe here. When it came time for bed, the girls went one way and the boys went another. In the girl's dorm were cubicles with beds and built in dressers and desks. I liked having our own areas but I didn't like being away from Easy. We didn't bring any clothes so they took us to this closet that was full of brand new clothes. We were able to pick whatever we wanted. We all picked out some clothes and took showers. I asked one of the house parents if we could see Lillian before bedtime to make sure she was ok. We rode downstairs with her on the elevator and she took us over to the little girls unit. I was paying attention to all the doors and exits. I wanted to figure out how to get out of here and back to Easy. Lillian was happy to see us, we all hugged and kissed and we promised her that we would see her in the morning. We went back up and chose our cubicles out of those that were available and climbed into the bed. The next morning we got up, went to breakfast and started meeting even more of the kids in there. After we had been there for 24 hours we could use the phone and of course Easy was my first phone call. I called his number and there was no answer so I dialed the Queen's Royal Inn and asked for my mom's room. The phone answered on the first ring and it was his voice. "Chris?" I said. "Angel, is this my Angel? Where are they keeping you?" "I'm on 13th and Lottie, on the corner." "Why did you let them take you?" he asked. "I didn't let them, there were police and a welfare lady. There was nothing I could do, they took all of us." "You need to start looking for ways out, this is messing with my money Angel. I'm going to have to find other ways to get cash, you know what I'm talking about." "I am, I'll find a way out. I've gotta go, these people are telling me time's up." "I love you Angel, you know what to do, make it happen." As much as I wanted to be with him I wasn't so sure

I wanted to leave this place, it wasn't so bad after all. Plus I still had to look out for my sisters.

Easy would call me every day asking if I had found a way out. He knew where the building was now and would drive by daily checking to see if I was outside or anything. After being there for about a week or so I saw that one of the girls went what they called AWOL. What is AWOL I thought to myself? When the girl came back to the shelter the next day I asked her about this AWOL thing. Absent without leave was what she told me. It was just another way of saying "she ran away". She showed me how to pop the lock to the back door that lead to the yard outside. She said that when you get back you get a 24hr restriction and then back to normal. I called Easy and told him what was up. He said to wait until the weekend and that he would come get me. Meanwhile I continued to develop more friendships and more trust in the house parents at the shelter. That weekend I made arrangements with Chris over the phone to meet him outside at 7pm so around 6:50 I gave the signal, I had one of my friends start asking the house parents questions to distract them and I headed for the door. I got downstairs and hit the door to the yard and went running across as fast as I possibly could. I knew they would be coming behind me at any minute. I didn't want to look behind me to see who was chasing me. I made it to the fence and through the gate and onto the outside sidewalk. I finally looked back and there was no one, no one was chasing me. Do they even know I'm gone? I walked down to the pharmacy where Chris said he would be and just as I got there he pulled up. I jumped in the car and right into his lap. We kissed and hugged for a minute then he pulled away with me still sitting in his lap. We drove to Ardmore and spent the night there, his mom and sister were used to me now and were very welcoming. We had dinner and helped his mom move some things around in the house, she was changing the look around. We drove back to the city that next morning. Chris took me back to the neighborhood where I used to turn tricks and said that I was going to have to do a couple to make up for the money we had spent. "Please, please don't make me, I don't want to keep doing this." He grabbed me by my hair and pulled me close to his face. "You do what the fuck I tell you bitch!" He screamed in my face. So I got out of the car and in about 2 hours had made the money he needed. When I was finished he took me back to the shelter and dropped me off at the gate. I was so disappointed. I didn't want to go inside but I also didn't have anywhere else to go. It wasn't that I didn't want to be there. It was that I didn't want anyone to know what I Just went and did. It was none of their business anyway. I walked around the building and into the front door. They processed me back in and I went back upstairs. I went straight to the shower and scrubbed myself down. When I got out of the shower everyone was going down for dinner. I told everyone about my trip, of course I left out the last part. Who wants to tell their friends…and oh yea, I turned a few tricks before coming back too. I skipped that one. I went on like nothing happened, like it wasn't me who did that. I left that girl on the streets, here I get to be a kid, I get to be 14yrs old kind of. I had only been there a couple of weeks and one morning I woke up, started throwing up and couldn't stop. I went to Jeanie, one of the house parents and told her and she said they would take me to the doctor. We went over to the emergency room and waited forever to be seen. I felt like crap and just wanted to sleep. After a while they took us to the back and they took blood and urine and did a few test. The doctor came back in and did a pelvic exam. "You are pregnant, young lady" "I'm what?" "You're pregnant, with child." I was pregnant, oh my God, I'm pregnant. That's all I could think and it's all I could say. Over and over again. I am fourteen years old and I am pregnant. I am pregnant with his child and now we will be a family. When I got back to the shelter I asked if I could make a phone call. I called Easy. "Hello?" "I'm pregnant!" I blurted out. "Wait, what, you're what?" I could hear in his voice he was stunned. "How do you know?" "I went to the doctor and they did tests. I'm pregnant." "Let me think about this, let me call you back." And he hung up the phone. I was so confused. I thought having a baby was a happy thing. We had talked about it, he said he wanted a child with me before. We didn't talk about when but he said he wanted it. A few days later he called and we talked about going to see his mom again to tell her about the baby. His mom already thought I was 16, now 16 and pregnant, but really, 14 and pregnant, what was she going to think of me now? I wondered. That weekend Chris called and picked me up but it was for work, not to go to his moms. He said that we would go back the next time so I continued to work until it was time to go back.

Life went on at the shelter and we did a lot of fun things that made me want to stay there. The only part that I didn't like was when they would try to get us to say bad things about mom. I didn't like her or the decisions she was making but she was still my mom. They let her visit a couple of times. But mostly we just did what the other kids did and tried to stay out of trouble, kind of. We had made up our own shelter band. We were all in it. My sisters, Stacey, Traci, all of us did something. We used various things to make music, Mark and Blue were the beat boxers, rappers, and drummers of the group. I was the scratcher, I had a red brush that I was scratching across the wall that made the perfect scratching sound. However, it left a huge red swish mark on the wall. The house parents weren't too keen on that one. I got a restriction for it but they let me continue to do the scratching as long as I stayed in the same spot, no new spots was the rule. Having fun with Blue made me start having a crush on him. The more things we did together the more I thought about having a real boyfriend my age but I was pregnant and even more confused than ever. Blue was getting calls from a girl who had gone home before I got there named Maya. When she would call I would get on the phone and mess with her and start a cussing fight with her. There were several times that she said she was going to find a way up there. One particular day we were going to go on a field trip to the swimming pool at the park. She had called and we were in an argument. I told her to meet me at the park and she said that she was coming but she never showed. It took a couple of weeks but she eventually stopped calling and Blue started being my best friend while I was there. I didn't look at it as a replacement for Chris because Blue was my age, which for me was abnormal. I was only used to men, not boys. But I needed to do something. I was going AWOL with Chris when he would call but that was only every week or so Blue started filling in the gaps. He was very scared of Chris finding out that we were becoming close. I knew the two worlds were separate enough that he would only know if I told him and I wasn't about to tell, I was too scared of the consequences. I didn't even want to do this but my urges weren't something I was able to ignore so I did what I felt I had to do. The first time we tried to hide away alone was a really awkward event. We had decided that we were going to meet each other in the community bathroom that was in the middle of the common area. Blue went into the bathroom first and I waited a while and then went in behind him. We sat down on the bathroom floor and just as we were attempting to get started Grandma Julie knocked on the door "Who's in there?" she said. We looked at each other with our eyes bugged out and mouth's open. We were busted...maybe. She knocked again "Who's in there?" "I am" I responded. I could hear some giggling on the other side of the door. "Who's in there with you?" she asked. I looked at Blue and we started laughing. We knew we were busted then. She asked again "Who's in there with you, Blue are you in there?" She banged on the door again. "Blue answer me" she said. We were arguing whether he should or not. I said go ahead, we were already busted, how were we going to get out. Blue wanted to wait her out. Well I knew there was no waiting out Grandma Julie. She would stay like the Washington Monument waiting for us to come out. Finally Blue answered. "Yes, Grandma Julie, I'm in here." About that time you could hear the entire group of kids outside the bathroom door bust out laughing. We were busted big time. We opened the door. Sure enough, everyone was there laughing. It was pretty funny though, you didn't get nothing past Grandma Julie. She gave us the only restriction she could which was 24hrs and that didn't stop a thing.

It was mostly fun in the shelter but about once a week they would send a worker to talk to us. They wanted us to tell them bad things about our mom so they could put her in jail. And as bad as I didn't want to live with her I didn't want her in jail either, she was still my mom. I had already told the other girls not to give them any info and every time they would talk to us I would make sure my sisters remembered what we were doing and why. We had already lost one parent in the divorce, we're not going to lose another. After talking to them we went back to the common area to hang with the other kids. I was getting bored and we didn't have a field trip planned for the weekend so we started planning an AWOL Just to get out and have some fun. We waited till after dinner to leave. We snuck down the back stairs and ran across the yard. The boys went over the fence first and we followed. We walked all over the hospital complex which spanned about 5 or 6 blocks. We were chilling in this courtyard when we saw the hospital police coming. We went to the edge of the courtyard to get away and realized we were on the second floor. The boys Jumped automatically, we Jumped right behind them and took off running as we landed. We darted across 13th street into the neighborhood area running for our lives. There were some smaller buildings on that side. We found a breezeway and collapsed on the grass. The boys checked to see if the police were still following us. They didn't see anything so they came right back and sat in the grass with us. It was a perfect truth or dare opportunity and as usual boy + girl was the end result. After everyone got done we walked back to the building we called home. They checked us back in and gave us 24hr restriction and as usual, it didn't change a thing. I had grown close with Kato and Blue and we often protected one another from other teens in the unit. One of the girls on the unit called Kato the N word and I was so angry. How dare she, she was white trash as far as I was concerned. I was going to let her know that she can't go running her mouth like that and not have consequences. The way I was being raised was with consequences, it was the only way to learn. While she was in the TV room I ran up on her, threw a sheet over her and beat the crap out of her. I had already been warned that they would move me if I kept fighting so I couldn't let her know who it was. I wanted her to know it was me kicking her ass but I needed to stay there more than I needed her to know, but I knew my

165

message would get across. I only had a minute or two to do this so when time was up I ran out of the door and came back in on the other side. She was crying on the floor and holding her face. "I can't see, I can't see." I rushed over to her, "What happened, who did this?" I asked with a shocked tone, knowing exactly who did it. "I don't know, I was sitting here and then a sheet and I can't see now." She said through her tears. I called for the staff to help her and sat there with her. I didn't want to help her at all, I wanted to help myself. I wanted to know that she didn't know who it was so I wouldn't be in trouble and it worked. They took her over to the ER and returned later. Her eyes were both black and her nose was swollen. By the time she got back some of the kids knew it was me but they weren't about to say anything, they were trying to get me to calm down. One of the reasons they were trying to get me to calm down was because I was pregnant. It still hadn't completely registered with me yet. One minute I would be in full compliance eating right and taking care of myself for the baby. The next minute I was fighting with any and everybody and didn't really even acknowledge that I was pregnant. My anger would take over and I was finally in a place where I could release some of it. Not that it was being released in the right way, because it wasn't. But it was still a release. As the weeks went by I had started feeling the changes with the pregnancy. I was able to ignore that it was happening at the beginning. I was too busy going on field trips everywhere to worry about being pregnant. But I was, and I needed to calm down if I wanted my baby to be happy. I was working on it, not for me, but for the baby. One of my workers noticed that my clothes were getting tight and said that she was going to take me shopping. We went to the mall and got a few maternity clothes. I had never really seen them up close before. The pants had stretchy material across the front. I thought that was the ugliest thing ever. I didn't want anything to do with those. I got some maternity tops with leggings, I couldn't do the stretchy thing. That weekend they had a great outing planned. We were going to the big water park. I had always dreamed of going there. We were overly excited on the bus ride to the park. The house parents had packed us lunch, we were going to spend the whole day there. We ran from ride to ride to ride. Blue and I went back to the bus in the parking lot before lunch time. We were getting pretty good at sneaking away for some alone time. Some of the kids knew because they would be lookouts but the staff, they were easily out numbered. We were all worn out from the day and quietly rode home on the bus. It was only a few days later that they announced that we would be having a guest come to the shelter. He was a famous boxer and was coming to talk to us. When we were being told they asked if we had any ideas about what we could plan for that evening. I asked if we could cook for him. Easy's mom and Grandma Julie had taught me how to cook pretty good so they said we could do it. We planned out the menu and they gave it to the kitchen to make sure we would have all of the ingredients. Fried chicken, mashed potatoes with chicken gravy, green beans, and sweet corn bread. The morning of his visit we all went down to the big kitchen to get the food and any pots and pans we would need. We carried it all back upstairs and went to work. By the time he got there we had the whole place set up. He brought his wife with him as well, she was so pretty. All of us girls were talking about how pretty she was. It was a great night, the kind of night you want to have every night. There were a lot of memorable experiences while I was in there. This was one of the only places I could just be a teenager, a pregnant teenager, but a teenager. A regular 14yr old with friends and outings and fun.

One of the best was the trip to Lake Tenkiller Camp. We loaded up the bus one morning and drove for hour's way out in the country. The camp had cabins all over and a big dining area for everyone. The girls were on one side and the boys on the other. There were days in the woods and days at the lake. The evening before it was time to go some of us decided that we were going to take a midnight trip to the dock. We snuck down to the dock and dared each other to Jump in. We were all scared because you could see the fish swimming Just under the water. These fish had long sword like things at the front of their heads. We all imagined they would stab us in the water. Piranha were also an issue. We had all seen the movie and weren't about to take a risk on that one. We hadn't seen any but that didn't mean they weren't there. The guys grabbed some fishing nets from the pier and started trying to catch one of the fish with the sword face. We were all frightened for them. What if the fish was too big and pulled them in. How would we explain to the staff that they got eaten by the fish? They eventually caught one, when they pulled it up out of the water we ran like crazy. Yelling and screaming, remember we were supposed to be quiet. That wasn't happening. By the time we got to the cabins Paul and Sarah were outside wondering what the screaming was. We ran into the cabin and slammed the door shut. The boys came running behind. Sarah called for us to go back outside. "What the mess are y'all doing?" Paul asked. "We were just having fun on the last night, we didn't mean to scare the girls." Kato said. Paul started laughing and "Those girls were really scared huh? Let's have some fun with the other cabins." We went and got the last of the tooth paste, shaving creams and shampoos and started pouring it on everyone who was asleep. Several of the boys had shaving cream put in their hands, nose tickled, and spat in the face. By the end we had all the kids up and it was 2am. We finally crashed for a few hours then up early for the ride home. It was a fantastic trip, I didn't want to leave. The summer was coming to an end and they started sending us home one by one to mom. I was the last to go because of the pregnancy and that suited me fine. When I was finally released back to mom I had just had my 15th birthday and was 4 months pregnant. There was no party to be had, she didn't have running water, and Chris wasn't keeping me gone enough. More often than not he was coming to get me for work and not just to spend time with me and our baby. He was buying more gold and cars because he was starting to make more money. I didn't ask and didn't want to know how. He showed up in a Blue Cutlass one day. It was one of the cutest cars I've ever seen and it was dark blue, my favorite color. I ran out to the car and hoped in. "I got this one for you Angel. When you get your license, this will be yours. I've got to get some things done and then it will be yours after my baby gets here" he said as he rubbed my tummy. Sometimes he would rent a hotel room for us so we didn't have to be at moms. I didn't know why we couldn't go to our apartment and I didn't ask. After all, being in a hotel without working was a treat. We were laying in the bed at the hotel and he reached into his pants and pulled out a ring and put it on my finger. It was a ring with a heart on, he said, "This is for carrying my heart in your body." I immediately starting hugging him and crying. He was so wonderful to me. So thoughtful. He really was thinking about me when we weren't together. I would worry about that often but his actions would always let me know I was worrying for nothing. He loved me, he protected me and we were a family. I was pregnant with his first born. He was so excited about the baby coming. He wanted a boy as much as I wanted a girl. We took as long as we could to leave the hotel, I hated it when he had to bring me back to moms but I was glad he came to get me daily. It had been almost 4 weeks and I was coming up on my 5th month. There wasn't much change with mom or Chris. Matter of fact it was getting worse quick. Mom was not working so I was having to pay back Easy so that there was food in the house, more than the bread that the food bank gives. I talked to my case manager and asked her about what I could do. I wanted to have a safe place for me to be while I was pregnant like the shelter and for the baby when it got here. I remembered that there was a group home for teen mom's next to the Juvenile shelter. I was hoping she could find somewhere like that for me. I didn't want to keep turning tricks while I was pregnant. That wasn't good for the baby at all. I didn't tell her about my problems with Easy, just the ones with mom. She said that she would see what she could do. Staying at moms was like torture to me, I didn't want to be there. I kept my things packed up and lived out of bags forever because I didn't want to unpack my things at her house. I couldn't and didn't trust her. I started living everyday like it was going to be my last day there. There was no way to clean things, there was no way to flush the toilet, and the gas would be shut off soon. I had to go. My case manager finally came through for me. She took me to a lady's house name Karen. She was a foster parent to babies but had never had a teenager before, let alone a pregnant one. She had two boys of her own that were becoming teens but no girls of her own. I talked with her for about an hour, basically an interview. I told her all the good things I wanted to do and skipped all the bad unless she directly asked. She liked me and said that I could stay there with her until the baby was a couple of months old and that she would teach me all the things I was going to need to know. I was so happy I couldn't wait to move in. It was the middle of the week and I had to wait until the following Monday for some reason. I didn't tell anyone what I was up to because I didn't want Chris to find out and stop me. He was coming to see me on a regular basis and he was working with other girls now because I couldn't make much money pregnant so he didn't have as much time for me anymore. Monday finally came and my case manager came to pick me up. She knew the situation with mom, I told her that Chris was a possessive boyfriend but nothing more. She agreed to act like she had to take me, that it was the state's decision because I was pregnant. We put all my things in the car and she took me to Karen's house. On the way over I was looking out for Chris. I was afraid that he would see me in the car and chase after us. I never knew when he was coming or when he would bring me home so there was no way to track him. I sunk a little lower in the seat and we talked about the foster home on the way there.

~Chapter 13~

Making Greedy

Karen lived in a big old two story house in the historic district. There were wooden floors and wooden bookshelves and a staircase. There was a fire place and an island in the kitchen. And my room was huge with a king size bed and my own bathroom. I felt like I was in a dream. I had just turned 15yrs old and this was a great late birthday present. They even had cake for me since I didn't get any other kind of party. After a few days I called Chris and told him that the state had taken me again. I had started calling him by name because we were going to name our son after him. I wanted to get used to his real name, we can't have our son calling his daddy Easy. He was not happy about where I was and was very upset about them taking me while I was pregnant with his child. I assured him that I was ok but that I didn't know where I was, only that I was in a neighborhood staying in a two story house. After about a week there I was able to get back into school. I was enrolled and had started months prior but staying with mom with no way to clean made it harder to go to school. My case manager had enrolled me in Emerson Alternative High School. This was the high school for all the girls who got pregnant before graduating. So everyone in the school either had a baby or was about to have a baby. That made it a little easier to deal with. Everyone was so busy with their own kids it didn't leave much room for drama. Shortly after arriving at Emerson I found out that the same girl from the shelter Maya that I had told to meet me at the pool was also going to this school and was pregnant. We finally came across each other and decided that we should be friends and not fight while we're pregnant. And friends it was. We only had one class together but we would sit together most lunches. I was getting my grades back up because I was going consistently. I was good at the work and mostly made A's so it wasn't the work, it was being there or out working that made the difference in my grades. I really needed this now, I needed my education for my child. After school every day I would stand waiting in line for the school bus to take me home. Our bus had pulled up and we were getting ready to load. I was about to take a couple of steps forward when I felt a hand grab my arm. It was him, it was Chris. I was so scared, he took me by the arm and walked me over to his car. I got in and he told me to show him where I was staying. He yelled and screamed the whole way about how the state wasn't going to have his first born and that he should have access to see me when he wanted because I was carrying his baby and I belong to him. I took him to Karen's house and he parked down the street. After he had calmed down screaming about the state he asked about how the baby was doing and if I needed anything. He talked to my belly for a while and then let me get out and walk to the house. The next day when I went out to the bus stop he was there. He said he was going to take me to school but he didn't we went to the apartment. When we were on the way he was talking to me about aborting our baby. He thought the state was going to take our baby and he didn't want the state to have his baby. "We're too far along for that I'm over 6 months" I said. "I know what the fuck I'm talking about" he said.

He went on and on about it throughout the day, he wanted to have his son but if he couldn't no one would. It was exhausting trying to convince him an abortion was not only something I wouldn't do but it was impossible. We eventually took a nap and ended up oversleeping. He told me to hurry because it was time to go back to school. I got dressed and we went to the car. I had been there for my whole school day. He drove me to Karen's house and we waited for the bus to drive by. While we were waiting he told me that if I told Karen about our contact that he was going to burn the house down with everyone in it and I believed him. I didn't want her to know because she said that was one of the stipulations for staying there was that I stay away from him. When I got home Karen knew immediately something was wrong, I'm sure I looked a mess. She asked me what was going on and I told her that I had been throwing up all day and didn't feel good so I wanted to go to bed. I prayed for a long time that God would protect my baby and that he would be ok. The next day I told Karen I was still feeling bad and she said I could stay home from school. I knew Chris would be waiting for me and I knew he would be mad but I wanted to protect my baby. The next day I had to go to school and I made myself purposefully late so Karen would have to drive me. I was worried the whole day about what was going to happen after school. Even though I was staring at the clock when the bell rang, I Jumped. I knew he would be there to get me. I walked as slow as I possibly could but the outside was coming whether I wanted it to or not. I could see his Orange Cadillac from the first step out the door of the school. By the time I got over there he had gotten out of the car. He opened the door for me and I got in, he got in and we drove away. "How's my Angel doing?" he smiled at me and leaned in for a kiss. He scared me when he acted that way when I knew he was upset. My body would freeze when he was upset. I knew he was capable of hitting me at any moment. He hadn't done it yet, more hair pulling and shoving than anything else. I didn't want to upset him anymore than he already was and after the other day I wasn't going to challenge anything. "I'm ok" I said in a low tone. "How's the baby doing?" he asked. "The baby's ok, my belly doesn't hurt anymore." "Did you say anything to anyone?" "No" I said quickly. "You better make sure the state doesn't take my first born or I'll kill you" "I promise Chris, I won't let them, I love you and our baby, and we're going to be a family right? All I have to do is stay in this place till the baby is born and then things can go back to normal. I promise." I said trying to calm him down. "I love you too Angel, I Just need you out of there, you belong to me. I need you out of that house. I'm sorry about yesterday, I panicked thinking about them taking my son. I didn't mean any of that." "I want my son, I want my son with me." "I'm learning a lot about how to take care of the baby and I need that Chris, I want to be a good mother." I plead with him. "I'm proud of you Angel, you're trying to do this right. I've gotta give you credit for that. It's time for you to go, gimme some sugar." I leaned in and kissed him and he kissed my cheek. I got out of the car and walked to the house. When I got in the house I pretended to still be sick and went straight to my room for the night.

A couple of weeks later Chris picked me up from the morning bus stop and we went riding around town. "I had to move, do you want to see the new place?" "Sure," I said quickly assuming that this was my place also. We drove over off of 10th street and Penn and he pulled into the driveway of what looked to be a duplex. We walked in and I could immediately tell there was another woman there. This wasn't Aprils stuff either. I was upset but I couldn't show it. When we went into the bedroom Chris started kissing on me and leading me to lay in the bed. We got undressed and made love. All my worries and stresses went away when I was with him like that. It was like our skin on skin contact calmed everything down. Plus I had one thing no one could ever have, I had his first born son. That was irreplaceable. He took me to the school around lunch and I checked myself in. I was not into my school work that day. I wanted to know who the other girl was if it wasn't April. Only weeks later when I was almost 7 months pregnant we got another surprise. I was starting to suffer from high blood pressure and they decided to admit me into the hospital for a while. I was in full panic mode,

I didn't fully understand everything they were talking about and I was so worried about my baby. What I did understand was that my baby wasn't getting the oxygen he needed. In order for him to get what he needed I had to do exactly what the doctors said, and that I did. I needed to call Chris, I needed to call his father to let him know what was going on. I called day and night, it took me three days to get in touch with him because he didn't answer the phone. When he did he was upset and screaming at me but there was nothing I could do. I told him where I was and he came up to see me but he had April with him. I didn't want to see her or them together so I said I wasn't feeling well and they left. I was there for a while being monitored and then they sent me home with strict instructions. I had orders to have absolutely no salt, I loved salt. At school me and Maya would get the fries at lunch and salt them to death. I would even put salt on the ketchup that of course had tons of salt already. That was probably part of what got me in this position in the first place. I also had to lay on my left side and not get up for anything. When you lay on your left side your heart operates better and it reduces the blood pressure. I did exactly what they said. I was so worried about anything harming my baby. Karen started having the teachers come to the house and school me so I would be able to stay on track with school. This was my second time trying to finish 9th grade. I made good grades and Chris would help me when I needed it but I missed too many days the first time and had to wait until the new-year and try again so I was determined to finish this time. It was important to me and Chris that I graduate, he said we could make lots of money with a good job at the right place so getting through the 9th grade was only the first step.

While staying at Karen's I learned more information than I could have ever imagined. She taught me way more than how to change diapers, administer medication, and put the baby to sleep. She was the closest thing to a real mom I ever had. She stayed at home mostly so we were together all the time. Karen had a husband and two sons. One was a year younger than me and the other was two years under the oldest one. And we had some little ones from the state also. That taught me a lot about babies and toddlers. I would help Karen with the kids and sometimes when they cried she would leave it to me to figure out what was wrong so I could learn by experience. Her husband had a lamination business and we would run errands for him from time to time. Karen had a sewing machine and said I could use it to make the bedding for the baby. I wasn't sure at that time if I was having a boy or a girl so I went with purple. I made the bumper pads, comforter, and pillow. We would go garage sale hunting for clothes. The state didn't give you money to buy baby clothes. We found some great stuff. It took a little while to get comfortable at their house but I finally did. One day we were sitting on the couch watching the news. The first teacher was about to fly up into space and bring back with her stories of wonder. We were all glued to the TV when all of the sudden we saw something on the TV we couldn't register. The shuttle had exploded in air just over a minute after takeoff. I can't think about being at Karen's house without thinking about that moment. We were getting closer and closer to the babies arrival. I was still living on my left side and ballooning up bigger and bigger. It was time to start learning what to do before deliver was upon us. Karen signed us up for birthing classes. I had no idea what to think. Karen played the dad for the class. She was very supportive and made sure I paid special attention to the most important parts. The more my belly grew, the more I felt him moving around, the more excited I got. I couldn't wait to hold my baby. Over the next couple of months I learned a ton of stuff I would have had no clue of, not only about the pregnancy, birth, and baby but also about me. Karen was the first one to assert that I shouldn't be with Chris. She allowed him to come over and drop off some baby shower gifts and she was not happy at all. She wanted different things for me but Chris and I had already made a baby. It was too late to turn back now, the baby was going to be here any minute. Karen already had a bassinet that was perfect for the antique lace cover we found. It was girly but it was beautiful. Lace was ok for baby boys too. We had worked hard to make sure we had everything I needed for the baby. Chris dropped off a box of pampers but I was making an effort to do it the old fashioned way with cloth diapers.

It started, it was subtle at first and I wasn't sure what was going on. It felt like my back muscles were being twisted and the twist would slowly move around the bottom of my belly to the middle. Similar to what they said it would be in the birthing classes but they didn't say anything about it hurting so much in the back. I went and told Karen and we started timing the contractions. We would feel my belly get hard as the contractions were coming. The stronger the contraction the closer to concrete my belly felt. I started to get nervous. Although I had gone to class and Karen and I had practiced, I was still scared to death. I was a little girl myself. I wasn't ready for this at all. A whole real live baby was going to come out of me, and my belly was big! I had watched videos and stuff but I was still worried about how my big ole baby was going to come out of little me. The contractions got to 5 minute apart so we headed to the hospital. After getting strapped up and everything…the contractions stopped. I couldn't believe it. I was so ready to have my baby, to hold him. I was disappointed getting my clothes back on and all. We went home and the wait was on. I continued to have irregular contractions for the next few weeks. Then one morning they got regular and they were stronger than they had ever been. When the contractions got to 5 minute we started heading for the van. By the time we got to the van and hit the road they were 3 minute apart. I remember laying down in the first row of the van seats. Rich was driving and he was trying to do his best to take it easy but there was nothing that could make it easy. Going over the rail-road tracks was the worst. I felt every tire move across every rail. We got to the hospital and got all strapped up and everything and the contractions didn't stop this time, they just got harder. Each one was harder than the next and they kept building higher mountains on the monitor. The doctor came in and checked and I was only at 2cm and the baby was still high up. My back was killing me more than anything else. We had brought a can of tennis balls like they suggested in the class but that Just wasn't cutting it. I was hurting so much, I couldn't stop crying. Nothing we put behind my back would relieve any of the pain. The birthing class lady said if you have back pain you could use a tennis ball can to help. My foster dad Rich, being the strongest in the room, had taken the can and was pressing against my lower back really hard to help give some relief. He held his arm there for the longest time and it was helping when nothing else would. He would take small breaks when he had to but he kept putting the pressure on to help me with my labor. Karen was keeping me focused and helping me stay on track with my breathing. The nurses came in and were looking at the print out from the monitors and said the baby's heart beat was becoming irregular because my blood pressure was going too high. They had me on my left side for most of the labor and it still wasn't helping much. They had to switch to an internal monitor on him they said. "Internal monitor, how?" I asked. "We've got to connect it to the baby's head to monitor closer" the nurse said. I started crying again, I didn't want them to put anything in my baby's head but I also didn't want them to not be able to monitor him. I asked her to show it to me and then I was able to see it was a tiny monitor that just went under the skin. When they put it in they said I was still only dilated to 4cm. I was in so much pain and we had been there for hours upon hours. I asked the nurse if I could have an epidural and she said I had to make it to a 5cm first and they would be back to check. They, when I say they, I mean about 9 they's. I almost hated to see them coming. The county hospital was a teaching hospital so every time someone came in to do something they had a crew with them and everyone else wanted to do it too. Well that got old real quick. I was hurting too much with back to back contractions to have everyone and their uncle checking my cervix. It was another couple of hours and finally I was at a 5cm. After the nurse checked me she ordered the epidural but because of my blood pressure they had to do a timed bleeding test. "What's a timed bleeding test and why can't you give me an epidural. I want to be done with this." I cried out to her. "It's where they take a little punch razor thing and make two incisions in your skin to time the bleeding. It won't take that long and then we can get you that epidural." Another nurse came in with this pill box looking thing and laid it against my arm. She pushed it and it popped down. I felt the pressure from the movement but I didn't feel the razors cut my skin. Thank God because I was already in enough pain. It was a three minute test that seemed like 20. My contractions were strong and were not stopping, they were moving up and down. When the test was over the nurse checked me again and low and behold I was almost a 10, that fast. Only problem was the baby was still high up. I was still so small being only 15 and my hips were not letting him through. My contractions were incredibly strong, it felt like my body was going to explode at the bottom from the pressure. The nurse said the words I didn't expect or want to hear. "It's too late for the epidural, you're going to do it natural" WHAT? No epidural, I couldn't imagine the pain getting any worse. My nurse checked again after a while and said that I was a full 10 but that we were going to have to push the baby down or do a C-section and I did not want a C-section. I thought I was already as scared as I could be in the situation and she added to it. The nurses helped put me in the pushing position and began the task. While I pushed the nurses put pressure on my belly to try to help him down the canal. It was not easy but I pushed, and pushed, and pushed. I pushed for over an hour. I was pouring sweat, my body had almost numbed it's self from the extended time in pain but the increase in pain stayed ahead of it. I had no idea it was going to be so painful to have a child. I had seen them wincing on videos and a moan here and there but this was ridiculous. I was in serious pain and the only remedy I had available was not "available" to me. After several hours of pushing he was finally crowing and they took me to the delivery room.

Karen stayed right by my side and Rich was there to take pictures. They put my legs up in stirrups and started washing down my legs and privates in the brown cleaning stuff. They hung big blue paper towels over me and one of the nurses asked if I wanted to see in the mirror. I said that I did so she moved it over. I didn't notice until later that it wasn't aimed right and by that time I didn't care. I was hurting, bad. I was trying so hard to get the baby out. I'd never felt pain like that and didn't want to anymore. I wanted to go back in time and do some magic to get the baby out. Anything but this. They asked me to push again and the doctor said that they were going have to do an episiotomy. I remembered that word from the classes and it wasn't a good word. By the time I registered what he was saying he had been handed what looked like a big pair of gardening shears and he went at it. I could hear the shears cut through my skin. I'll never forget that sound and the pain that went with it. The next push I could actually feel him moving down now. That had done it, it was working now. Within a couple of pushes the doctor said it, "The head's out". One more push and out he came. I didn't hear any noise and looked over at Karen with what I'm sure was a very panicky face. "Hold on baby, they're working on him" she said. About that time he let out a big ole scream, loud. He was clearly pissed about what was going on and I don't blame him. I started laughing and smiling and Karen did too. Then the nurse handed me the most precious thing on earth. There he was, my baby, my son. I looked into his eyes and he looked at me. It was love at first sight. He was a quiet baby. Not much noise after that first, what the hell is going on? Rich was taking pictures and the doctors continued to do what they do down there. I couldn't tell you what else they did. All I can remember is holding my son, looking at my son, and touching my son. He was real, this wasn't a play baby, he was a real baby boy, my baby boy. I tried to feed him like the nurses asked because I was going to breast feed but he didn't want it right away. After a while they took him to do all the things they had to do and moved me to my room upstairs. Karen stayed with me until they got me up then her and Rich went home to get some rest. I couldn't sleep at all! I kept calling to the nursery to have them bring him to me but they were taking too long. I got up, unplugged the IV thing, and walked to the nursery. They were mostly just sitting there. "Can I have my baby please" I asked at the desk. "What is your room number, can I see your wrist band?" the nurse asked. She verified everything and then gave him to me in a cart thing on wheels with a plastic bin on top. I don't know why but I thought that they would keep them in the traditional kind of bassinet. You know the white weaved one with the moon shaped hood over one side. I called Chris and told him that I had the baby and that yes, it was a boy. He was so excited he started yelling "I'm a father, I'm a father!" He said he would come to the hospital soon. It was about two hours later when I heard that distinctive sound, the dancing horses coming down the hall. I sat up in the bed and did my best to fix my hair. I had ballooned being on my side for months with little to no movement. And the pregnancy acne had hit explosion mode while I was in labor so I'm sure I looked peachy keen. Chris walked in and I started smiling, sitting there holding our son, his first born. He walked over with a huge smile and talking baby talk all the way over to our son. And right behind him was April with Samuel. "Hi Angel" "Hi April, hi Samuel." What the crap are you doing here?? Was what I wanted to say but that would have gotten me in trouble so I stayed quiet. April asked about the labor and I told her about doing it natural. Chris was happy to hear that, he didn't want our baby drugged up during birth. After a while he sat Samuel up in the chair and let him hold our son, then he handed my baby to her. I didn't want my baby to be a part of that life so having her hold him was not top on my list, it wasn't on my list at all. Not that I think she would have hurt him or anything, I know she wouldn't but this moment was for me and Chris. Not me, Chris, and his girls. They stayed for a while and Chris held his son till the last minute and they left. I went through the baby stuff that Chris brought with him and changed my baby's clothes. The second night Chris came by his self. He got in the bed with me and we laid with our son between us. "We're a family now. You don't just belong to me now, we're a family" I took that to mean we were seriously bonded now, like married, not just because he bought me but because we have a child together. "You can't keep staying with that lady now Angel. My son's got to be with me." "I'm not going to be there long but I've got to learn how to do this. Please let me stay" I begged. "I want to be able to come see my son." "I'll get some things worked out, I promise" Chris stayed until visiting hours were over and the nurse had to ask him to leave. He kept kissing my cheek and she finally pulled him by his arm to make him leave. I kept my son in the room with me Just about the whole time.

On the last day they brought the paperwork to do the birth certificate. Chris had insisted that he be named Christopher after him since he was the first born, first son, and just because Chris said. I had already started calling him Greedy. Every time I would start feeding him it was hard to get him to stop. And when I would pick him up for burps or to play with him he was constantly looking for the milk. Greedy was it, of course he had 14 other nicknames from me and various others but Greedy stuck. Karen had helped me put everything together for Greedy. We had a bed, high-chair, bassinet, and the whole nine yards. All he had to do was get here, and here he was. We had finally come home from the hospital. It was a great event bringing him home. We had everything ready. I walked him in the house and laid him in his bed for the first time. He looked perfect in it. I sat on the bed and stared at him for what seemed to be forever. I watched his back move up and down with his breathing. I was so nervous and he was so fragile. Karen promised me that I can't break him, that his limbs are kind of rubbery at first. I was careful holding him anyway. He finally woke and I changed him into the cloth diapers. While he was sleeping I went through all his little bitty outfits and chosen the one I wanted him to wear for the day. I held him close to me and walked to the living room. I was so nervous and unsure about keeping him safe. I sat there for hours just holding him. "You're going to spoil that baby and then you'll be sorry" she would say. After about a week I asked Karen if she thought Chris should be able to see Greedy. She said as bad as she hated to say yes…yes. "But not over here" she quickly added. So the plan was that I would take a visit to my mom's house because that was the only place Karen could legally let me spend the night because I was in state's custody still. While at my mom's I could see Chris and he could see Greedy. I called mom and told her when I would be coming over with the baby. She was excited to see him and so were my sisters. That weekend came and Karen took me over to the address I had for mom. The house mom was staying in was super small. When I got inside I called Chris to let him know I was there. About an hour or so he pulled up and came in. I didn't have a car seat with me so I couldn't go anywhere, I think Karen did that on purpose. He sat there holding and talking to his son for over an hour. Calling out 9 thousand nicknames and couldn't settle on one. Chris went to get some food for me and left after he dropped it off. He said he would be back tomorrow. The house was only a one bedroom so as usual I had to sleep on the floor with my brand new baby. Greedy was 20 days old, now normally I wouldn't remember that however, that night was the first time he rolled over by his self, that's the only reason I remember it was 20 days after he was born. I was freaking out that morning when I woke up. I knew I had left him on his belly and he woke up on his back. It took me a minute to figure out what happened. My baby was having milestones. Chris came over that morning and picked us up. I didn't expect to go anywhere and wasn't supposed do either. I was nervous about driving without the car-seat but didn't have a lot of say in the matter. I was still a kid even though I had just had one. We rode out and got some burgers as usual but then we went back to mom's house. I expected him to take me to the apartment but he didn't. When we got back to mom's house we sat in the car for a couple of hours. Mom's house was not the cleanest on the block and neither I nor Chris wanted to have the baby in there if we didn't have to so we stayed outside. When it got late we went in and mom, Tyana and Lillian had gone to bed. We had the living room to ourselves. Chris laid on the pallet on the floor with me and rubbed Greedy's back till he fell asleep. After the baby was asleep Chris started rubbing on my body. It had only been 3 weeks and the doctor said I was supposed to wait 6 weeks. I was scared but I couldn't say no, I belonged to him. He climbed on top of me and started pushing his self into me. It hurt and burned all at the same time. He had talked earlier about how he thought it would be different since the baby had been through there. After he finished he told me that "my body still felt good but he didn't feel my heart" he wanted me to leave Karen's so he could have full control again. He told me that I would be able to get a welfare check and food stamps if I lived on my own and he would be there to help with Greedy too. I couldn't say no so I told him I would find a way to leave. Even though I didn't want to leave at all. I was so confused. I wanted to have the family with Chris that he said we would have but I didn't want to leave the stability I had found with Karen and her family. I loved her and she loved me. For real. And there was still so much to learn. How do you learn 18 years of info in a couple of months? Chris left and I fell asleep. The next morning I woke to Karen calling to say that she was on her way. When I woke up to answer the phone I noticed that Greedy was already up. He was sitting there quiet and looking around. Karen came and got me and we went back home.

Over the next several weeks I studied Karen, how she worked with the babies, the toddlers, her preteen and her teenager. I was trying to soak up as much as I could in the time I had. Given my own childhood it was crucial that I find other ways to get the info needed to raise my own child. She was part of the map that I needed to get through this thing called life. We were sitting on the couch one day talking about raising Greedy. She was the greatest at advice, she said. "When you pull up at someone's house they will all look outside and say the same thing but in different tones. They will be excited "Hey, there's Sarah, and she's got the kids!" Or dread you coming "Oh, there's Sarah, and she's got those kids." She was great about giving little stories like that. Simple, but covers huge ground. I so enjoyed staying with Karen, Rich, and the boys. I only have one regret, one day, one action that I took. One day while I was still pregnant Karen had gotten all the items needed to make strawberry shortcakes. She got those little cupcakes that come 6 in a pack and there were 5 of us so that left one. After we did the dishes Karen left the extra cake on the counter. Everyone had gone to bed and I had gotten up in the middle of the night hungry. Of course I remembered the cake and so I ate it and went back to bed. The next morning I woke to Karen yelling at the boys asking who ate the cake. She was upset. I started to confess but then wasn't sure if she was going to ask me to leave because of it and I couldn't take a chance with that. When I came into the room she asked "Sarah did you eat the cake that was left on the counter" "No" I said. Immediately her oldest son said "She's lying, look at her she looks guilty I can tell she's lying. Look at the fingernail marks on the paper where it was, I don't have fingernails." He was so upset and I had lied. I know for some this would not be such a big deal however, the oldest son, the one who knew I was lying and tried to tell everyone else, he was blamed for it. Not only was he blamed for it but he was scheduled to go on a golf day with his dad and my lie caused him to get grounded and miss his day with his dad. I cried in my room several times over that one. I stayed in my room most of the day because I felt bad that he was in his and not out golfing with his dad. I hoped to have the chance to make it up to him one day, however his dad died a few years ago in a plane he was flying. Lesson learned; be careful how long you wait to tell a person you're sorry. I didn't ever want to leave Karen's house but the time came.

~Chapter 14~

She's Prettier Than Me

My social worker helped me get on welfare and food stamps and I moved into an apartment Chris had for me. We had a nice little furnished duplex, the landlady lived in the bigger half of the house. She didn't like Chris at all and would complain when he would spend the night. I'm sure she could hear every creek of the bed. The first weekend I was back Chris took us down to Ardmore to show grandma the new baby. From the moment we got there until we left I think the only time I had Greedy was feeding time. Between his mom and his sisters, that baby was spoiled rotten. We drove back to the city and Chris dropped me off at my apartment. I would stay up all hours of the night playing with my baby boy. We didn't have to be anywhere so when he was up, I was up. One day Chris had come by, when he was getting ready to leave, he asked me to get him a bottle because he was going to take Greedy with him. I got the bottle and gave it to him with a diaper. I carried the car seat out and put it in the car for him. I cleaned house while he was gone. There were some things I wasn't able to do with the baby so this was good timing. When Chris got back to the house he honked the horn and I went outside to get Greedy. When I walked outside I seen that he had someone in the car with him. It was a girl but it wasn't April. The first thing I noticed was that she was very pretty. She had long brown hair and beautiful eyes. Her lips were full, like I'd always wished for. She was around my age but a little older, I could tell she was American Indian. The second thing I noticed was that she was holding Greedy in the front seat. My blood began to boil and I know it was visible. Chris was getting out of the car and seen that I had a sour look on my face. He asked "What the fuck is your problem" as he was getting Greedy through the window from her. "Why isn't he in his car seat Chris?" I asked as he handed me Greedy, knowing any other question would be the wrong thing to do. Well that question was apparently the wrong thing to do. Chris swung at me with an open hand I tried to move fast enough but it didn't work. His hand hit me so hard on the side of my head that I fell to the ground. My ears started ringing, everything went into slow motion. When I hit the ground I was trying to hold on to Greedy more than I was trying to break my fall. I landed right on my behind but I didn't lose hold of Greedy. He started screaming before we ever hit the ground. "Don't ask me no fuckin questions dizzy bitch" I cowered down on the ground expecting the worst. I'm sure if I wasn't holding Greedy he would have laid into me. He grabbed my arm and stood me back up real quick "Take yo ass in the house dizzy bitch, and don't ever question what I do with my child, that's not your child, that's my child" he screamed at me. He came stomping after me and grabbed the baby. He walked back to the car and handed the baby to her. That "*her*" that was sitting in my man's car. Chris walked around to the driver side, got in. I was crying out to him to please give me my baby back. About that time neighbors started coming out and he drove off. There were a lot of first that day. That was the first time I seen Brook and the first time he had ever actually hit me, and the first time he took the baby for punishment. He had done many other things pull my hair, choke me, throw me around, but had never hit me, especially with the baby in my arms. I don't know why it was new to me but it was. I had watched him beat the crap out of several different women many different times but I seriously thought he wouldn't hit me. I went inside and cried until I couldn't cry anymore. Her first impression seeing me was him hitting me. That was not what you do to your number one. I was losing my place with him. Just as I thought it was being strengthened by our son, it was being torn apart by a new girl. A couple of hours later he brought my baby back. He didn't say anything to me, he handed me the baby at the door and walked off. Greedy was upset too cause his momma was and he could feel that. We rocked until we both fell asleep. The next day I talked myself into believing that he pushed me down instead of hit me. I protected him to myself instead of protecting myself from him, and life moved on. When the first of the month came around Chris moved me from that apartment. He was worried that the landlady would eventually bring in the police. While we were moving I found out that my new place was April's apartment first and that Fred from the first apartment we lived in was living downstairs. I wouldn't have picked it but, it was a garage apartment that he had already furnished, and it was a decent apartment. I was still 15yrs old so I couldn't legally get an apartment of my own so I couldn't be choosey. When I was moving in we had to move the rest of Aprils stuff out and take down the clothes lines she had hung in the living room. I Jumped up and grabbed one of the lines to pull it down like Chris had just done the other one. Lucky me, the nail came right out of the ceiling and right into my arm, Just above the wrist area. I started freaking out yelling and crying. It was a 4 inch nail and most of it was in my arm. Chris turned to see why I was freaking out. When he seen the nail sticking out of my arm he grabbed my hand with his hand and the nail with the other hand and jerked it out. The blood shot up like a water hose had been turned on. "Put your fucking finger on it!" Chris yelled. He went down to the car and came back with some gray tape. He took a wad of toilet paper, put it on the hole and wrapped the gray tape around it. "Now let's finish this shit." He got up and went back to work and so did I. My arm was throbbing and when it would hang down it throbbed harder. The toilet paper wasn't enough and I started bleeding from under the tape. I went to the bathroom and was trying to shove more toilet paper under the tape when Chris came in. "Here" he said as he stretched out his hand. I gave him my arm fearing what he was going to do. My instincts were right. He ripped the gray tape off my arm. All the hair went with it. My arm was in pain inside and out. This time he took a wash rag and folded it then taped it in place. He taped it tighter, almost too tight. I went back to work getting everything put in its place. When we were done we went back to the other apartment and started packing there. The next morning we got up and started moving the boxes and stuff to the other apartment. It only took a couple of trips because I didn't have much, no furniture to speak of. Finally I was settled in the new place. There was a little back room that was Greedy's bedroom at first but he never slept in there and quite Frankly, I never felt right about that room, there were too many noises in there and it was too far away. I eventually moved his bed to the bathroom. I know, the bathroom?? Well this bathroom was actually almost bigger than the bedroom and where the door set it put his bed only feet from mine. I was good with that and so was he. We started living as close to a normal life as we could for the dysfunction we were in. Life was ok for a couple of weeks then things started changing again.

Chris came one evening and said I had to go with him and to leave Greedy there in the apartment. I was not ok with that, I was trying to be a good mother. "I can't leave him here alone, please don't make me do that. What if something happens?" "Nothing's going to happen put your shit on and let's go." "Chris please" He grabbed me by my neck raised me off the ground and threw me on the bed screaming "Get your shit on and let's go!" When I landed on the bed where Greedy was it made him fall off the bed. He landed on the floor and immediately let out a scream. I jumped down at the same time as Chris to get him. Chris picked him up first and was apologizing to him and trying to calm him down. I was so anxious and scared I thought my body was going to explode. Chris got him settled and laid him down in the bed. I didn't want to let him go to sleep but

Chris didn't leave me much choice. He was cussing me the whole time he was putting him down. Saying that it was all my fault and if I would have just got my shit on and gone then he wouldn't have fallen. He said that if there was anything wrong with Greedy he was going to bash my head in. I got dressed and we left, leaving Greedy in his crib. Chris drove me out to NE 23rd, the whole way he yelled at me about the baby and how I was going to fuck it all up like my mom and he was going to be kicking my ass. He knew exactly how to make me feel worthless and he enjoyed doing it if you ask me. When we pulled up in the parking lot that was the point in time where I knew what was going on. Chris had set up a trick for me. I was so upset, I wanted to cry and almost started until Chris seen me watering, grabbed my face and said "I wish you would." I knew what that meant. He told me what room to go to and I went and knocked on the door. It was an older tall lanky white man. Looked like your typical guy, nothing special. He started repeating some of the things Chris had said about my qualifications. The more he quoted the sicker I got to my stomach. I seriously believed that after having his child he wouldn't make me do this anymore. I was wrong, I wasn't gaining ground I was losing ground. I pulled the trick and came out with the money and gave it to Chris when I got in the car. The guy had given me an extra $20 that he said was for me but I gave that to Chris too. As bad as I needed money I didn't want a child molesters money anymore, plus if I got caught with money that he didn't give me that was a reason for him to punish me. I know they knew every time that I was a young girl, for sure under 18. That was actually one of Chris's marketing tools, under 18. I was thinking about Greedy the whole time we were gone. I was imagining all kinds of weird crazy things that could possibly happen. That "What if" game that my little sister played that drove me crazy. Well I was playing it with myself. What if he chokes? What if the house catches fire? What if he wiggles out of the crib somehow? When we got to the apartment I Jumped out of the car before it completely stopped. I wanted to know that my baby was ok. I ran up the stairs to his room and swooped him up out of the bed. He was still sleeping and grabbing him startled him but I couldn't let go. I looked him over to see if the fall had left any bruises or bumps and he didn't have a scratch on him. Chris didn't even come up, he left that night and didn't stay with me like he usually did. I knew if he wasn't spending the night with me then he was at April's or Brook's and that night I didn't care. I soaked in the tub, scrubbed myself down and went to bed. I had Greedy in the bed right next to me. I started thinking of ways to make extra money without having to turn tricks. I couldn't think of anything that didn't lead to jail. I was almost old enough to get a real job, my 16th birthday was coming up. I didn't know how much people made working but I knew it was money, and I needed money to keep him happy. Plus school was already here and I needed to figure that out too. I spent the majority of my time taking care of Greedy and teaching him everything I could. I started singing him the ABC song when he was a baby and as he got older he was making letter noises to it with me. He was the smartest baby ever. Life went on as normal as it could for a while, my birthday came and went. There was no sweet 16 for my birthday, not even a cake. I helped Greedy sing it to me and the festivities were over.

It was time to get dressed for work. Chris would still make "appointments" for me from time to time and I was still scared every moment I had to leave Greedy alone. It didn't matter to me that he was sleeping the whole time. I was supposed to be with him at all times. One night Chris had made an appointment for me but it was only 7 in the evening and Greedy was wide awake. I tried to put Greedy down but he wasn't having it. He was crying because he didn't want to be in the crib. Chris said it was time to go and started pulling me away from the crib. I started crying and that made Greedy cry more. Chris picked him up by the arm and started spanking him on the diaper and yelling for him to shut up. Of course that scared him and made him cry even harder and me too. Chris put him back in the bed and picked me up by the arm and started dragging me down the stairs. I didn't catch my footing till we were at the bottom. I had hit my ankle on the way down and it was hurting bad. When we got downstairs he practically threw me in the car. He cussed me all the way there yelling at me to stop crying. By the time we got there I had stopped crying but I looked like crap with swollen red eyes and I had a limp from hitting my ankle and it was swelling fast. He told me what room to go to and I started limping over to the door. Chris Jumped out of the car real quick and ran up on me. "What the fuck is wrong with you?" he yelled through his teeth trying not to be loud. I turned my ankle where he could see the swelling. "Oh you a stupid bitch, why the fuck did you do that?" I didn't say anything, I was so afraid of what he would do. I kept limping to the door. I knocked and a man opened the door. I walked in with my head down. I didn't want him to see my face but I couldn't hide the limp. "What's wrong with you" he asked. I showed him my ankle. "I twisted it on the way over here." About that time he seen my face. "Yea, I don't want to do this" he said. "You can go now." I tried to straighten up for him to get him to go ahead with it so I could get the money. "Please, I'll do extra, don't make me go, please." I begged "I'm not paying for a beat up prostitute" he said as he pushed me toward the door. I had just turned 16 but the age didn't matter. Like he said, I was a beat up prostitute. I walked back outside with my head hanging down, Chris got out of the car and met me half way. "Did you get the money that fast?" he asked. "No, he didn't want me" Chris grabbed me and shoved me to the ground. "You ain't worth shit to me" he said. He walked over to the car and was getting in. I got up and tried to get in the car but he pulled away. He left me there, he left me there. How was I going to get back to my baby, how would I get home to him? I didn't know what to do. I was afraid of what he was going to do to me if I left the area where he left me. I stood in the parking lot for a while thinking he might come back but he didn't. I started walking home but I was way on the other side of town and I was not familiar with the area at all. My ankle was killing me, I could barely walk. I thought about calling the police for a ride because I needed to get back to Greedy but what would I say. And most of all what would keep them from taking Greedy away from me. Nothing, so I did nothing but walk. I walked until the sun came up. I cried the majority of the way. 99% of the people drove by, the only two cars that stopped looked like serial killers so I Just kept walking. When I was walking up the driveway I could see that Chris's car was there and the trunk was up. April was coming down the stairs with my dish drainer in her hand and they were putting my things in his car. I didn't even care I struggled to get to the top of the stairs with my ankle and seen that all my stuff was gone. The only piece of anything left in the apartment was Greedy's bed that Karen had given me and a pile of my clothes. I ran as fast as I could to the bed and Greedy was laying there sleep. I grabbed him up and started squeezing him tight to me. I looked around as I was holding my baby, he had taken everything. I heard the car start up and I looked out the window and he was gone. Most of my dishes were gone, some of my food was gone. I only had a face towel and no big towels. Everything was gone. I used a t-shirt, got some ice and put it on my ankle. I kept the ice coming, freezing more as I used it. I didn't move around much, I Just held Greedy most of the time and kept ice on my ankle. It was a couple of days before he came back. When he did he Just came and got Greedy and left. Now I was all alone in an empty apartment. I figured he took Greedy to April, so while I was upset that he was gone, I knew he would be ok. I stayed in the apartment, I wanted to take a walk or something to get away from the boredom but I didn't want to not be there when he got back. I spent my time cleaning things that were already clean, sleeping and laying with my foot up so it could heal. It was two days before he came back. I could see into the car from the window above when he pulled up. He didn't have Greedy with him and I couldn't help but start crying. I tried to straighten it up before he got up the stairs. I was sitting on the floor in the living room when he got up there. He had a bag and a bible in his hand. He opened it and started reading to me, he would always reading about punishment. "Though hand join in hand, the wicked shall not be unpunished, but the seed of the righteous shall be delivered." I was the wicked of course and he was the righteous that put forth the seed. He handed it to me to read out loud, I read for a while in Proverbs where he liked selecting the verses that made you look bad and him look good. It was all about obeying and being obedient or suffering punishment because he was the Alpha and Omega. After a while he took the Bible and shoved me to the ground and kicked me in my behind. "You got too much room in this mutha fucker for someone who is as worthless as you" he said. He told me to go to the bathroom, he handed me the bible then he shut the door. I could hear him start nailing on the door. He was locking me in. I hadn't been locked in since before we were taken to the Juvenile shelter. I slumped down on the floor and wanted to cry but nothing came out. I heard him leave and tried to budge the door. It opened just a bit. Enough that I could tell that he had put a lock on the door and he had slid the dresser over in front of the door. I remember thinking at least I have a toilet and water from the sink. I didn't have a cup but I did have a bottle so I used that. It was two days before he returned. When he did it was Just to yell at me, smack and push me around and degrade me. We read the Bible together again and even though I would try to think of him as the wicked and not me but it didn't work. He made me feel so worthless. I kept asking about Greedy and he kept saying it wasn't my son it was his and I didn't deserve to know about his son. He told me to get my shoes on and that he was putting me out. I couldn't stay there anymore and I didn't have a son, he did. I begged him not to put me out and to let me see my son but he didn't care. He grabbed my hair and stood me up and marched me down the stairs and out to the front yard. I fell to my knees in the front yard, he grabbed me by the hair and drug me to the street. He said I couldn't be on the property because it was his even though it was my welfare check that was paying the rent. That part didn't matter, I had just turned 16 and no one was going to rent an apartment to me. I got up and started walking away, I walked down 10th street for a while then back over to the apartment. My ankle was better but it still hurt with every step. I stayed in the back yard because number one I had nowhere else to go and number two I needed to be there when he came back. It was another two days before he came back. I didn't eat the first day because I was trying to lay low and not be seen unless it was by Chris. The second day Fred had walked outside before I could get around the corner. "Hey Angel, what you doing over there?" Fred asked. "I'm waiting for Chris to come back, he has Greedy." "He told me you wasn't living there anymore and he told Charles and he's about to rent it out." "No, he can't do that!" I said, "This is still my apartment, it's not the first yet! Fred will you please call Charles and tell him not to rent it. Tell him to give me some time to work this out, please." I begged. Fred had a look on his face like he wanted to help me but didn't know what to do. "You can stay here at my place for a couple of days if you need to" he said. "You know Chris would trip out if he even heard of me being in your house, I'll Just hang around here if that's ok". "Well let me get you something to eat then." I was seriously hungry so I took him up on his offer. I took the plate of chicken he gave me and went to the back of the apartment. I ate it quick and took the plate back around to Fred. It was a few hours later when I heard Chris pulling into the driveway. When I heard him park I came from behind the apartment and Just stood where he could see me. I wanted to approach him but I was afraid to. I didn't want to make the situation any worse than it already was. Chris got out of his car "What the fuck are you still here for?" he asked as he walked to Fred's door and started knocking. "Please let me see my baby" was the first thing out of my mouth. He turned sharply and marched over to me real quick and shoved me down. "You ain't got no fucking baby bitch and don't be asking about what's mine" he yelled. Before he finished Fred had come out and started walking over to where we were. "Hey hey Chris, what's going on brotha?" "This dizzy bitch gotta go that's what the fuck is going on." "Come on now Chris, I've known you two for a while and Angel a good girl Chris, I know she is. What she gone and done that's this bad?" Fred asked. Chris was looking at me on the ground crying when Fred was talking to him. "I can't have a bitch that don't do what I say" as he kicked me in the side and then looked back up at Fred. "I got MY son and this bitch can go back to her sorry ass momma" "Please, Chris, Please let me see… before I could finish he was on top of me choking me and screaming "You ain't got no fucking baby, that's my baby" Fred grabbed Chris and started pulling him off "Chris, you don't wanna go to jail, let her go Chris, let her go!" When I was younger, around

10 or 11, we would play the knock out game. Crazy stuff I know but what I learned from that was what the point of no return felt like. That point where even if they let go you're gonna pass out. Well he had me right at that moment and what I also knew was if he held me for even a few seconds after I pass out, I'm dead. Right in those seconds, he let go. My mouth was buzzing from the lack of oxygen, my eyes felt like they had popped out of their sockets, my head and ears were throbbing and ringing. But I could still hear him yelling over that "Angel, Angel, wake up!" My body was limp from passing out but I could start to feel him tugging on me. I remained limp, I was almost disappointed that he didn't kill me. If I can't have my son, why even be here. All the sudden I feel a big splash of water in my face. Fred had grabbed the water hose and was hitting me right in the face. I gasped for air and rolled over to avoid the water. Chris swooped me up real quick "I love you Angel, I love you, don't you go nowhere on me". It was an instant turn around. When he thought he killed me he loved me. Before, he hated me. He carried me over to the apartment door and opened it and we went upstairs. He laid me down on the living room floor. Every moment I wanted to ask for Greedy but I didn't want to re-live the same thing. After we were done he said I could stay there and for me to take a shower and stuff. Chris left and I started looking around to see what was left there. Pretty much nothing, but I did find one of Greedy's blankets. I picked it up and smelled it and just held it to my face for a while. I took a shower then waited at the window, with Greedy's blanket. I was praying that he would have Greedy with him when he came. As scared as I was for him to return, I knew it was the only way for me to get Greedy back. It was a few hours later and the sun had gone down, finally I saw his lights turn in. I couldn't see into the car very well until he was getting out and I didn't see him. Chris came up the stairs half way and called for me to come with him. We got in the car and started heading for the east side and I knew what was up. I still wanted to ask about Greedy every moment and it was killing me not to ask but I kept it in so I could hopefully get him back. We went to the usual spot and I "did what he said" and prayed that my

reward would be more than a place to stay, I prayed for my son. I went back to the car and gave him the money. Chris was in a better mood and was showing affection. All I was doing was praying. He took me back to the apartment and dropped me off. I took a shower and took my place at the window with the blanket. I couldn't tell you what time I fell asleep but I woke up right under that window. I didn't have anything in the apartment to tell me what time it was but by the sun I figured it was around 9 or 10 in the morning. There was nothing in the apartment so I went down and knocked on Fred's door. He asked about me and gave me a sandwich and I hurried back upstairs. It was a while before Chris finally came. And I could see sitting in the front seat was Greedy. My heart almost jumped right out of me and out that window. If I had the ability to fly I would have flown down to him. I raced for the door and almost killed my ankle again trying to get down the stairs. I opened the door and Chris had Greedy in his arms walking toward the door. I anxiously waited for him to give him to me but he walked right past me and up the stairs. I followed right behind him and kept my eyes on Greedy the whole time. Chris took Greedy to the back room where there was carpet and put him in there on the floor. I was right behind him and thought I was going to be able to pick him up. Chris turned me with his hands and took me to the living room to lay on the floor together. Greedy started crying half way through and Chris got up and went to the back room. He spanked him and told him not to cry but Greedy was still too young to understand and kept crying. Chris came back to the living room and started up with me again. After a while Greedy cried his-self to sleep. Every time I thought we were finished Chris wanted more and I wanted Greedy. I continued to do what he asked, hoping he would leave Greedy with me. It was several hours of going between cuddling and him screaming and yelling at me about how stupid I am and how I'm not worthy. That "if I don't get it right God is going to punish me by taking our son" and if that happens he will surely kill me. By this time it was dark outside and Chris got up to take a shower. He had me sit on the toilet next to the shower so he could keep an eye on me. After he got dressed he went into the back room but he came out empty handed. He walked over to me and gave me a kiss goodbye and said he would be back tomorrow. It seemed like it took hours for him to get down the stairs but he finally did. As soon as I heard the door shut behind him I ran to the back room. Greedy was laying on the floor sleeping, I couldn't not pick him up. I grabbed him and it startled him but I could tell he was happy to see me too. He hugged me and we gave each other kisses. I took him to the living room and we played until the both of us fell asleep. Greedy woke up crying because he was hungry, Chris had only left one bottle. I went back down to Fred's and he gave me milk and some food. That afternoon Chris came back and he had some of my stuff, over the next few days he brought everything back and things went back to the way they were.

~Chapter 15~

Bang Your Head

Months later Fred moved out and I moved downstairs, it was 25 bucks cheaper a month. I liked it better too. There were no stairs, the back room wasn't there and Greedy had his own room. The living room was small but on two levels because half of it used to be the garage. The kitchen was a strip with the fridge at the end and I made the small dining room into Greedy's room. The bedroom was a good size and the bathroom was inside the bedroom. Chris had gotten me new furniture because this one wasn't furnished. I felt like the Queen of the land. I had never had new furniture of my own. It was a couch and loveseat and they came covered in plastic they were so new. Coffee tables, end tables and even two lamps. He was doing great financially at this time. Both me and April were on welfare so our checks paid the rent and we had food stamps to fill all three houses with food. He still had me doing "appointments" basically like a call girl, April was still working the streets, she had a hand full of regulars and Brook was still working as a stripper in the clubs. Things were going very well for Chris the money was coming in every day. I was in my apartment one day when I heard a car pulling into the driveway. I looked outside and it was a really nice red car. It wasn't Chris in the Cadillac. I wondered who it was so I kept looking out of the window. The door opened and Chris popped up out of that nice car. I ran to the door and opened it. "Wow, Chris, this is a really nice car." I looked over and April was in the car and Samuel was in the back. "I just bought this beauty. The guy at the dealership wanted too much for it but I talked him down to a real nice price, and paid the man cash." I didn't dare ask what that price was. "Come on, get Greedy and let's go." He was so happy about the new car. I walked in a got Greedy and we got in the backseat with Samuel. Chris headed straight for the highway. He was talking about all of the things he was going to do to the car. New paint job first, new cloth cover for the roof, new carpet on the floors. Chris kept all of his cars in perfect shape and perfectly clean. We rode around for about a half an hour and then he dropped me back off. For a while that's all he would drive. One day he came to get me and already had Brook and April in the car with him. We would all go shopping together sometimes. We would get along with each other with him around because the consequences were not worth being a bitch to each other. One of Chris's favorite stores was the Langston's Western Wear store because he could get his Levis jeans and snake skin cowboy boots there. He would buy us all jeans and sometimes a top or two. There was a boot shop across the street where he would have the tips and taps added to his boots. He would take his boots there every month to get them cleaned as well. And one of his other favorites was renting and copying movies. Video stores were the new thing and Chris wanted to have a library of videos like the store. He bought video recorders to set up at everybody's house and would have us all tape the video's he rented. When we were about half way through the process of creating his library the Beta came out and we had to start getting the Beta version of everything also. Chris loved watching movies and we spent tons of money making sure he could watch whatever he wanted. His favorites were all the Richard Pryor movies, The Ten Commandments with Charleston Hesston and the Charles Mansion movie Helter Skelter. We watched those so many times I could say most of the words with the movie. I was good at memorizing things. That's part of what helped me make almost straight A's in school. I was still trying to finish my 9th grade year. I failed the first time because I wasn't there enough. I had been going to school again to try to do 9th grade. I was at the pregnant girl school when I was with Karen but I wasn't always able to go after I moved with Chris, so that year was a wash. I was hoping third time would be a charm. When I was in school my grades were great, I Just needed to be there. I needed to finish 9th grade. My chance to finish what was no longer my freshman year was fading away fast.

Chris decided to move Brook out to the NW side of town because she was working over there. He didn't like that she was still in the neighborhood where her family lived. They didn't like that she was with him. April and I were helping move all of the stuff to the new apartment because Brook was at work. I was in the front seat of the Lincoln with Chris and April was in the back. We were headed down 12th street. April made a smart remark from the back and all the sudden, Chris started swatting at her in the back seat trying to hit her. She was dodging to get out of the way and then he practically jumped in the back seat of the car while it was still moving. He was punching her over and over with his legs in the air. I was trying to Jump over to the driver seat and grab the wheel without getting kicked by his boots. Before I could get the wheel, the car went up on the steep median in the middle of the road. I yelled for help, I grabbed the wheel to pull it back down and Chris finally turned back around in the seat and took control of the car. We were about a half of a second from hitting a car that was on the side of the road. When I looked back I could see that April was bleeding from her lip and her eye. I did my best to keep my head forward because Chris didn't want you to have any communication with the other girl who's getting her ass whooped. We got to the apartment and was moving stuff in and while Chris was downstairs getting more things, April and

I crossed on the stairs. "He's yours Angel, you can have him, and I can't do this anymore." I didn't say anything back I Just kept going with my stuff. April had set me up before and had me say things to her in confidence that she then took to Chris so I didn't want to say anything that was going to back fire on me. We finished the move and Chris took April back to her place while I cleaned the furniture and the rest of the apartment. When Chris got back we went shopping for new plastic runners for the floors and a few other things. When we got back, we ate dinner then put the runners on the floors. By the time we got done it was midnight so we went to bed. When we were laying there talking Chris was telling me how much he trusted me and how much I had grown and matured. He knew how to cut me down and he knew how to lift me up. "So since I'm your number one I'm supposed to tell you everything, right?" "Yes, of course Angel, what are you talking about?" "Well, when I was walking by April when we were bringing the stuff in she said "He's yours Angel, you can have him, and I can't do this anymore." "Oh, she did huh, dizzy bitch!" I don't know why I didn't think he would but he got up, got dressed, put his boots on, and left. I don't think it takes a genius to figure out where he went and what happened. He came back and was still heated. He woke me up and preached to me for a few hours about being obedient and how that was a sin and that the wages of sin was death. He was the Alpha and Omega and that even if we say things out of his site he can still hear us, he will still find out, and we will be punished to the ends of the earth. That night I wasn't sure if he had killed April and this was what he was trying to say or that he would kill me. Either way wasn't good. I sat there like a statue listening to him. I was afraid to move or do anything to upset him. He laid down in the bed and we eventually fell asleep. The next morning he praised me for being loyal and obedient and telling on April. I didn't feel like being praised. She received more punishment because of me, that didn't make me feel good at all. We went shopping and got Greedy some things and then went back to my apartment. Chris didn't stay with me but a couple of days a week now because number one he didn't like to hear Greedy cry and number two he had three full time girls to satisfy and still had other girls here and there. It was more than a week before I seen April again. She was alive but wasn't looking that great. Her face was still bruised with a cut by her eyebrow and you could tell that she was favoring one of her arms. He had picked us both up to come over and clean the apartment. This is something he did on a regular basis. One of us cleaned the apartment everyday but sometimes he would have us clean together. While we were cleaning he was on the phone with his mom and they were talking about someone coming to the city. After we cleaned Chris took us home and told me that he would be back for me later. I cleaned up my house and got Greedy dressed and myself as well. I had no clue who was coming because he didn't say much but I sure was curious. It was late in the evening by the time he showed up. He had a black woman with him and I thought it was one of his sisters or cousins or something. I got in the car and he introduced her, "Angel, this is my wife Teraya." Yea, his wife! Come to find out, he had married her when he was younger back in Ardmore. She had moved to California when they separated and that was when he came up to the city. We rode out to the apartment and when we got there Brook was already there. When we all walked in she had a sour look on her face and her and Chris went to the bedroom. You could still hear what he was saying because he had started yelling at her and she was yelling at him. His plan was that Brook would go to her mother's house for the night and he and his wife would stay at the apartment. It didn't go over too well with Brook. She was resisting and that just pissed Chris off. You could hear things thumping around and her screaming while he was yelling. The door flew open and Brook went running out of the apartment. He came out and chased her for a minute then came back to the apartment and got us. He told me to drive the Cadillac and him and his so-called "wife" got in the Lincoln and headed down McArthur Blvd. A few blocks down the street we seen Brook walking along the road. Chris pulled over sharply and I did my best to follow without wrecking the car. He Jumped out of the car as soon as he stopped and ran up to Brook. He started punching and kicking her. I don't know why it shocked me but it did. I was so scared I was shaking. She had fallen to the ground and he was stomping on her everywhere. It was after dark and he had a white jogging suit on and that made him practically glow in the dark. It only took a minute or so before someone pulled over. It was an older couple and they yelled for him to stop but didn't get out of the car. The next vehicle was only seconds behind and was two younger guys, they jumped out of the truck they were in and started running over to her. When they did Chris ran back to his car, pulled off and I followed him. We went back to my apartment and he told me to keep the Cadillac for the night and he would be back tomorrow. He left with April and Teraya. I worried all night long about her. I wondered if she was ok. It was a pretty bad beating. I was also worried that the police would be there to arrest him when he got back to the apartment. The police did get involved but I didn't ever know to what extent. Brook stayed with her mother for a few weeks until things calmed down and so she could heal. From what April said he had broken her collar bone that night and that her family didn't want her to ever be with him again. But there was an issue, she was pregnant. And oh yea, did I mention that April was pregnant too? They were both just a few weeks pregnant and only a few of weeks apart in their due dates. Brook continued to dance and had moved to another club off 39th & Meridian. Life was as normal as it could be for a little while but things never stayed that way. With both of them pregnant the money was starting to slow down and Chris's frustration grew. He decided to move back to the old neighborhood so once again we were packing up everything and moving it. It was a nice sunny day and we loaded up all three cars. He was driving the Lincoln, April was in the Cutlass and I was driving the Cadillac. In the back seat of the Cadillac was all of his stereo equipment. He had the best stereo equipment around. He had all the pieces that made the music great. He bought them individually. This was more expensive but it was how the higher end items were bought. His speakers were the best as well. The only time there was no music playing in the house was when we were watching a movie. All of us had stereo equipment at our houses so that whoever he was with, he still had his music. He had a huge music box for the car that was filled with all of the current artist and some of the oldies. He would take it everywhere he was. Each car had one so he had all his music everywhere and it was very important to him. I was driving as careful as I could with all his prized possessions in the back. When we were getting on the highway April was in front of me and slammed on her brakes. When she did, I did, and the stereo in the seat slid down on top of the one on the floor. I spent the rest of the ride trying to reach back and put it back in the seat while still driving and not looking suspicious to anyone else. I was in a panic and was trying my best to keep it together. I wanted to start crying right there, I knew this would be bad. If he knew I had scratched his equipment he was going to beat my ass. We only had two lights between the highway and the new house so there was no time to try to push it back up on the seat. When we pulled up I went to that door immediately to see what the damages were. When I opened the door my heart sank and the lump in my throat grew. There was a huge gash in the wood of the other piece of equipment made from the metal corner of the one that fell on it. Not Just an indention but a full blown deep scratch about 3 inches long. I hurried and put it back in place, grabbed the scrapings and wiped them from the corner of the metal one. I grabbed the record player that was in the other seat and put it on top of the metal one. I carried that in the house on one hip and Greedy on the other hip. When I got in Chris gave me other assignments and I wasn't able to go back to the car to get the one with the scratch. I was going to hopefully stack them and put them in the entertainment center hoping he would never see the scratch and I wouldn't have the consequences. I was unpacking the kitchen cabinets when I heard him yell from outside "What the fuck is this?" I ran to the door and seen him standing next to the Cadillac, my heart sank again. "What's wrong?" I yelled. "Bring your ass here" he yelled. I walked over and he was holding the wood covered receiver. "What the fuck is this?" he said again. "I don't know, it was already like that. It was like that at the apartment. I didn't know that you hadn't seen it" I said hoping he would buy my story. "Brook" he called. Brook came jogging out of the house to see what he wanted. "Did you see this scratch here before? Weren't you the one who put these in the car?" "Yea, I packed em and I didn't see that. But I Just pulled them out of the cabinet and they were on top of each other so I wouldn't have seen it if it was there. Isn't this the one that you sent to that man to get fixed? Maybe he scratched it." She said. Chris's focus quickly shifted to the old man he had fix the receiver for him "Old dizzy bastard, Imma go up there next week and get in his ass. Let's finish this shit." We all went back to what we were working on. I was so relieved. I don't know if she saved my ass intentionally or on accident but I didn't care at that point. I was off the hook, I may not be beat today. Brook and April were both pregnant so they couldn't lift much so most of that was me and Chris. And the more I moved around the more Greedy cried. He was Just over a year old and wanted me to hold him, but I needed to move the stuff. Chris had always been impatient with Greedy's crying and by now was spanking him several times to try to get him to stop crying, which only made him cry harder. I think Chris figured out that if you make babies cry harder they pass out sooner. I hated it, I wanted to run over and attack him. He had no right to spank him, even if he's the father, he's too young. If he would have let me hold him and talk to him for a minute I could have calmed him down. But I couldn't, I had to keep doing what I was supposed to. So we stayed on focus and we got finished with the move. The new house that Chris had found was kind of like a house/garage apartment. It was built into the side of the raised grass yard and was basically an apartment on top of a two car garage. It was your basic 4 square living and bed in the front with kitchen and bath on the back. And of course we put those plastic runners through the whole house. In the garage Chris had set it up where the car was on one side and on the other we had hung some blankets and curtains and made a little chill out room in the garage. He had a fold out couch, a TV with a collection of movies, and a few end tables. It wasn't a bad place to hang out and watch movies. "Angel!" Chris called. "Yea!" I said as I stuck my head out from the garage. He was on the stairs above me that go to the front door of the house. "Take Brook to work, take the Cadillac. You still got the keys?" "Yes, is she ready?" "Here I come!" She yelled as she came down the stairs. She stopped to kiss Chris as she went by him on the steps. "Be careful, ok." he said as we were getting into the car. Brook threw her bag in the back and we headed down Miller and turned onto 10th street. "Did I save your ass back there or what Angel?" "What do you mean save my ass?" I asked. "Did you scratch that equalizer?" "No, I didn't do anything. It was in the back seat, how could I have scratched it?" I didn't want her to know even if she did know. That was just ammunition to use against me later and I had fallen for that enough times with April. "Girl, you are crazy, I would not let something like that happen!" I exclaimed. We pulled up at Meridian and there were a line of cars at the light. There was a guy in a truck next to us gawking. Brook started messing with him. Waving and blowing kisses at him. We were cracking up laughing. He was almost twice our age. "Rev up the car like ur going to go but don't, watch him" she said. I revved up the car and when I did he took off not looking ahead and slammed right into the car in front of him. Both of us looked at each other with that surprised with bugged out eyes. She was facing me "I'm not looking, I'm not looking! Is he looking?" I peeked past her and he was slamming his hands on the steering wheel. Only seconds later the light did turn green and we took off laughing. We laughed all the way to the club. I let Brook out and headed back to the house. I was still laughing about it. I loved hanging out with her. She was so much fun, always joking around, unless she was mad. But mostly we got along. I loved watching her draw. I wanted to be able to draw like her. She was really talented. She had drawn a picture of an American Indian Chief with all the feathers and weathered face. It was beautiful! She had it hanging up in the bedroom and I would always stare at it, and anything else she was drawing.

Sometimes when we were chilling in the garage if it got too late to walk back to my place he would stay in the garage with me on the fold out couch while Brook stayed upstairs. One night when we were chilling in the garage watching movies Brook came down to ask Chris what time he was going to come to bed. Chris had just started taking off my clothes when she walked into the makeshift room. He was upset that she hadn't announce herself and then he started accusing her of trying to eaves drop on us and being "out of pocket". Being "Out of pocket" to Chris was anytime you did anything he didn't like. While he was yelling at her she yelled back at him and said she was taking her shit and leaving because she was tired of seeing him with me and April. Chris Jumped up and grabbed her by the neck and threw her down on the fold-out bed where I already was. He was screaming at her "If you leave you ain't taking shit. And you ain't taking this baby either. Chris grabbed her legs while she was kicking at him and spread them open. Once they were open enough he started stomping on her between her legs. He was stomping repeatedly and screaming that he wanted the baby to die. Brook tried her best to get away from him but it wasn't working. At one point she grabbed hold of me and was using me as leverage to pull away from him. Then he thought I was helping her so he started reaching across and kicking me in the side and back. I struggled to get away from her and she was struggling to get away from him. She finally broke free and was running for the door. He grabbed her about half way and was swinging at her with a piece of wood from the garage. I put my head down, I didn't want to see it anymore. I knew what was happening to her was going to happen to me too and I didn't want to see it. Closing my eyes always made the boogie man go away when I was scared. Closing my eyes now didn't make him go away. It didn't help at all. Greedy had woken up by this point and was screaming because of the fight that was going on. "Take that fucking baby upstairs and get your ass back down here" I ran out of the garage and up the stairs with Greedy. I could still hear her fighting and trying to get away and I could hear him still attacking her. I put Greedy in the kitchen were Chris had made an area for him with the baby gate and I ran back down stairs. I wish I would have ran down the street with Greedy into oblivion. That's what I wanted to do but fantasy wasn't working today. When I got back down to the garage he was on top of her. He was stomping on her all over. I stood at the opening of the room but I didn't want to be there. Chris stopped with her and ran over to me, grabbed me up, and threw me onto the bed with her. He was yelling that we were worthless and that we will both regret turning on him. He kept pacing back and forth at the foot of the bed screaming at us, stopping to kick and hit us every few words. He had worked up a sweat and finally walked out to take a break. Brook and I laid on the bed, both of us crying but scared to comfort one another because of what he may think we were trying to do. After a few minutes went by he banged on the floor from above, which was a prior signal to come up so we both got up and walked upstairs. When I walked in Chris was holding Greedy and had calmed him down. Brook was in a lot of pain and took a while to get into the house. About the time Chris was going to go out the door for her she came in the door. She sat in the seat closest to the door and stayed there for a while. Chris decided we needed to clean again so I grabbed the rags and started oiling down the furniture. It was clear that Brook was in pain when she moved and all I could do was pray that he never went all the way with me like that. I was in pain also, but nothing like her. I wanted to help her but I couldn't even help myself. Chris calmed down and after we finished cleaning he took me and greedy back to our house and dropped us off. I was happy to be alone that night. From this point on it seemed like every few days someone was getting hit, kicked, slapped, or something. With April and Brook getting bigger in their pregnancy they were not able to make as much money and April's money had all but stopped, she was a month ahead of Brook in the pregnancy. All she had coming in was her welfare check. Brook was still dancing but only here and there partially because of the pregnancy and at other times because of bruises from Chris. I recall this one night in her last few days at work at the club. She had called Chris at my house because there was a drunk guy in the club that kept messing with her. Chris told me to come with him so I did. When we got there Chris went inside and in what seemed to be less than a minute Chris came back out and was in the middle of a fight with an older big white guy and they immediately went to the ground. I was so scared, I thought for sure the police were coming. They rolled back and forth and I could see that they were throwing punches at each other. Chris's punches were landing and his punches were flying all over the place. It was only seconds when Chris was on top and the guy was out like a light. Chris put his hand up at me as if to say "wait a minute" and he walked back in the club then right back out again with Brook. They got in the car and we drove away. The guy was still laying on the ground and no one else had come outside to see that he was there. Brook told the story as we drove home. The guy had come up to give her a tip on stage a few times and when he would go to give her the tip he kept trying to stick his hand where it didn't belong. She told the manager but he didn't do anything, that's why she called Chris. We were almost home when he realized the stone in his ring was missing. We turned around and went back. When we were coming up the street we seen there was an ambulance at the club. Chris turned down a side street before we got there and we went to the house. Later that night we went back to the club with flashlights and was trying to find the stone. We never did find it but I think we touched every rock in that parking lot.

We all stayed at the other house that night. I stayed downstairs with him and Brook stayed upstairs. That next morning I walked back to my place. On the way home I saw that one of the neighbors had put some stuff on the curb. There was a fish tank and I wanted it. I grabbed it and put it in the stroller, carried Greedy and we finished our walk home. I cleaned it all up and couldn't wait to get some fish for it. Later that day me and Greedy walked up to the TG&Y store up the street. They had a small fish department and you could get 3 guppies for a dollar so I got a few and we carried them back home. We talked all the way home about what their names would be and how to take care of them. Greedy was really excited about the fish. I had set the tank up in the corner of the living room and we put the fish in when we got home. I was proud of my little fish. It was a couple of weeks later when I noticed that one of my fish was hanging low in the belly. We were going to have baby fish!! I went and got a little net thingy for the baby fish to live in and the whole 9 yards. I put the pregnant fish in the net and sure enough days later there were about 20 little fish swimming around with mom. I moved her to the big tank and started nursing my little school of fish. I had never had a fish tank before and I thought I was doing great with my little fishies. I wanted to have my sisters come over so I could show them. I would get to see them every once in a while. My oldest sister Amanda had recently moved into an apartment building not far from me and she would walk over sometimes to see what I was up to. Chris would see her from time to time and had asked about her working with us. I was always afraid to respond to that question. I didn't want my sister to be part of this. I didn't want anyone to be part of this. He had different ideas. The money was starting to slow down and he wanted another girl to help. He told me to call my sister and have her come over so he could talk to her. I didn't want him to talk to her or even see her for that matter. I reluctantly called and hoped that she wouldn't answer the phone. "Hello" "Hey Amanda, what are you doing?" "Oh, sitting around." "Imma come pick you up, ok?" "What for?" I didn't answer her question, how do you answer a question like that. "I'll be there in a few minutes, put your shoes on." I hung up the phone, we got in the car, and headed over to her place. I was hoping something, anything would happen. I was willing to be in a car wreck to avoid making it over there but I was too chicken to make it happen. We arrived quickly and I didn't have time to come up with anything to avoid this. She rode with us back to the other house and we went into the garage. Chris closed the door to the garage. I didn't know what he was going to do, I was so nervous I could feel my legs shaking standing there. I was trying to control it enough that it wasn't so obvious. What if Amanda tells everyone? What if he hits her? What if he wants to have sex with her? The "what if" game was in full effect. Me and Chris were leaned against the back of the Lincoln that was in the garage and Amanda was standing in front of us. "Do you want to make a lot of money?" He asked her. "Sure I do, what kind of job?" She said as she smiled. I knew that smile would be short lived here. "Do you know how to dance?" "Yea, a little" she let out

211

that goofy laugh of hers as she said it. "Take your clothes off." "What?" she said as she tilted her head to the side. You could see she was trying to reframe what he just said to her. I know she was thinking "Was that what he said?" She wasn't alone, I was trying to reframe it also. I didn't want to hear what I Just heard, I wanted to un-hear it. I understood that it was going to happen. What I didn't understand was how it would feel when he said it to her. How I would feel seeing my sister hanging out with my child's father, my boyfriend. Or having sex with her, what if he has sex with her? What if he started making her do appointments? I didn't understand what hearing those words would do but that didn't keep it from killing me on the inside. I wanted to pretend that I was not even there. I wanted to go back to our little town in Arkansas. I wanted to be back in the old house with Amanda at the head of the class in our bedroom, teaching us our ABC's. I didn't want us to be there with him, I wanted to be anywhere but there. I didn't want to hear him say that to her, but I did, and I started rationalizing it. How else would he know if she could be a stripper without seeing what her body looked like? She had already had three children. I knew that he wouldn't ask her twice without consequence so I leaned forward and cut into the conversation. "Hurry up, we don't have all day, do you want to make some money or what?" I was taking a huge risk I was hoping that I wasn't going to be setting myself up for punishment. She started unbuttoning her pants and pulled them down. I wanted to run over and pull them back up but I couldn't. I couldn't do anything except stand there and watch, petrified. She wasn't going to say no, she pushed them to her ankles and rose her shirt in the air as she came up. He started giggling and she did also. I wasn't sure if he was doing it to make her feel comfortable or what. I was so confused. "You have the same body as Angel. Y'all have almost the same body", his giggle turned into a hysterical laugh. "I've never seen sisters before naked, I didn't think you would look so much alike." By this time he was bent over slapping his knee and making that sound, like he was out of breath, he made when he laughed too hard. Meanwhile, I was hoping my face wasn't displaying what was going on inside my head. I think I went past confusion. While there were similarities, but I didn't think we looked alike at all. The situation was going from bad to worse. Chris raised up and off of the car. He grabbed her hand and raised it above her head to turn her around so he could see the back side of her as well. She was giggling as he was doing it and jealousy came flaming from inside. I didn't want it to, I didn't want to feel this about her. I felt the tears start to well up in my eyes, trying to hold back all seven hundred and twenty eight emotions that I didn't understand but were still going on at that time. When he stopped her he dipped her down like they do in dancing. Was he going to kiss her right here right now? Was this really happening? This cannot be real, this cannot be happening. I was screaming but it was all to myself. It was all in my head, I had no one I could scream at except myself. He raised her up without kissing her but my feelings didn't change at all. "Put your clothes back on I want to take you somewhere." After she was dressed we got back in the Cadillac and rolled down 10th street. He stopped at the chicken fry place and got us sandwiches on the way. When he started to turn into the parking lot of the strip club I thought I was going to throw up. I was nauseas from all the emotions and no release. This was happening more and more as time went by. I was getting physically ill from the array of abusive and confusing situations, like the one at hand. I couldn't believe what was actually happening. We parked and they got out. I wanted to go in with them but I had Greedy and couldn't he was barely over a year old. Not to mention the fact that I was not quite 17yrs old yet. I watched them walk inside through the side view mirror. He opened the door for her and swatted her on the ass as she walked in the club. I saw her look back to laugh and smile at him and that enraged me more. The energy in my body felt so strong, I felt that if I kicked the dashboard I would end up with my foot in the engine. I was furious, I started hitting everything around, the door, the seat, the dash, everything. I wanted to scream but I couldn't bring that kind of attention to myself. I was so mixed up. I wanted to protect her from what was going on and I also wanted to fight her because of what was going on. I had an obligation to him to help bring in girls but never thought it would be like this. After a while Chris came out by his self. "Where is Amanda?" Was the first thing that hit my thoughts? Now protection mode was back on. He got in and didn't say anything. He started the car, backed out and left the parking lot. He looked over at me as he was looking at traffic to pull out. The look on my face prompted him to speak. "She's alright girl, you look like I done killed her. You worked in the club, you know she'll be ok. Don't start no shit Angel!" As he spoke he began to get upset. We went back to Brook's house because she was at her mom's. All I could do was think about Amanda and what was going on. Some of the girls in the club would fight, some would offer you drugs and get you messed up so they can steal your money. I didn't want any of those things to happen to her. I didn't want her to be in this situation at all. Chris and I got in the bed and watched a movie after. When it was around 1am he got up and showered. I got up and got in right behind him. I tried to hurry because I had to get Greedy ready too. When I got out of the shower I grabbed some clothes from the dresser. I heard Greedy laughing so I walked out to see what they were laughing at. There was no they, it was Just Greedy. He had left without me, he went to get her by his self. The tears were unstoppable. If he's alone with her the chances of something happening are great, on both sides. They could end up in bed together or she could end up being beat up for not making enough money. I laid down with Greedy and rubbed his back until we both fell asleep. He came in about an hour later and plopped down on the bed "Wake up" he yelled. He tossed a wad of money at me. "This is yours, you get the first night, buy what you want." I didn't want that money, I didn't. I put the money on the dresser and moved Greedy to his bed on the floor. I stayed silent. "What's wrong with you?" When he asked, it caused the waterfall to gush out, I couldn't hold it. I blurted out "What if we find someone instead of her?" "What the fuck is wrong with her? I've already put my time in this and you brought the bitch over here." "You asked me to" I said in a high pitch. That was all it took. He reached up at me, grabbed me by the hair, and slammed me to the ground. He jumped out of the bed and started kicking me. I knew the best thing I could do was to get up at that point. I started raising up and when I did he grabbed my hair again and flung me across the bed. I landed up against the dresser and fell to the floor. Before I could even register that I was on the ground again he was pulling me back up by my hair. He threw me around the room for what seemed to be hours but I'm sure it was just minutes. Everything was going in slow motion until I landed against the entertainment center in the bedroom. When I landed I knocked it backwards which caused the TV to fall on top of me. It crashed into me as I was trying to catch it. "If my TV is fucked up, I'm going to fuck you up." He picked it up off of me and set it back on the shelf. I crawled away from the front of the TV and laid on the floor with Greedy by the bed. He pushed the power button and I prayed that it would come on. That rainbow flashed on the screen and the TV came on. He straightened up the video recorders and put a movie in. When he went to the bed he didn't even look my direction. It was as if I wasn't worth a look. I laid there on the floor while he watched his movie. I wanted to get up in the bed because the floor was not very comfortable. Greedy had a stack of blankets and I had nothing but thin carpet padding. Scared of what may happen, I didn't know if it would be ok to get in the bed and I didn't want to be in the bed with him anyway. It would mean one of two things, either he would attack me again for making a decision or he would want something from me. The safest place was the floor. My head was throbbing with an incredible amount of strength. I put my hands into my hair and felt all the knots in my head. There were so many I would have to count them to know the total. Each time he would take me airborne by my hair it would pull the scalp up and cause a huge knot on my head. My leg was hurting pretty bad also. When I landed on the dresser the edge was at my thigh so I had this long thin bruise but boy did it hurt. I fell asleep on the floor and was still in the same position when I awoke the next morning. When I got up I quietly went to the bathroom to take a shower. I climbed in and let the hot water run over my skin. I leaned my head back into the water and closed my eyes. I could feel the water making its way through my hair to my scalp and down the length of it.

I felt something moving down the back of my leg and looked down to see what it was. It was a huge amount of hair. I had hair falling out all over the place. All the hair he had pulled out the night before was streaming down my legs and was so much that it started clogging the drain. I picked it up and tossed it in the trash. I started to flush it but I wanted him to see what he had done. I was hoping that if he seen the results of what he was doing he would not do it again. It made no difference at all. He didn't care, I wasn't the money maker anymore, Amanda was. When I got out of the shower he was awake. He took his shower and got dressed. He said I could go home and for me to clean my house. I walked down the street while he drove away. He started picking her up every day for work and dropping her back off at home after work. This went on for almost a week and then the unexpected happened. Chris had gone up to the club to pick her up and they said she had already left with a white guy. Chris drove back to the house and burst in yelling about my dumb ass sister. I Jumped off the bed and met him at the bedroom door, well his hand met my throat at the door. He picked me up by my throat and we landed on the bed. "What the fuck do you know about this?" "I don't know anything, I don't know anything" I said in a broken tone as I tried to shake my head. I had no idea what he was talking about. I tried to speak again but instead I Just gurgled from the pressure of his hands. "I don't like disrespect Angel" he said as he started releasing and raising up off of me. I stayed in the same position afraid to move. My heart was already beating fast as heck from him coming in so loudly, now I could hear it in my head. "Your dumb ass sister left the club with some white mutha fucker, get your shoes on" he said as he walked out of the house. I picked up my shoes and Greedy and headed for the car. We drove straight to her apartment. I went in to check on her and see what happened. I knocked on the door and her old boyfriend was there. She had separated from him a few weeks prior and all the sudden he's back into the picture. "Can I talk to you out here?" I said as I pointed to the hallway. "No, she can't, we're back together and she's not doing that anymore." "Shut the fuck up, no one's talking to you" I barked at him as I walked past to get to her. I got up on her ear and started whispering "If Chris ever asks you what happened, tell him that I tried to get you to come back. I don't want him to make you do anything else." She agreed and I headed back to the car. When I walked out of the building it was like breathing new air. She was saved and didn't have to be a part of the situation anymore. I had to stay conscious of my face, I was happy inside for a moment and needed to be upset. I opened the car door and plopped down in the seat. "He's in there with her and they are back together. He said she isn't dancing anymore" "Fuck what he said, what did she say" She Just stood behind him and didn't say anything, she wouldn't speak to me. Chris got pissed, peeled off and headed to the house. The whole way home he was cussing, shoving me, and slapping me for letting this happen. It was my fault she ran, I was supposed to get her to stay. "I didn't do my job!" I didn't want to do it! Not with her. So I didn't knowing there would be consequences. We got to the house and he hit the weight bench as soon as we walked in the door. He was pushing the bar up and down with such force the weights were shaking and starting to inch off. He wasn't talking much yet and I was staying quite to hopefully avoid the wrath. After he worked out he showered and got dressed again. We left the house and rode around town for a little while and got something to eat while we were out. Shortly after dark we rolled over to the club. Chris noticed that the same car that was at Amanda's house was parked in front and of course he headed right in. I waited imagining all the scenarios that could be playing out. And of course I had a session of "what if?" I heard the door slam open and out he came. He looked like he had just been in a fight or at the least a serious argument. Right behind him were the club bouncers. "Don't come back here" one of them yelled. When we were pulling out he gave me the details. Her boyfriend was in there with her and prevented him from being able to talk to her. She told him how much money she made and now he wanted the money.

That next day I was playing with Greedy right outside the front door when his man in a truck backed into the driveway.

Chris came in right behind him and got out the car and started thanking the guy for meeting him there. He walked into our apartment and instructed the guy to take everything. "Take everything?" I said as I looked in Chris's direction. "Yes, take everything, I bought this shit! If you can't pay me for it, he can. Now, get out of the way." He said as he walked by with the lamps in his hand. This was my punishment for losing Amanda. He was going to leave me with nothing again. When he was done the only thing I had left were a few dishes and my bedding. Not the bed, but the bedding. I was embarrassed, sad, mad, and oddly enough ok with it. I didn't want my sister to be mixed up in what I was tangled in. She didn't need to be with him. She needed to be raising her own family. Her boyfriend started taking her to the club for work and staying there the whole day so that Chris couldn't get to her. We went there three days in a row and pretty much the same thing would happen. The club eventually fired her because her boyfriend was there too much. After that third day, he had that man bring my furniture and stuff back. It took a little while but he eventually stopped yelling at me about it. It was time for Chris to get his hair braided so he had me drop him off over in the south side projects to have it done. I had to keep the Cadillac to take Brook to work. On the way back to the house I was driving by the carwash with extra time on my hands. It will be a nice surprise for Chris. I turned on my blinker and slowed down to turn. As soon as it was clear I whipped the Caddi into the lot. I pulled carefully into the stall. I was really short so it wasn't easy to see over the long hood of the Cadillac. After I parked I got out and used the money changer to get quarters. I soaped it down and rinsed it off. Taking special care when drying it off. Chris would take the car regularly to get it washed and waxed. You had to rub it a specific way. I looked at my watch and it was much later than I thought. I jumped in the driver's seat and started up the car to head out. I got to the edge of the lot and was patiently waiting my turn to go. When I sped out into the traffic the back of the car started to fishtail because the tires were still wet. In my efforts to correct it I landed over the curb and on the grassy side area. I was shaking to death. I got out of the car and could see that I had bent one of the rims. I was so scared. I picked Chris up and told him what happened. He was upset but glad that I was ok. He said I could have been killed. We drove back to the house to drop off the Cadillac. It was the weekend and I had made some money so we were headed to the mall. We rode in the Lincoln and I was dressed to the nine's. Chris had his hair braided and was wearing his snake skin boots, Levis, wife-beater, and jacket. Greedy was in jeans and a cute little button up shirt. He looked like a little grown man. We were a great looking family, everywhere we went people were staring at us. We spent a few hours and a few hundred in the mall that day. He dropped me off at my place when we were done. I hadn't really been there in days. I brought in the new stuff and hung it up, and made us something to eat. After I put Greedy in the play pen I turned on the stereo and started cleaning house. I had a stack of 45's that I loved to listen to when I cleaned the house. I had all kinds of music. Chris would take me to the music store with him all the time and he would let me buy music for myself sometimes. I was jamming to a song and yelling it out "Bang your head!" I was dancing around the house having a fun with Greedy. He was coming up on one, and one of his favorite things to do was jumping up and down in the play pen. When the music was on, he was jumping. I jumped back into the living room with my air guitar and started playing the solo part as if I were on stage with the band. Greedy was laughing hysterically. All the sudden I hear huge kicks on my locked front door. It only took a second to see it is being kicked in. On the third kick Chris comes in flying. In one swipe he sends the record player across the room before I even knew what was going on. He ran up on me and slapped me across my face so hard I flew immediately to the ground. "Answer the fucking door when I knock!" he screamed over me. "I didn't hear you because the music" I blubbered at him in my crying. I was still holding my face because it was on fire. My ears were ringing, I was so stunned I was frozen. "Why the hell did you have the music up like that?" "I was cleaning the house" I cried out. "You don't need no fucking music to clean a house" he screamed as he stomped on the record player with his boots breaking it into pieces. He moved to screaming over me and kicking me as he screamed. He raised his foot in the air and I thought he was going to fully Jump on me. As his foot came down it slanted just enough to pass over me. He stepped past and over to my fish tank and literally pulled the front glass right off of the tank. All the water, my fish, rocks, plants everything went on the floor. "My fish just had babies" I said. Chris came down on me in a fury of fist that were hitting me everywhere. I tried to keep my head dunked down so he wouldn't hit my face. It was still stinging from the huge slap he started with. He raised up and I thought that he was finished but he wasn't. Chris had never beat me this bad. He had never slapped me in the face like that either. He had pushed me around, and pulled my hair, he hit me in the head, a couple of months ago, while I was holding Greedy and knocked me down but never like this. This is what he did to the other girls not me. I was completely crushed, I wasn't special anymore. I was crying out for him to stop and Greedy was crying also. Chris picked Greedy up and took him to the bedroom and shut the door. When he came back in he continued to yell at me about not answering the door and having him stand out there knocking because "You're in here listening to white boys scream." "I'm sorry" I said. By the time I had finished saying the ree part his hand had connected with my face again. "Nobody told you to talk you dizzy bitch" He grabbed me by the hair and threw me across the room. I landed up against the couch and he was on top of me before I could even get straight. He grabbed one of my legs and I instantly knew what was about to happen. I started kicking my other leg trying not to let him get a hold of it but it didn't last long. Chris got my other legs, spread them open, and his boot was quickly stomping into me. As soon as his foot was headed that way I twisted and his boot scraped my leg going down. He was still able to reach and when his boot landed the pain went through my entire body like an atomic blast. I could barely breathe it hurt so incredibly bad. I started kicking, twisting, and pulling my legs together to try to get away. I couldn't hear what he was saying because the pain had taken over. He finally released my legs and I folded. I eventually passed out from either exhaustion, pain, or both. I woke the next day in the bed with him. Greedy was crying and I tried to get up to get him. My body was so sore I could barely move. Chris Jumped up and grabbed him and brought him to the bed. Greedy kept a tight grip on me when he hugged me. I saw him looking at my bruises and I quickly covered them up. We laid there playing with our son for a while then Chris got dressed as I dressed Greedy and they left together. I laid in the bed replaying what I remembered from the previous night. I had tear streaming down my face, I didn't even attempt to wipe them because I knew they wouldn't be stopping any time soon. That night was the changing point. After that night I knew I couldn't stay, I'd have to start making plans to go before I couldn't. By this time in the relationship I had heard him say to all of us that "he's going to kill one of us bitches" and I believed him. I prayed that he wouldn't kill me before I was able to escape.

For the next few days I could hardly move I was hurting so much. All I wanted to do was lay around and let Greedy play beside me in the bed. I still had to get everything cleaned up and it was not easy but I did it. Chris came by the next day and had me get up and cook for him. I did my best to act like nothing was wrong and everything was ok but it wasn't. He stayed with me that night also, we never talked about what happened but he knew there was a difference in me so he started keeping Greedy with him most of the time. The next day I walked to the laundry mat to do the laundry and call a couple of people to try to get out of my situation. I was going to need help and I only had a couple of people I could even ask so I was praying everything would work out ok. First I called my girl Maya the one I went to school with at Emerson. Her Pops answered the phone and said that she was in Enid Oklahoma for a couple of months but he gave me the number where she was. I called and told her about what had happened and that I needed help. Maya was staying in a home for pregnant teens and couldn't let me stay there but at least if I could find a way to Enid then I would know someone there to help me get started again. I called my only other option, Stacey. We met in the Juvenile shelter as well.

She had a son around the same time I had Greedy and most importantly, she had a car. It wasn't much of a car, it was an old green Chevy and the interior was falling apart but it rolled and that's all I needed. I told her what was going on and she was willing to help me also. I was getting a welfare check and that was the only income I had any access to. I'm sure I was making more than a thousand a month with the appointments but I didn't see any of that unless I needed something or he wanted to buy me something but that was all on his terms, not mine. So the plan was set, on the first I would cash my check, pack my bags and head for Enid…as long as he didn't catch me and kill me. I still had almost two weeks to make it to the first. I was trying to think of ways to get more money so I thought about asking Chris to buy some things that I would be able to take back to the store and get the money back. I didn't know what I would ask for but I had to get thinking on it. Over the next few days I took inventory of my belongings and decided what would come and what would stay since there wasn't going to be room for much. I rearranged things so that what I needed was always in the front so I could grab and dash when I needed to. We were going to have to do the move in less than 10 minutes to make sure that Chris didn't show up and kill us all. He knew when the mail ran and was accustom to taking me to cash the check and paying the rent his self. I prayed every day that somehow God would help me get away. Every few days I would call Maya and Stacey to make sure that they were still on board and everything would be ok. I had just picked up the phone to call Maya one day when Chris walked into the laundry mat. I saw him walk in out of the corner of my eye I and hung up on Maya in mid-sentence. "Who were you talking to?" he asked. I couldn't tell him I was on the phone with Maya because I wasn't allowed to have any friends. "The phone just rang so I picked it up. The lady calling Just wanted directions to the laundry mat so I was giving them to her" "Get your shit and let's go" Chris said with a crappy tone. "I Just put everything in the dryer, it's not done yet" Chris walked over to the dryer opened it and said "Get your shit and lets go" I grabbed the pile of wet clothes and put them back in the laundry basket. I carried it to the car while

Chris grabbed Greedy and the stroller. When he got in the car I wanted to ask him why he was making me leave but questions were out of the question with Chris so I Just rode the short ride to the house. When we got inside you could tell that he had been there. All of the cabinets were open and for some reason the fold out couch in the living room was out. Chris had been searching my house. Why, what was he looking for? After I sat the basket down I began laying things around where they could dry. Chris came in with Greedy, went straight to the bathroom and called me in there. I had asked the night before for some household supplies and like I said earlier I was hoping to return the items for the money. "Why did you ask me for soap, toilet paper and shampoo if you have some already?" I didn't know what to say but I knew if I didn't start talking quickly then I was going to be in deep. "I was getting low on everything so I Just asked for it all so you don't have to buy more later." "Bullshit" He yelled as he pushed me out of the bathroom and on the floor. "Get up and get in the car" he said. I got off the floor and went to the living room to get Greedy and we went to the car. Chris drove us to the house down the street and we all went inside. Brook wasn't there, she had gone to visit her mother. Chris had me start cooking some stew, which was his favorite meal. While the stew was cooking he wanted the house to be cleaned again and the furniture wiped down with oil. I went to work doing all the tasks he asked. Later that evening we watched a few movies and when it was time for bed he told me to take Greedy and sleep downstairs in the garage. After I got settled downstairs I started trying to figure out what he was thinking and why he was making me stay here instead of me and Greedy's house. Did he figure out that I was trying to leave? I haven't packed or moved anything out of place. Yes, I asked for the extra stuff but I seriously didn't think that would let him know I was leaving. Chris was very smart, especially street smart and he could figure out almost anything. The first was still a week away and I was going to have to start thinking of plan B if he kept making moves like this. That next day when I woke up Chris was gone and the upstairs was locked. I locked up the garage door and Greedy and I walked back to my place so we could clean up and change clothes. I had gotten in the shower and was about to wash my hair. I was leaned back in the water with my eyes closed when Chris came in. "Who the fuck said you could go anywhere?" He startled the crap out of me because I thought I was alone. He jerked the curtain open and started grabbing at me. He got my arm and threw me out of the shower. "Get your ass in the car!" I grabbed my dirty clothes and started putting them back on, got Greedy and went to the car. When we got back to the other house Brook was there. We walked in and she came from the kitchen. "Why are they back over here?" she asked. "Ask another mutha fuckin question" Chris said in a serious tone. She didn't ask anything but she rolled her eyes as she walked off and Chris lost it. He started hitting and cussing her about questioning him and about keeping a straight face. He said he would remove her eyes before he would let her look at him like that. Greedy started crying and that distracted Chris so he got off of her. We both spent the rest of the evening listening to him lecture and read from the bible about obedience and wicked people. When I was younger and he would do this he had me convinced that those wicked people they were talking about was me. I read that bible so many times it was to the point where when I was bored I could just think about the bible and almost read it from my head. I didn't want to read it, I didn't want to have anything to do with it. He was the one who made me read it all the time. As I grew older I was starting to see that those wicked people he said I was a part of was actually more like him. Greedy kept crying off and on because Chris expected him to stay in the playpen for hours and he wasn't ok with that, he was used to me holding and playing with him. Chris told me to take Greedy home and come back. My face must have said it all because Chris walked over, slapped me, picked up Greedy and said "Come on Bitch". We got in the car and took Greedy to the house. I put him in his room and moved everything out that I thought he would be hurt by I gave him two bottles because I didn't know how long I would be gone and I didn't want him to be hungry. Chris was outside honking the horn for me to hurry. When I started to leave Greedy started to cry of course and so did I. When I got in the car Chris yelled at me to stop crying and started cussing me about being a big ass baby and crying all the time. We went the few blocks to the other house. I got out of the car to walk into the house, I wasn't walking fast enough and I was still crying. Chris ran up behind me and kicked me in the back so hard that I actually took flight. There was a tree in front of me and that was what broke my flight. When I landed on the tree and bounced down to the ground my entire lower body felt like it had pins and needles, like it was instantly asleep. He had done it this time, I knew I was hurt bad. I started panicking on the inside, how would I raise my son if I'm paralyzed? I was trying to mentally calm my body down so it could operate but I had to calm me down first and I didn't have time for that. I tried to get up but my legs were too wobbly and they weren't cooperating. Chris grabbed me and was trying to make me stand up but it wasn't working as well as he would have liked. He kept dropping me back to the ground. The less control I had over my legs the more upset he was. He started punching me in the side and stomach to try to make me stand straight but of course this was making me bend and move which was making me fall again. It was horrible, the more I tried the more I couldn't do what he wanted. Chris eventually drug me into the garage and started beating me more. Those snake skinned boots were all I could see coming at me, kicking and stomping. He kept saying if I was going to continue to be "worthless" then he would sell me to Roach, his other pimp friend. Roach was older, ugly, and beat his women in front of anyone. I didn't want to be beat or pimped but since it was already happening I didn't want to switch to anyone else. I wanted to get it right and that was next to impossible. Chris had a way of making you feel like it was your fault that he was beating you. If I did what he said or if I was smart enough to follow his directions then I wouldn't have this problem. I always tried to go by the rules, if I disobeyed a rule it was because I didn't know or it was for a damn good reason. But reasons didn't matter, I was punished whether I knew what was going on or not. There were no areas of the punishment that were fair and tonight was no different from any other night. He was asking questions I didn't have the answer to so I would be hit for not answering. Like, why am I so stupid? How do you answer that? If I did know the answer I would be hit for not speaking. I fell asleep while he was preaching to me. When I woke up I was down stairs by myself. I walked upstairs and he was just coming out the door. "Get in the car!" I walked toward the car but my mind was so far away. What about Greedy? Were we going to get my baby? I got in the back of the car, Brook was already in the front seat of the car. We left the house and he went straight for 10th street. I started crying and my brain quickly spiraled out of control. I wanted my baby. I didn't like leaving him alone. I was so upset with myself. How could I let this continue to happen? How could I stop it from continuing? I felt so powerless and worthless. I was ready to just die, I wanted to die right where I was. If this was "life" then I wanted no parts of it. I wondered why I was the one, out of all my sisters and all my friends, why am I the one. Why does it all happen to me? I started convincing myself that I was the chosen one, chosen to be abuse, chosen to be worthless. I didn't want to be any of that, I just wanted out of it all, however that was to occur. He drove to the gas station and filled up. We stayed in the car while he went into pay. When we had marks he would make us stay inside the house fully or inside the car if we did get to go somewhere. I'd do anything to be home, lock me in the house, but with my baby! I didn't want to go with him, I didn't want to do anything except get to my baby. He headed back toward the house and pulled up at Brook's place. "You can go home now." Was the only statement I was happy to hear from him. I started to get out of the car to walk but he said to get back in and he gave me a ride. We went inside the house and I went straight for Greedy's room. He was asleep on the floor with toys all around him. I could tell that he had cried his self to sleep, his little eyes were swollen. I went and made a bottle before waking him. Chris picked him up and I handed him the bottle. Greedy started eating without even waking up. Chris laid him down on the couch with the bottle and told me to go to the room. He followed behind me and we undressed and got in the bed. He was holding me and rubbing his hands through my hair. "I don't like having to do those things to you Angel but you've gotta listen better. You can't disobey me or question what I do. I'm a man and I know what's right, you are a little girl, you don't know anything. Just follow what I say and you will stay safe." He held me for a few hours and kept telling me that he loved me and didn't want to put his hands on me but I keep making him. Chris stayed with me most of the day and the next night because I kept getting sick. I was getting dizzy and nauseous and still had the headache from hell. The next day, after Chris left I went to the pay phone and called my friend Stacey to make sure that we were still on for the trip, which was only a day away. Stacey said her and Ronnie, her boyfriend, and the owner of the car, would be there tomorrow. I had to wait for the mail to come for my check then I was leaving. I started reviewing everything in the house making sure things were all setting in the right places so that I could grab everything quickly and be gone in a matter of minutes. And truly minutes was all I had. I quickly rearranged the closet in my bedroom so that the few boxes I had were easily dumped so I could use them for getting my stuff. I hated that I wasn't going to be able to take everything. Mainly Just our clothes was all I could take. Clothes and pictures, those were the most important. Chris came over later that afternoon and picked us up. We rode around town with him for a while, went to Burger King and got some cheeseburgers. We went over to Langston's and got some new jeans for him and picked up the boots he had at the boot shop. It was a typical day, with one exception, I hoped it was my last day with him and not my last day on earth.

The mail usually ran around 11 or so, sometimes earlier. I set up Greedy's toys out in front of the house around 10 in the morning so it would look like we were Just playing but I was waiting for what would seem like one of the longest moments in time. I sat there playing with him for the first hour staring down the road, listening for the turn of every vehicle praying it wouldn't be Chris. As usual when you need something to happen quick it takes forever. I could finally see him, the mail man was coming down the street. I started collecting Greedy's

227

toys and waited for the mailman to hit my driveway. Watching him walk down the street was like watching molasses drip from a tree. He finally got to my house and I waited for him to put all the mail in the box. I ran behind him and pulled my mail out. Yep, the check was there. Now to make the much awaited phone calls. I practically ran to the laundry mat where the phone was. I called Stacey first and she was headed over. I called Maya second and she said she would start looking for an apartment so when I got there I would choose and pay. I ran back to the house and started throwing everything in the boxes. I kept the boxes in the closet and the shower to hide them from Chris if he came in the middle of everything. My heart was racing so fast. I was sweating like a pig and knew if I got caught it would probably be the last event of my life. I heard a car pulling into the driveway and my heart stopped. Either this is Chris and I'm possibly dead or it's Stacey and I'm going to escape. I threw the box I was working on in the shower and ran to the window to see who it was. It was Stacey and Ronnie. They were getting out of the car. I opened the door quickly "Come on, y'all we gotta be fast. "Ronnie grab the two boxes in the shower. Stacey grab Greedy and I've got the rest of it." My heart was pumping so hard I bet you could see it through my shirt. If Chris pulls up, he would have us blocked in and there would be nothing we could do. Ronnie surely wasn't going to fight him and Stacey wouldn't stand a chance. In less than three minutes we were pulling out of the driveway. That was actually one of the scariest parts. Brook's house was Just a couple of blocks away and so was April's. One quick move and I'd be dead. We made it out of the driveway and then on to 10th street. We had turned on to the street when there he was. I could see him coming a few blocks away and so could Stacey and Ronnie. "Get down, get down" Ronnie said. I dunked down in the back seat hoping not only that he didn't see me but that he didn't recognize Stacey. She had only seen him a couple of times before and he had never seen her in this car. My prayers were answered, he drove right past us. "He's gone, but he turned on your street" Ronnie said. My heart dropped into my stomach. What will he do when he sees I'm gone? He's going to be furious! We were away from the house but we weren't out of the city yet. I still had to cash my check at Whitakers grocery down the street. Chris knew where I cashed my check and I was praying that he wouldn't come right behind me to Whitakers. Ronnie didn't even park, we had reviewed what we would do if Chris pulls up. First if he doesn't recognize him and come toward the car then honk twice to let me know inside that he is coming. If he recognizes them and comes after them, they were to lay on the horn and I would come running. The plan was for me to Jump in the car and we would hit the highway which was only a few blocks away. I'm not sure how we were going to out run him but that was the plan. I looked around and didn't see Chris so I got out of the car and ran in the store. When I got to the window there was one person being helped and I had to wait. Every little noise that came from outside and the door was making me Jump. I was wishing for the best but was certainly prepared for the worst. Every time the door would open I would look to see. It was finally my turn and she went pretty fast. I didn't even count the money, I Just grabbed it and ran for the door. When I got right outside the door I looked to make sure that he wasn't in the parking lot and then made a b-line for the car. Ronnie was pulling the car toward me as I was running at him. I jumped in and we sped out of the parking lot as if he was indeed chasing us. We went straight for the highway and there was nothing in the way. It was a little more than an hour to Enid and we talked about everything that had been happening on the way. I was grateful that Stacey was willing and able to help me. When we got to Enid we found the place where Maya was staying and picked her up. I was so happy to see her. We hugged for the longest then she went with us to get the apartment. Maya had already decided which one. It was close to most shopping and cheap. When we were driving over I thought we were in the wrong neighborhood. All the houses over here were huge, it looked like the historic district or something. We found the house finally. It was on the corner so it had the wrap around yard and it was beautiful. It was one of those old two story wooden houses with a porch and a fancy front door. My place was around the side and was above their two car detached garage. It was a one bedroom with a kitchen and fully furnished, perfect. I signed the lease and gave the lady her money and the place was now mine and Greedy's. Stacey and Ronnie had to get back to the city so they didn't stay long. Just long enough to take my things upstairs and take me to the store for a few things. Maya and I arranged the apartment and put things away. We sat and talked for a while then she had to go.

~Chapter 16~

A New Place

So here we were, getting ready to start a whole new life in a whole new place. We didn't have a TV so I Just read the books I had to Greedy, taught him everything I could, played with him and cleaned the rest of the time. The family that lived in the house in the front was nice. I don't remember the lady's name but I had been there about a 2 days when the vomiting and headache got worse. I went to the neighbor's house to use the phone to call for an appointment. I was starting to dial when I felt it. I ran for the bathroom but barely made it into the door when the vomit began to spew everywhere. I was not doing well at all. Vomiting, dizzy, weak and still scared to death. She helped me off the floor and I tried to start cleaning but she wouldn't let me. I was mortified. What kind of neighbor throws up all over someone's bathroom? The shower curtain, the sink skirt, all of it was splattered. I kept apologizing over and over. She helped me to the car and took me to the emergency room. She had little one's of her own and couldn't stay with me but at least I was there. They did a series of test and said that I had a severe concussion and they wanted me to stay the night. I couldn't do that, I didn't even have anyone to watch Greedy while they did the CAT scan let alone someone watching him overnight. I refused so they discharged me and they told me to take it easy and set me up with an appointment to see another doctor and then we were done. The security officer walked me to the front of the hospital and we walked back home, it wasn't that far. I continued throwing up for the next couple of days but it was getting better. And really I don't care if I had to throw up every day to be out of the situation I was in, it was worth it. I didn't have a job or any responsibilities outside of Greedy so I was able to devote all my time to him, and that's what I did. We spent every moment together learning, he was a great student.

There was a park down the street that I started taking Greedy to so we would have something to do outside of the apartment. It was your typical park with lots of open space, nice trees and a playground. Greedy would play for hours. He almost always fell asleep on the way home. One day when we were at the park I met a nice lady who was there with her kids. She asked about me living in Enid and how that came to be. I didn't want to tell her the whole story but I did tell her I was running from an abusive situation and that's why we were alone. "Well how old are you honey, you look like a baby" she said. "I'm 17" I replied. I hadn't quite turned 17 but it was only a couple of months away. She offered to take me to church with her and I took her up on that offer. I wrote down my address and described the garage apartment to her. We were going to church. I hadn't been in a church in a long time and for a reason. I wasn't real keen on the church thing but it was somewhere to go and something to do. I can clearly remember the last time I went to church, I was about 11yrs old. The visiting pastor we had at the Nazarene Church for revival called me into the church office. He said that the shorts I was wearing to church were too short and while explaining it he used his hand to demonstrate how easy it would be for someone to get at my private areas. I should have been shocked but I wasn't. At that time there were others molesting me so I had the idea that molesting children was normal and everybody did it. It still didn't feel right but when it's going on all around you, what else would a kid think. So I Just didn't go back to church again. I looked through all my clothes trying to find something that would be appropriate for this church thing. I didn't have any dresses that weren't street dresses so I settled with some jeans and my favorite shirt. I still had two days to go to Sunday but I was ready. I told Greedy where we were going, he didn't really know what I was talking about but he was my only person to talk to. My interactions with the neighbor and the church lady were only a few. The days passed slowly and finally it was Sunday morning. I got up with the sun and started getting Greedy ready and then myself. We were ready about an hour head of time. I heard a car pull up and the nice lady was at the door knocking. Greedy and I went down the stairs with her to the van. She had her whole crew in there. We arrived at the Church, it was an Assembly of God Church and a pretty big one too. They had what I thought was a neat daycare system. There were numbered lights on the wall behind the pulpit and if your number lit up you knew your child needed you in the daycare. That was one of the things I remembered about that church. The other, left me a little freaked out. We were sitting in Church listening to the pastor preach when all the sudden a lady in the congregation Jumped up and started babbling out loud. The preacher stopped and we all listened, some in excitement, me in fear. I had no idea what was going on. "What is she doing?" I whispered. "She is talking in tongues." I had read about this in the bible but had not seen it before. When I was little we went to a Baptist church and they didn't do that. I was staring at her in amazement. What was she saying and why did she Jump up in the middle of the sermon. What the crap was going on? After a couple of minutes she sat down and then right after she sat down another lady on the other side of the church stood up and started decoding what the other lady had said. I was wondering how she knew, was this some foreign language. Then she plopped back into her seat like nothing happed. Her neighbors were not acting like anything was going on, I was so confused. The pastor went right back into the sermon without addressing them or explaining what had Just happened. I was so wrapped up in what had just gone on that I couldn't pay attention to the pastor. I was seriously wondering what had Just happened? Was this real? Are all those stories in the bible real? And if so, what does this mean about Chris. Chris never talked in tongues, does this mean he isn't sent by God? I was hoping church would give me answers but it only gave me more questions. We started going to church with her on Sunday's. After the second Sunday I decided to write to mom to let her know that I was ok. I didn't know if she was worried about me but I thought my sisters might be. I wrote the letter with a few details as possible. I asked her to not let Chris know that I wrote to them. But that I was Just writing to let her know that I was ok. The third Sunday we went back to her house after church and we made plans to go swimming at the public park in a nearby town. Greedy had never been to an actual swimming pool before so we were excited to go. The pool was about 30 miles away with nothing but open fields on all sides the whole drive. We got there and it was much bigger than I had anticipated. We stood in line to get in and headed straight for the water once we were inside. We played for hours. It was so much fun, and relaxing at the same time. I was starting to feel like we had made it, I could relax, we were going to be ok on our own. God was watching over us. A few days later the nice lady came over to take me to the grocery store. The first of the month had rolled around again and I couldn't carry too many bags with Greedy's stroller so she took me. We both shopped and then used our expert female organizing techniques to get it all in the car with the kids too. It was packed in there but the job was done. When we got to the apartment she helped bring up the groceries and I put them up after she left. I was so tired, I cooked dinner for us, read Greedy a few stories and we went to bed.

I had decided since it had been a month that I would call my house and if the phone was still connected and Chris answered the phone I would let him know we were ok and then hang up. I called the number and it rang several times. I was Just about to hang up the phone when I heard a deep voice "Hello?" It was my mom half asleep answering the phone. Why is she answering my phone at my house? I thought to myself. I didn't tell her I was leaving because I was afraid that she would tell Chris. "Hello, Mom? Why are you answering my phone?" She answered acting like she had been crazy trying to find me. "Where are you, where have you been, we've been looking everywhere." I bet the "we" she was talking about was her and Chris. "Why are you at my house?" I asked. "Chris told me to move into your place. He said he had paid the rent and didn't want the money to go to waste." I don't know why I asked, I knew I wouldn't get the right answer. I knew better, he had her move in so that if I called or came back he would be able to get to me. She asked where I was and I Just told her that I was far away. She asked me to call back later to talk to Lillian. I didn't call back that day. I had to think about what was going on and what I was going to do. The next day I called early in the morning. I knew Chris like to sleep in so that would be the best time to call. "Hello?" It was my sister Tyana. "Hey, it's me." "Chris was here all night." "Are you serious?" "Mom told him about the letter and I tried to take it to the room but he wrestled me down for it." "Did he hurt you?" I asked in a frantic voice. I was envisioning her with a bruised face. "No, he was laughing and tickling me but he was serious. He got the letter and read it." "What did he say?" "The only thing he said was "Dang" he read it a couple of times. He was trying to figure out where you were." "I didn't write the return address cause I figured mom would give it to him." "Where are you anyway?" "I can't tell you Tyana, if you slip up and tell mom, she's going to tell him and I'm going to be in serious trouble." "Mom's asleep in there with her boyfriend, I'm not going to tell her that you called." "Thanks Tyana, I love you." "I love you too". I sat back and thought about the conversation. He was coming over daily trying to find out where I was, and now he was starting to get physical with my sisters. I was so afraid of what was going to come next. If I'm not there then he has full access to them and mom's not going to stop him from taking one of them like he did me. I did my best not to drive myself crazy thinking about it. I packed up Greedy and we went for a walk through the neighborhood. I didn't have a TV for distraction, nature and Greedy were the only things I had, and I was grateful for those. A few days later I called in the morning again and the phone was answered on the first ring. A deep voice said "Hello?" It wasn't mom this time, it was Chris. I didn't even have to say hello. I was in full panic mode on the inside. The hesitation to speak after he said hello was enough to let him know it was me. "Angel, where are you. I love you Angel, where is our baby, let me talk to him. I put Greedy on the phone without even responding to him. I could tell he was asking him questions. Out his mouth it comes "I like Enid daddy" my heart sank. I grabbed the phone and said he had ran away. "Where are you? Are you in Enid?" No, that's not what he said, he was talking about a cartoon." I was trying to say anything to try to make him forget what Greedy had just said. I told him I had to go and hung the phone up with him still talking. I sat up all night staring outside and jumping at every car light that turned down our street. It took a day or so but I finally calmed down. It was only a few days later, after we had gone to bed that everything turned upside down. Both of us were fast asleep when a BOOM, BOOM, BOOM startled me awake and I Jumped up out of the bed. Someone was beating on the front door. It was still dark outside so I looked over at the clock and it was after 1am. I opened the bedroom door and I knew things were about to get really bad. The view from my bedroom door was a straight shot to the living room door. That door had a window in it and I could see the shadow of the person on the other side of the door. It was Chris. I didn't need to see him in the light to know who he was. He had come for me. My body froze right there in that moment. I think time stood still and went into a speeding fast forward mode all in the same millisecond. What was he going to do? Was he going to kill me? What about Greedy? How did he find me? Would my neighbors help? I had 14 million questions running through my head. The door was only about 10 foot steps away and I was wanting it to be 100 miles away. I knew if I didn't open the door he would kick it down. I walked over and slowly turned the knob bracing for what was going to come from the other side of that door. Chris slid his hand between the door and frame as it opened and helped it open the rest of the way. He walked around the living room and looked in the kitchen and bedroom. "Nice little place here. Where's my son?" he said with a little anger in his voice. I pointed to the bed in the room and he walked over and picked him up. Greedy was sleeping and stayed sleep. I was frozen, I stood in the middle of the living room barely able to breathe. I was waiting for him to attack me right then and there. Chris walked into the room and laid him down on the couch. He walked over, took my hand and led me to the bedroom. "Did you find yourself a little boyfriend down here?" "No, I've not been with anyone, I haven't had sex." "I'll be the judge of that" he said. Chris played with Greedy while I packed my things to go back with him. I waited the entire time for Chris to start beating or yelling at me but he didn't. He was actually slightly apologetic. He said he understood why I ran and that I needed to be more careful about the things I say to him if I don't like the results. I got the Cadillac all packed up with as much as I could take and we headed back down I-35 to the city. When we got there we went to Brook's house. He had moved her from the place on miller into a duplex on Young's Blvd. She made a pallet on the floor for Greedy and I slept on the couch. The next day Chris got me an apartment around the corner but still in eye's view from Brook's front yard. It was right next to the laundry mat I always used so at least it was convenient. The apartment was furnished so I Just had to put up the clothes and groceries and we were good to go. Chris came back that night and took Greedy with him. He came back only a few minutes later and he brought his cowboy boots. I was a fool to think that he wasn't going to punish me for leaving. Chris started yelling at me about leaving him and taking his son and how stupid I was to think that I would get away with it. He took off his belt and started swinging it at me, he was hitting me over and over and over. My whole body was on fire. I couldn't even tell you what he was yelling, I couldn't hear through the pain anymore. At some point he threw the belt and started punching, slapping and kicking me. I tried to run out the door but he grabbed me and pulled me back in. Chris got on top of me and was holding his hand over my mouth to shut me up but it was not giving me any air to breathe either. He was yelling for me to be quiet. I was as quiet as I could be for how much I was hurting. I did my best to hold it in but my best wasn't good enough. He stood me up and grabbed the belt again. He made me bend over and grab my ankles like I was a kid, like my step dad did. He said for every sound I make I would get a lick with the belt. I tried not to make a sound. I had snot running back up my nose and my body reacted and sniffed. SLAM, that belt hit so hard it made my whole body tingle, there was nothing on my body that wasn't reacting to that. I tried not to make a sound but I couldn't help it. Then we moved into a vicious circle of belt lashes. The more he hit the less I could control the sounds coming from my body. The less I controlled the sounds and the more he hit me. The more he hit me the more the sounds my body couldn't keep from coming out. It seemed to go on forever. He finally stopped and sat down in the chair. "Go cook me something." I walked into the kitchen with my ass, arms and legs still throbbing from the pain and started putting food together for him. I was a zombie, I was the walking dead, in that moment, and I started wishing for death. I cried my last tear that I had in my body. I didn't want to keep doing this. The only thing that stopped me from slitting my throat while cooking was that little boy. I couldn't do it because I didn't know what would happen to him, where would my son go? Who would take care of him? I decided I had to stay, I had to stay for my son. After I gave him the food he started running down the new rules for me. Basically stay in the house and don't walk out unless it's on fire or I'm with him. He said that Brook and April would be watching too and that if I tried to leave him again that next time he wouldn't be so nice. He locked me in the backroom and left the building. I took a look at my wounds and it wasn't as bad as I had seen in the past so I didn't complain plus it would do no good to complain. He brought Greedy back a few days later. It was almost my 17th birthday so I considered that my birthday present. Me and Greedy stayed locked inside the house most of the time except for when Chris would come get us. We would go riding around with him and he spent most nights at my house for several weeks. I would like to say it was because he was in love with me but I know it was because he wanted to make sure I wasn't running away again. He was back to being nice most of the time but he was constantly reminding me that he would not tolerate another situation with me. Chris had started making appointments for me again after my bruising went away. I hated them more now than ever. I was about to turn 17 and the older I got the more I knew about how wrong this was and the more I wanted to do something different. The old lady who owned the apartments I was staying in had complained about the noise in my apartment. The noise of course was Chris beating me. She didn't want that going on at her apartments and she wanted us out. Chris had started looking for another place close by. I had just gotten my welfare check and was holding on to money to get the next place with. The old lady was at my door asking for the rent. I told her that I would bring it to her later but I had full intentions of moving that night or the next day. I did my only load of laundry next door then went back to the apartment to pack up. Later that evening when Chris got there he asked for the money. I went to the drawer to retrieve it and it was gone. The money was gone. I threw everything out of the drawer. I went through all of the drawers pulling them completely out of the dresser. The money was gone. Not Just any money, this was Chris's money. There was only one thing that could have happened. The old lady had to have come in and stole it. Of course the first thing to hit his head was that I had stolen the money to escape. Chris seen the panic in my face and realized that I didn't take the money. But did that stop him from taking it out on me? No. He slapped me around for leaving it in such a stupid place and then he left. I was anticipating this being a much more severe beating because it was about money. He had been ramping up through the years and I didn't see this as any different but it was. I waited for him to come back and start again but he didn't. He came back a few hours later and told me to start packing everything up in the car. Chris paid for the new duplex around the corner and made sure to let me know I would be paying him back. As I had got older I realized more what was going on and especially what was right and wrong. I didn't want to turn tricks for him anymore but I had to find a way to replace that money or he wasn't going to let me stop. I worked up the nerve and talked to Chris about letting me get a real job because I was old enough now. I was surprised but he said I could. The next day he watched Greedy while I walked around the neighborhood applying for jobs. After I finished at Taco Mayo I walked over to the Del Rancho and got the job there that day. Del Rancho was set up like Sonic with the drive in ordering stations. And they had the best chicken fried steak sandwiches in the world. The owner was a little old lady named Connie. She was nice as could be or she could be mean as hell but mostly she was nice. I got assistance from the state with daycare and Greedy loved going there to play with the other kids. He was almost two and he wanted more than momma to play with. There was a van that would pick him up and bring him back home in the afternoon. It felt great to be working a real job that didn't involve being with men I don't even know. I still had to turn a few tricks here and there but it wasn't as many times a week as I used to. Chris said that when I start making that much in tips at work then I wouldn't have to turn tricks on the weekends. I was excited about the prospect of things changing and us finally having a stable family together. It wasn't an easy job but I was more than willing to do it. Connie had a grand-daughter that was my age, 17. She would come by after school sometimes and wait for her mom. Her life was so different than mine. I was supposed to have that life, but I didn't. I would help her with her homework sometimes and she would ask about what school I went to. I told her I had already graduated early. I didn't want her to know that I was a dropout and a prostitute. I kept that part to myself and just talked about work. My life was work and this was the new job. At the drive in restaurant the customers would give us tips for bringing out the food and I would split my tips in half and stash one half in this little white monkey Greedy had and the other half went to Chris. I was stashing money to leave again. Every time things started getting better they would quickly get worse again. This time I had planned to Jump on a bus with Greedy and leave the state hoping he wouldn't find me. I had no clue where I was going to go but wherever it would be, it would be far. I continued working and giving my money and food stamps to Chris and things were ok for a little while. I had kept in touch with Maya and we were plotting together for a way out of this again. After some careful planning and making sure he was in a good mood I asked if I could go see my friend Maya from school. Number one he didn't know she was the one who helped me last time, he thought a social worker helped me. Number two I told him that I was working on bringing Maya to him to work on the streets. With that prospect in mind he let me go with her overnight to her house. It was a seriously long drive to her parent's house in Jones, it was in the country. I met her parents and we talked about my situation and my desperation to get out. They said they would pray for me but didn't agree to help me. Maya and I stayed up all night long talking. She was telling me all about her boyfriends and school. I didn't have any good stories to tell so I did most of the listening. We did what teenagers were supposed to do, we fell asleep right before the sun came up. We only got a few hours in and then it was time to take care of the horses out back. That next day her dad was supposed to take me home on his way into work but he Just got up and left. I called Chris and told him what happened and that I would be home in the afternoon and he was not happy. He wanted to come get me but I didn't know where I was at and didn't want to tell him. Later that afternoon we learned that Maya's dad had to leave on an unexpected trip out of town for his job and wouldn't be back until the morning. I had to find another way back home. I didn't even know anyone else who owned a car. Maya got a hold of a friend of ours from the Juvenile Center, Kato. He was going to college at the time at Central State in Edmond. He drove out to get me and it was already after dark. Me and Greedy hopped in the car and I thought we were headed home. Instead we went back to the campus. He had borrowed a friend's car and didn't have permission to go to the city. I waited while he found the guy and told him what he needed to do. We were finally on the road, rolling down Broadway extension to the city. I was already nervous about what I was going to walk into because we were coming up on midnight. All of the sudden the car started sputtering and it died. We had ran out of gas. We started walking up the ramp of the highway and since neither of us knew where we were we certainly didn't know which way to a gas station. We chose to go right first. We thought we seen some lights. After about 30 minute and a couple miles of walking it turned out to be the lights of a warehouse parking lot. We turned back the other direction and started walking toward the other side of the highway. We walked for what seemed to be 2 hours or more. My shoes had made blisters on my feet, Greedy was heavy as heck and didn't want to stay on Kato's shoulders so I ended up carrying him most of the way. We finally seen a Phillips 66 in the distance at Western Ave and I felt Just a little bit of relief. Me and Greedy stayed at the gas station while Kato walked back to the car. The only thing I kept thinking about was how bad the beating was going to be. It wasn't whether I was going to get one or not, just how bad it would be and if I would survive. He came back and picked us up and we were on our way home. By this time it was after midnight. We turned onto my street and I was relieved to not see Chris's car in front of my house. Kato pulled up in the driveway of the other duplex. It was so quiet outside you could even hear the little limbs in the driveway breaking as he drove over them. Kato put it in park while looking toward the front door, then he looked over at me. He knew who Chris was and what he was capable of. "Do you want me to help you with your stuff?" he asked, hoping I would say no. "No, you'd better go, thanks for the ride." I knew I needed help but I didn't want to get him killed. If Chris ever seen him carrying my bags that would be all it would take for him to have a reason to go off on him. I grabbed our bags, picked up Greedy from the back seat and kicked the door closed with my foot. Kato was watching as I walked away from the car. I started walking for the front door praying he wasn't here. Kato was still sitting in the driveway waiting for me to get to the door. The second, and I mean the second my foot hit the first step, the porch the light came on and the door was opening. He was there. My heart, stomach and everything else sank. I could hear Kato pulling off real fast, I didn't want to look back. I kept my eyes on Chris and was frozen on that first step. "Bring yo ass in the fucking house!" as he reached to grab the hair on the top of my head. With a hand full of hair he pulled me into the house and flung me down on the floor. He kicked me hard in the ass from the back. It felt like his boot had literally went inside me. I rolled over into a ball and pushed Greedy away from me so he wouldn't get hit too. Chris grabbed me by the hair again and started dragging me through the house yelling about me being out fucking other people without even getting paid for it. He was screaming that I would "never have a friend again" "never leave this house again to visit anyone" "if it's not about money, you ain't going nowhere!" Greedy was chasing after us crying and saying "No, daddy no!" he didn't want to see his momma hurting. "Get yo ass in the living room and sit down" Chris said to Greedy as he pointed to the living room. Greedy reluctantly went to the living room but I could still hear him crying. Chris slapped me around a few times then went to the living room. I heard him pick up Greedy and tell him it was going to be ok. "I'll be right back, don't move" Chris walked out the door with Greedy in his arms. I wanted to run out after him, I wanted to run and grab my baby and keep running down the street until it ran out. But I was frozen, like a block of ice sitting there waiting to melt away. Waiting to turn into nothing, with no trace or sign I was there. This was it, he's going to kill me this time. It was only about 3-4 minutes before he was back so I was pretty sure he had taken Greedy to Brook's house. When he came back he didn't even speak he Just slapped the hell out of me. I fell to the ground where the bed and dresser met. He picked me up by my hair and started pressing my face into the bed where I couldn't breathe. I tried to calm myself so I wasn't using as much oxygen but it wasn't working. When I thought I was about out of air he finally pulled me off the mattress. He was calling me dizzy bitch and filthy whore then he spit in my face. He hadn't done that to me before, I had seen him do it to several of the girls but he had never done that to me. I know, I should be more hurt by the fact that he's beating me on a regular basis but being spit on, in the face. "Bitches who are spit on are considered to be the lowest of the low" this is what Chris had told me in the past about other girls. He would beat them and then spit on them as they were laying on the ground when he was done. I was so fixated on the fact that he had spit in my face that I can't even recall the end of the beating. I can' Just remember him spitting in my face and me understanding what that meant to him and what it meant to me. While I was thinking about him spitting on me I didn't realize that he had gotten the scissors until he started cutting on my hair. "You won't go outside now bitch, you won't be showing out now you fucking ho." He was saying as he was cutting chunks out of my hair. I was trying to move away from him but he kept cutting at my hair. He grabbed my head and put me in a head lock with one arm and started cutting at my hair again with the other. There were two different times where he cut my scalp with the scissors as he was cutting. I couldn't do anything but cry. He was making me so ugly. I already felt ugly, now I'm hideous. Chris finally let me go and I dropped to the ground. I had nothing left in me. If I wasn't already broken I was surely broken now. Ugly inside and out now. "Clean up this fucking mess" he yelled as he walked out of the house. I laid there on the floor for a while thinking about what I looked like, crying and feeling helpless. I got up and started cleaning up after my beating. I never minded cleaning house but I hated to clean up after a beating. You knew how and why each piece of furniture was out of place, you could usually still feel the sting of the landing while you're cleaning up. I cleaned up everything else and left the hair for last. When I was growing up I had long and pretty hair. My mom would comb it and put pony tails and plats in my hair. My sisters would all play with my hair. It was really thick and long most of the time. I remember my first hair-cut. It too was not the traditional beautician. My sister Kathi and I were playing upstairs in the room across from Daddy's shop in the big white house in Marvell. I should have known when she wanted to cut my hair under the sheet, that we had a problem. But she was my older sister and I trusted her. She said she was going to give me a stylish haircut like the new lady on TV, with the long feathered hair. I envisioned exactly what I would look like with it and gave her the go ahead to chop away. When she was done we went downstairs and it was Lillian who saw me first. She was around 4yrs old and immediately started to cry. I must have looked pretty bad. I went to momma and she took me straight over to the only hair cutting place we had for girls. It was a lady about mom's age with a big dark bun on her head. She cut my hair into the best shape she could. I don't remember if Kathi was grounded for that but I do remember feeling ugly because of it. I had long beautiful hair and it was all gone. After that I never let anyone else cut my hair. I would trim my own ends and I Just let it grow. When Chris met me it was really long. At some point when I was working on the streets I had gotten lice and when I was pregnant in the Juvenile shelter they had a beautician cut it off to kill the lice and remove the eggs. That was pretty traumatic, but nowhere near traumatic as this. My hair had finally started growing out, it had taken me almost two years to get it past my shoulders and now it was gone again. I gathered the hair from the floor and walked into the bathroom to throw it away. When I walked in I caught a glimpse of myself in the mirror. Hideous didn't cover it, I looked worse than I could have ever imagined. I stared at myself for the longest. My hair was 14 different lengths with the shortest being less than an inch. I stood in the mirror and cried. I was so ugly and beaten down, I had pretty much resigned myself to believe that I was going to eventually die at his hand and no one would know about it or even care. As the weeks went by I stayed in the house when I could. I only left for work and the good thing was I only had a couple of days on the schedule. It was part of the uniform to wear a hat over my head. I used one of Chris's Do-rag's to cover my neck so that helped hide it until my hair started growing back. After a week or so I didn't have to wear the long sleeves anymore because the bruising was going away.

I was healing up Just in time, I had to go to the food stamp office and renew my food stamps. The daycare wouldn't watch Greedy for that. I couldn't ask Chris to watch him because that would be telling him what to do. So I asked my sister Lillian to watch Greedy for me so I didn't have to take him with me. Getting there by bus was hard enough but doing it with a toddler was even harder. Chris didn't like my family being around Greedy. He always felt that they were white trash and he didn't want Greedy to be any part of that. I handled things at the welfare office and headed back home. I lived a few blocks into the neighborhood so I had to walk that part after getting off the bus. I walked down park place to avoid seeing Chris if he happened to drive to the house. I had gotten about half way to my old apartment where mom and them were staying when I heard a car come around the corner behind me. I didn't think anything of it until the car slowed down behind me, it was Chris. He pulled up beside me and rolled down the window. "Where the fuck is my son?" "He's right here at mom's house, I'm getting him now." I was hoping he wouldn't say anything, he sped off and pulled into her drive way. I ran the rest of the way to try to get to the door with him instead of after him. I was too late. When I was coming up the driveway to the back I heard him and Lillian screaming at each other. I walked in and Chris was holding Greedy and screaming in Lillian's face about Greedy's face. I looked at Greedy and there was a small scratch on the top of his nose. I looked over at Lillian "What happened?" "She shouldn't have my fucking son, that's what the fuck happened." "Fuck you Chris, I was playing with him on the couch and he just lunged to the floor, he landed on his face, that's a carpet burn. I didn't do anything!" Lillian said quickly. She was pissed with a bad attitude as well. They screamed back and forth for a while I was so scared that he was going to hit her. He turned to me, "Don't bring my son over these people's house again, ever!" he screamed in my face. He got in the car with Greedy and pulled off. I talked to Lillian for a few seconds trying to calm her down and then headed to the house. The screaming match continued at my house except it was one sided. I didn't participate in the argument. I sat there, defeated, completely defeated. What else could I do? I didn't feel like things would ever change. He finally left but life didn't change much at all. It was the same ole, same ole, day after day. I was 2 days away from my 17th birthday and I was not that excited about it. I didn't have birthday parties anymore that was long gone. I didn't get too many presents from Chris these days either. Speaking of he had just pulled up in the driveway. He was in the little blue rabbit that he had gotten a couple of months before that he traded in the Lincoln on. That was what April usually drove. When I looked out the window I could see that she was in the passenger seat. Chris ran up to the door and I quickly opened it. "She's in labor, were going to have the baby." I grabbed my shoes and Greedy and headed for the car. Brook was in the Cadillac right behind them. April was in so much pain I don't think it mattered who was coming. We got to the hospital and Chris got out with April at the entrance. I took the car and parked it. When we walked into the hospital I knew right where to go, I had already been through this and knew the way. We got there and Chris was in the waiting room. He said they were getting her hooked up to everything. I sat with him for a while and talked to Greedy about having a baby sister. The nurse came and got Chris and they were in there for quite a while. When he came back I knew the baby had been born. He was grinning ear to ear. "Well, what did she weigh? How did it go?" I had questions and he had no answers. He was so smitten by his baby girl she was all he could think of. After a few minutes the nurse came out with a beautiful baby in one of those carts they put the plastic bassinets on. She was so pretty. I wanted a girl too but it was against the rules and really I didn't want to get pregnant so I figured I would be good with Greedy having a sister with April. Brook said she wanted a girl also. Chris quickly talked over her and said "Boy, Boy, I'm having another Son." We left after she left with the new baby. We took the Cadillac home. Chris had started driving the rabbit more to throw off the police because they knew his Cadillac too well. Me and Brook watched her boys while she was there. I had Samuel and she had Lil Man. He was born a little while after I had Greedy. There was always debate about whether Lil Man was Chris's son or not. But this child here, there was no mistaking. She looked exactly like a Sharp when she was born. I could see Greedy's face in hers. Chris had decided her name would be Christina. After she came home we would go over to her house at least once a week to see the baby. April had a little nursery set up for her with a bed and stuff. She showed me the lock on the door that she used to keep Samuel and Lil Man out of the room when she had to leave for work for Chris. April was pretty smart about the ways to keep the kids as safe as possible in the situations we were in. And right now that was helpful because we had several children showing up in the picture. Christina was about 2 weeks old when Chris and April took a trip down to Ardmore to show his mother the baby. I didn't get to go because they had all the kids with them and because I had to keep an eye on Brook, she was in her last month too and could have the baby at any time.

Christina had just turned a month old when baby number two was on the way into the world. Once again, I was chilling at the house when Chris ran in to say Brook was in labor and headed to the hospital. April came and picked me up and we went to the hospital together. There were four kids between us and two were toddlers, we needed to be together to team up on them. We got to the labor and delivery waiting room and waited for Chris to come tell us something. I noticed there were other women in the room also. I thought nothing of it until Chris came in. He said hello to them and that they could go back now. Who were they I thought, then it quickly hit me, they were Brook's sisters or something. I don't think they were very happy to see us there. I probably wouldn't have if it were my sister or daughter so I understood, but what they didn't understand was that we spent years together at this point. I'd watched her belly grow through the months and we were waiting on this baby just like they were. We were going to love on this baby just like they were. When they came back they called him out into the hallway to talk. He came back in the room and said that me and April had to go home. They gave him the ultimatum that we go or he goes with us, but that we were not welcome at the hospital. April drove us home and dropped me and Greedy at our house. "Let me know if you hear something" I said as I was getting out of the car. I took Greedy in the house and we played until he fell asleep, I was only a few minutes behind him. That morning Chris came in and told me it was another Girl. They had named her Channell after his baby sister. I knew Brook was mad about the name. We had talked about it after the first time Chris brought it up to her. She didn't want to name her that. She wanted to name her Brooklyn after herself, not him or his family. As usual he won the battle and the name was set. Brook did the same as me, never called her by the name that Chris put on her. She always called her Brooklyn. In the end the name didn't matter, what was important and matter was that she was here and she was healthy. For the next several weeks he would often have us all in the same house at the same time. He liked seeing the kids next to one another, the girls were identical. They were almost like twins. I think Brook was under the impression that when she had the baby that me and April would go away, and that was not what was happening. The more we were together the more upset she was getting. We didn't have fights or anything like that, you could tell by her actions and tones. Everything was subtle, and that was exactly what we were keen to. I tried to avoid going over if I could, I understood how she felt. I didn't want them with my son either but what I learned was if he was with them they treated him well and we would do the same for her child.

Changes were starting to happen everywhere. My oldest sister had moved into the duplex in front of my old apartment where mom lived now. Chris started spending more time away because he was trying to bond with two babies in two households at the same time. My place became the refuge from the crying babies. He would come over and just want to sit quietly. We would all lay on the bed. Usually the first one to talk would be Greedy and it was always something that made us laugh. One day we were laying there and he said "big birds have big balls!" we were laughing ourselves into hysterics and he was laughing right along with us. He enjoyed being the center of attention even though he had no clue what he had just said. He knew the words individually and had just learned them because we were doing the "B's". It was still hilarious. Times like that made me miss my sisters. They lived only two blocks away but I was barely allowed to see them anymore. I had been over there one day doing Tyana's hair for her. I was sitting on the couch and she was sitting on the floor below. She wanted to have the ringlet curls so I was hooking her up. Greedy had been watching TV with Lillian. They were laying on a blanket on the floor. I was almost done and got up to go the bathroom. I was leaving the bathroom when I heard Greedy scream. I ran to the living room and Tyana was holding him. "What happened?" "He got up on the couch and sat on the curling iron." "Oh shit" I said as I looked at his leg where the burn is. "Oh my God, Chris is going to be so mad at me. He's not going to understand. He's going to burn me back." I was so scared. "Why are you panicking it was an accident, Chris will understand." "No he won't Tyana, he won't understand. I'm going to be in big trouble." I put ice on his leg trying to calm the burn down. It was red as red could be on his inner thigh. I felt so bad about the burn, I started thinking maybe I deserve to get beaten. I was careless enough to leave it there for him to get burned. It was my fault and I needed to be punished. Lillian finished Tyana's hair because I couldn't calm down enough to do it. I packed up Greedy and walked back to the house. I waited for Chris to come home and when he did I showed him the burn on Greedy's leg. "What the fuck did you do?" he said as he grabbed my face. "I didn't do it, I was at mom's house." I wasn't finished with my sentence when he slapped me. "You will never go to their fucking house again. Never, don't let me catch your ass over there. I'm telling you, one of these days I'm going to kill one of you bitches. Y'all piss me the fuck off" He picked up Greedy and left with him. I sat there in the same place for a while waiting for Chris to return to beat me. He didn't come back for a few days. By the time Greedy was brought home the burn was healed up. I didn't know if he had been to April's or Brook's and I didn't care. I was happy to have him back but I was sad at the same time. I didn't get to see my sisters much already, now I would never see them again. Being that close and not seeing my sisters hurt but it was for the better but the rule about not seeing them didn't last long. Chris had talked several times about pimping out Tyana and Lillian and since the money was at its lowest with both babies being born I wasn't surprised when it came up in the conversation again. I told Chris they weren't trust worthy enough and that it would only cause more problems. We had already been through the event with the oldest and it didn't work out well at all. You would think he wouldn't want to try that again but they were young and every time we would see them Lillian would barely be dressed and on a few occasions she wasn't dressed at all. Chris told me to go to my mom's and start spending time with them to get my sisters on my side. He would watch Greedy while I would go over there. I walked over and the second I got in the door I started a fight with Lillian. She was easily triggered. A while prior she had hit mom in the face and gave her a black eye. She felt bad about it but in the moment she didn't stop herself. So any mention of that at all would set her off. She would go on the defense immediately. "So, no black eyes today mom?" I said as I sat on the couch next to her. Lillian immediately started cussing and screaming "Get the fuck out of this house, you don't live here" "My momma lives here, I don't have to do shit" we went back and forth, back and forth. I finally walked out and walked home. I told Chris about the fight but I didn't tell him what started it. I told him that me asking about her working started it. From that point on I would act pissed when I would see my sisters so that they would stay mad. I didn't need them to be around. The only way I knew they wouldn't try to be around me is if they are pissed at me. It hurt me a lot to be a part of what was keeping us apart but it was necessary. I wanted out and didn't want them to be the next victim. I tried to stay distracted with the two new babies. The girls were growing pretty fast. They could sit up if you propped them Just right. I enjoyed playing with them and Greedy did too. The more I thought about and seen all the new baby stuff the more I started feeling weird. I started noticing some changes, changes in my body. I started counting the weeks since I had been back from Enid. I had a period shortly after he had brought me back but that had been over two and a half months at least. I cried thinking about the possibility of me being pregnant again, I had just turned 17. Chris had made it abundantly clear that NO

251

ONE was allowed to get pregnant again. He was still upset about Brook and April being pregnant at the same time. He said he would "Kick it out of our asses if we got pregnant again, and that he was going to end up killing one of us if we did" I did my best to Just move on with the day but all I could think about was being pregnant again. As much as I wanted a baby girl I didn't want to be pregnant, I wasn't allowed to be pregnant. Pregnancy would surely mean death. Within a few days, as I suspected, Chris was asking about my period. He had come over that morning to take me to work and started asking questions. "Why haven't you started?" He kept up with my periods somewhat to make sure he knew what was going on. After two babies back to back he was much more observant in that area. I hadn't had a period and he started adding up the days. I could see the moment that the realization hit his face, the light bulb went on, she's pregnant. "You dizzy bitch!" he yelled as he ran at me. I had Greedy in my arms and I dropped him to the ground just in time for Chris to tackle me. First we were on the ground together and he was kneeing me in the stomach. Then he got up on his feet and started stomping me in the stomach repeatedly with his snake skin boots. It was hurting so bad and Greedy was screaming crying. The daycare van was supposed to be there any minute to pick him up for daycare. I didn't want them to see what was happening to Greedy's mom, I didn't want Greedy to see what was happening to his mom either. Chris continued beating me and then we heard the horn from the daycare van. I was happy and scared that they were here to pick him up. Number one because I hated for Greedy to see me being beaten. Number two how bad was it going to get after that van leaves. Chris carried Greedy out to the Van and then came back inside. I had gotten up and was sitting on the bed. When he walked in he told me to stand up. As I did he kicked me in the stomach again so hard that I flew back on the bed. He grabbed me by my hair drug me off the bed. He started dragging me around the house as he was yelling at me about being pregnant. "Do you want to die? How fucking stupid are you?" he kept asking. I was trying to explain to him that I couldn't get any birth control and didn't have any other way to prevent it. Chris never was much on hearing your side of the story. He would mock what you had to say and scream louder at you. "I tried, I tried" he said in a mocking voice. "Fuck you, you dizzy bitch! Stupid fucking whore! Worthless piece of shit! The shit on my feet is more worthy than you! I'm going to end up killing yo ass one of these days if you keep fucking up like this!" I remember all the things he used to say, some of them I can still hear in his own voice. Before I had escaped that first time I had learned to tune out on him, go to a different place in my mind where he wasn't at but keep my eyes on him, he eventually got hip to that one. He would slap me back or use my hair as the catapult to throw me to the ground or across the room to bring me back to attention. Why would I keep doing it you ask…well this will seem odd but it's true. The physical abuse is easier to take than the verbal when you know you will be getting both either way, it was my only way to make some sort of choice for myself. I guess that was my teenage rebellion moment, I was still a teenager. He'd started making drifting off harder, since I had been back, he started having me repeat back to him what he would say to me. Hearing someone else say it to you is hurtful and can affect you, hearing it from yourself, oh, that will do you in. I could hear myself saying it when he wasn't prompting it. He would have me tell him how worthless I was and then say things like "Ya damn right you are, dizzy bitch, like you fucking know something!" We did that for a while that morning and he was making me stand while I did it. I could barely stand because my stomach was hurting so bad. He had kneed and kicked me more times than I could count. He finally got to the point where he had worn his self out. He told me to get in the car so I could go to work. Chris made sure that I always made it to work, beat up or not. I tried to put my hat on but it was too painful. When we were pulling up he took the hat from my hands and shoved it down on my head. "Now get the fuck out" he said with no remorse at all. After being at work for less than hour the pain in my stomach was getting to be un-bearable. Matter of fact, the pains were starting to act more like contractions than bad cramps. They were moving from my back around to the front Just like it did when I went into labor with Greedy. Connie let me sit down in the back for a while but it didn't help much. When I stood back up I felt something coming from my vagina. I went to the bathroom and sure enough, I was bleeding and I knew my baby was dying inside me. I told Connie that I was pregnant and having a miscarriage and asked if I could have the rest of the day off. I called my mom and told her what was going on. She didn't live that far so she walked up to the Del Rancho to go with me to the hospital. I explained to her what I was feeling and she agreed that she thought it was a miss-carriage too. As much as I didn't want to even be around her I needed someone, I needed my mom, I was hurting so much. We waited for the city bus to get there and paid our fee to get on. The plan was to take the bus to the emergency room because we didn't have a car or cab fare. After we got on the bus my pains increased and the bus driver asked what was going on. My mom told him that we were trying to get to the hospital and that I was in the middle of a miss-carriage. The bus driver said we had to get off, we had to get off the bus. He wouldn't take us to the emergency room but he would call an ambulance. I was in pain and mortified. He kicked us off. I don't understand why we couldn't have just ridden down the street, it was only a couple of miles. I didn't understand why he wouldn't take us. The ambulance arrived and people started coming out of their businesses to see what was going on at the bus stop, I was so embarrassed. I didn't want to be doing any of this. What would I tell the paramedics? I had to think of something to tell them, I couldn't tell them it was Chris. He would surely finish the job and kill me, my child inside me was already dead, and he was the reason. The paramedic was asking an awful lot of questions. I didn't want to answer any of them, I Just wanted to stop hurting. When he would ask I would cry more so he said he would leave that to the doctors at the hospital. I rode to the hospital in the ambulance and was quickly put in a room when I got there. The nurse came in and asked for urine so they could do a pregnancy test. I was pregnant, they confirmed it, and I was also in the middle of losing the baby. After the pregnancy confirmation she asked what I thought I might have done that would make the baby miscarry. Kicks to the stomach will do it, I thought to myself as she was listing off things that would cause a miscarriage. "Strenuous exercise, moving furniture?" "Yes, moving furniture" I said. Moving furniture was the excuse I gave. I wanted to tell her that Chris did it but I already knew how the system worked. I knew I couldn't trust her. After all the hoopla would be over, I would always end up back with him every time. If I told the nurse I would be dead. She left the room, hours had gone by and I was laying on the table in pain and alone. No one was there, mom didn't come in the ambulance with me, and she had gone home because I needed someone to be there when the daycare van came back with Greedy so it was just me. I was hurting too much to get up, the cramps were Just like having a baby. I yelled out to the nurses hoping someone would come and give me some kind of pain meds or something. I got no response. I laid there a while longer while the contractions went up and down, just like when I had Greedy. That's what I kept thinking to myself, just like when I had Greedy. I had finally had it. I couldn't wait for them any longer. I decided that I would get up and go get help myself. I waited for the current contraction to subside then I started trying to pull myself upright. My stomach was hurting so bad. The bottom hurt from the miscarriage and the top from Chris stomping on me. I felt another contraction coming on and laid back down. I pulled the gown up and looked at my stomach and could see the bruising coming up and there was a big scrape on my side from his boot not landing quite right. My ribs hurt pretty bad too and I thought about the possibility of them being broken. I pulled my gown back down real quick, if they find broken or cracked ribs they are going to want to know who did it. And as bad as I would like to tell them, I know he's more powerful than they are and I can't afford the price for that one. I waited for the pain to go back down and started raising myself up again. When I did, I felt something come out of me. I knew I had been bleeding, it was probably a clot I thought to myself. I raised the rest of the way up and I could see what it was. It was my baby, the baby had come out of me and was laying on the table between my legs. I was frozen, I Just stared at it. I couldn't

255

believe what I was looking at. The baby was very small, about as long as my pinky finger and as wide as two fingers. It was white but translucent at the same time. The head was the biggest part, about the size of a quarter. There were black dots where the eyes and nose were growing and a slit where the mouth was. The arms were up on both sides of the head and the little hands had partial fingers. The lower half of the body was unrecognizable. I could see the belly and the cord coming from the belly but there was just a jelly like mess below that. No legs or feet. I began to cry, I cried harder and harder. My cry soon turned into a yell, "Heeeellllp" I yelled at the top of my lungs for them to come in. The nurse came barreling in "What's the problem?" she said. "I had my baby right here, it's here on the table" I pointed to the baby on the table between my legs. The nurse made a face like she didn't think I knew what I was talking about. She put on a glove and leaned over to see, her face quickly changed and she yelled for someone else to come in. She grabbed one of the little banana shaped pans you throw up in and she slid the baby the rest of the way off the table. I watched her with the pan as she moved away. I didn't know what she was going to do with the baby. I wanted to know if there was any way to save the baby but I didn't know how to ask and had become used to keeping my questions to myself. The nurses said a few things to each other and then she walked out with my baby. I wanted to run after her and get my baby. What was she going to do with my baby I wondered? I wanted my baby and I didn't want her to throw her away. The other nurse with her started prepping me for the doctor to come in. The doctor came in and sat at the end of the table where my feet had been put in stirrups. I was already in so much pain I didn't know what he was doing and didn't care at the time. I couldn't even think about what he was doing. The pain was distracting but I couldn't stop thinking about my baby. I believe the baby was a girl even though they never said so. I had that feeling every time I would think of her. It was only about another hour in the emergency room and then they sent me home, without my baby. She was dead. I would never get to see her again. I would never know what she looked like as a child, as she grew.

When I arrived there were two of us, now, only one. I was leaving her there with them. I was leaving alone, without my baby.

After leaving the hospital I walked to the bus stop and waited for the bus to take me home. I thought about my baby the whole way home. I could remember clearly what she looked like there on the table. I don't know how I would have cared for two children but I was willing to do it. I was willing to do it for her. I got off the bus at my stop and started walking toward the house. I could see in the distance that the white van that takes Greedy to daycare was in front of the house and my anxiety went sky high. I had called while I was at the emergency room and asked them to take Greedy to my mom's house, I guess they didn't do it. The closer I got, the more I tried to look down the street for Chris to see if he already knew and was at my house. I'm sure he had been to my job and found out. I couldn't see at first but when I got closer I could see that Chris was standing by the van talking to the driver. I got sick to my stomach. I knew what was going to happen, he was going to kill me. I didn't want to finish the walk to the house but I had no choice, my son was in that van. When I was about a half a block away the van pulled off. Chris walked back up to the house. I walked in behind him hoping to find Greedy there. "What are you looking for dizzy bitch?" he asked as I looked frantically through the house. "Where's Greedy?" I asked. "He's at my house bitch, my son, that you abandoned today, is at my house!" he said as he walked up on me. "Where the fuck were you?" he screamed. "I was at the hospital, I had a miscarriage, the baby is dead, and I'm not pregnant anymore!" I said in an upset tone back at him. "What the fuck did you tell them" Chris yelled. "I didn't tell them anything. The nurse was listing off things that could happen and I picked one" Chris grabbed me by the back of my hair and leaned in so close we were touching noses. "Did you say my mutha fuckin name at that hospital bitch?" I started shaking my head no as fast as I could get it to go. "No, No, I never said your name, I never said your name" I assured him. He had absolutely no sympathy for what I had just been through. He threw me down on the bed and started pulling my pants off. I was still bleeding and hurting from the miscarriage and his beating but he didn't care. He climbed on top and raped me anyway. I was hurting so bad and there was blood everywhere. He didn't care he preferred to have the control over your body when he was mad. After he was finished he got up and started the shower. "Go cook me something, I'm hungry" he yelled from the bathroom. I cringed as I tried to rise up from the bed, there wasn't any part of my body that wasn't hurting. I scooted across the bed and braced myself to stand up. I was only 5'3" so I didn't have far to go but it was so difficult, it was hurting so much. I stumbled to the kitchen and got so dizzy I fell to the floor. I was still bleeding from the miscarriage and I'm sure Chris shoving his thing inside me wasn't helping the bleeding. I laid on the floor trying to get it together. I heard the shower turn off and I started pulling myself up. When Chris walked into the kitchen I was leaning on the counter with both hands over my head waiting for the dizzy to go away. "You forgot how to do what I asked?" "I'm not doing good Chris, I think I might need to go back to the hospital" I plead with him. "Fuck going to the hospital, you're fine, I Just examined yo ass, you're fine!" he laughed at his joke. I didn't find any humor in it, I was scared and hurting and he was cracking jokes. I started shaking my head in disbelief. I was naked, with blood all over my lower body, still bleeding, dizzy to the point that I couldn't stand well and was trying to cook him something because he was hungry. I was thinking to myself, but I accidentally said it out loud "You don't even care". I froze when I heard it come out of my mouth, breathing and everything stopped. I could even hear my heartbeat from the outside. I knew what was about to happen. Just as I looked up I saw it, his hand coming at me with rapid speed. His open hand landed on the side of my head and I went down. "What the fuck did you just say, I don't care, I don't care? I picked your ass up out of the fucking gutter. I fed you, clothed you, and gave you a mutha fuckin roof and I don't care!" He was standing over me butt naked screaming so hard he was spitting when he talked. He grabbed me by the hair and drug me into the bedroom. "Imma show you what a mutha fucker who don't care will do, since I don't fuckin care." Chris grabbed another hand of hair with his other hand and within that same second I was airborne. He had thrown me by my hair toward the bed but because my hair was so short now he couldn't keep hold and I flew from his hands and landed about 6ft up the wall, which was like a kick in the back of the head and tossed to the bed. He drug me down to the floor and I found myself between the dresser and him and that was not a good place. When he would kick me on one side my head would hit the dresser on the other side so it was like getting kicked twice every time. He was kicking me in the side of the head with his boots and it was hurting so bad. He was Just kicking and screaming "I don't fucking care, remember, I don't fucking care!" The knots were coming up already, all over my body. "God Please don't let him kill me today." That's all I kept thinking, please don't let him kill me today. I had resigned myself to the fact that he was going to kill me one day, I Just didn't want "today" to be that day. I was working on getting me and Greedy out for real this time. He eventually got winded and stopped for a while. I stayed in the same spot, afraid to move. My head was hurting so much and the screeching noise that would come in my head after a beating was there. I hated the screeching noise, it was sometimes worse to deal with than the head hurting. I was rubbing my head and feeling the knots and every time I would pull my hands out of my hair they would be full hands of hair coming out of my head. It was already short and this was thinning it out. I heard Chris leave out the front door, it was finally over. I stayed in the same spot for a while thinking about how I got there and where I should be. I should be in high school getting ready to graduate from a small town in Arkansas. Not laying on the floor bleeding and beaten. My father's selfishness put all this into play. There was nothing wrong with my parent's relationship except for his sexual appetite. None of this would be going on if he hadn't left mom. When I was younger I used to think abuse was just the way things were but as I got older I could clearly see that this was not the way it was for everyone. And I had decided it wasn't the way for me anymore either. I got up and started cleaning up the apartment. I had bled all over everything. After

I cleaned up everything else I got in the shower and that's when I realized how many other places I was bleeding from. I had several spots on my head start stinging when the water hit and although I can't see on top of my own head I knew I was cut. Probably gashes from his boots, unfortunately not the first time. I had so many knots on me I felt like the elephant woman. They weren't overly huge swollen to that extent but I was still lumpy all over. I stayed in the shower till the water turned cold. There was blood on the towel when I pulled it off my head. I wrapped another one around, took some Tylenol and laid down. I couldn't tell how bad it was by looking because I couldn't see but if it kept bleeding I knew I might need stitches or something. After arguing with myself I had decided that if there was more blood on the towel in the morning, if I make it till morning, then I would try to get help.

It was about 4am when I heard the front door open. I laid there pretending to be asleep. I heard the footsteps coming toward the bedroom and knew it wasn't Chris. Brook came through the door "Hey Angel, you awake? I came to check on you" she said as she started pulling the towel back from my head. "I think I'm ok, Just my head though, did Chris send you?" I asked. It hurt when she touched my head to check the cuts. "Naw, I snuck out" she said as she leaned over my head. "Yea, he got ya good Angel, there's a couple of them." "Do I look like I need stitches?" I asked. "Well this one probably needs something. You got some Band-Aid's?" "Yea, there in the bathroom" Brook went and grabbed the Band-Aid's and a razor. "What the crap do you need that for?" I screeched. "Band-Aids don't stick to hair dummy, I'm Just going to do a little part, OK?" "Go ahead" I said as I leaned my head down and she got to work getting the Band-Aid on. The bleeding had mostly stopped but it was laying open I guess. I never got to see it, I Just got to feel it. "I'm going to leave again Brook" I said in a quiet voice. "Girl, if he finds you again he's gonna kill you, you know that!" she said in a forceful voice. "He's going to kill me either way, I can't let my son keep seeing this, and I can't keep going through this." I exclaimed. "I know Angel, me too" she said. "You should come with me, my friend is working on a place way out in the country, come with me." I plead with her. "My mom's going to let me come back over there and my brothers will protect me. I'll wait till your gone then when he calms down again I'll leave" she said. "You should go now, if we leave at the same time he can't look for both of us" I said. "The hell he can't him in the Cadillac and April in the rabbit" she said. "Ok, your right" I sighed. "I Just want out" I said as I started to cry. Brook hugged me "I gotta get back before he notices, I'll bring Greedy back to you tomorrow, OK" she said as she was getting up. I watched her walk away and drifted back to sleep.

~Chapter 17~

The Beginning

That next morning I got up early with the sun and ran to the payphone at the laundry mat. I shoved my quarter into the pay slot and started dialing the numbers as fast as I could. Maya answered and I told her about him beating me into a miscarriage and then beating me again for going to the hospital and that he had taken Greedy. She said she would talk to her parents again and for me to call back when I had Greedy with me again. I walked back to the duplex wondering how I was going to get out of this with my baby and both of us alive. Every time he beats me it's getting worse not better. My savior is turning out to be my worst nightmare. How can a person who shows you so much love and affection then hit and kick you like you're a bag of trash. I'm not trash…I'm Angel and I'm going to get myself out of this for good. I spent the morning reshuffling things like I had done before when I was getting ready to leave the last time. I was in the kitchen when I heard the front door open and immediately heard little feet running my way. "Mommy, mommy" Greedy yelled as he ran for me. I ran his direction too and swooped him up. It hurt my arms to hold him but I would do it a million times, just to hold him. I hugged him for a while and Chris stood there staring at me. You could see a lot of the knots on me and some of them had bruises to accompany them. I had one right at my hairline that was pretty big. Greedy reached up and touched it "You got an owie mommy" "Yes baby but momma's ok, momma's ok" I said as I hugged him close to me again. "Do you work today?" Chris asked. "No, I'm not on the schedule today, I work tomorrow though" I replied. "What time?" he asked. "9:00am" "I'll be back in a little while" Chris said as he was walking out the door. I sat there and held Greedy and played with him in my lap on the couch for a while, enough time to let Chris get back to his car and leave. I kept peeking out the house and looking to see if his car was gone from in front of Brook's house. As soon as I seen he was gone me and Greedy left for the phone. I put Greedy on my shoulders and ran to the laundry mat to call Maya. When she answered I didn't even let her finish saying hello. "Did they said yes, I've got Greedy?" I said in a hurried voice. "Yes, my mom's going to come get you right after work, she leaves work at 5 and she works on 23rd and Shartel so it shouldn't take her more than 15 minutes to get there. Do you have your things ready to go? She asked. "Yes, I've got everything ready" I said. "You aren't going to be able to take much Sarah, Just your clothes, we will get more later but there isn't any room in the car." "I'm good with that Maya I Just want to get out, thank you so much for helping me, you're the only one who can help me for real" I said as I started to cry. "Just be ready at 5 and watch for her car, it's a white 4 door car, and you know what she looks like. She's gonna honk she's not getting out. "No, no tell her not to honk, he will hear that and look outside. Tell her I'll be looking, I'll be running out the door the second she pulls up, I promise." I exclaimed. "Just be ready, and I'll be prayin that he doesn't walk up on y'all" "You and me both girl, I love you, and I'll see you later." "I love you too girl". I ran back home, it was around 11am and I had 6 hours to wait till she got there and 6 hours to pray that Chris didn't come back. I played with Greedy when we got home to get him ready for his afternoon nap.

When he finally passed out I got up and finished organizing things. I put all of our best clothes in the laundry baskets like they were dirty and wrapped some of the other things we needed in the clothes. I got to take a few of my pictures but most of them stayed on the walls. I was only able to take about one fourth of our clothes. I only had two laundry baskets and I couldn't let Chris walk in and find anything looking ready to go except dirty laundry. I took Greedy's favorite couple of toys and books and had them out on the floor ready to leave. And then we waited. That was one of the longest waits of my life. When 4:50pm got there my heart started increasing the beats. I double and triple and quadruple checked the baskets and kept looking out the door to see if Chris was coming. I could see that his car was in front of Brook's house I was hoping he was watching a movie or something. Every 30 seconds I was looking out the window waiting for Maya's mom to show up. I think I looked out that window a hundred times. My anxiety was through the roof and I was trying to calm myself down so Greedy would stay calm. There she was! Her white four door car was slowing down to stop in front of my house. I looked in the driver seat to make sure it was her mom and when I confirmed that I opened the door as fast as I could. Freedom was on the other side of that door. I stuck my head out and looked down the street toward Brook's house and then looked at Helen, Maya's mom. "No one's coming, hurry" she said from the window of the car. I ran out to the car "Lay on the horn if you see him coming" I said as I handed her Greedy through the window. I ran back into the house and grabbed Greedy's toys and threw them in the laundry basket, put the other basket on top and ran back out to the car. "Pop the trunk" I yelled as I ran to the car. I quickly put the baskets in the trunk and took of back to the house to get Greedy's car seat. I had it sitting by the door all the time for when we would go places with Chris so it was an easy grab. I looked back into my apartment and the pictures of me and Greedy still on the walls and closed the door. I didn't even lock it, no reason to now. I ran for the car, Jumped in and Helen hit the gas. I stared out the back window the whole time we were going down my street waiting for Chris to come yelling, but he never came. I prayed as we were coming up on each and every light that they would be green and we could keep going. I kept my head down low and had Greedy's winter cap on him so it didn't show any of his head and only part of his face. I was scared of Chris driving by and seeing us. I didn't start feeling any relief until we got on the highway. Then I started to breathe a little bit. "Girl you look rough" Helen said. "I'm so grateful that you came to get us, Thank you so much. I promise I will work to pay you back." I said. "You don't need to worry about anything right now except being safe. I'm a nurse so I'll take a look at you when we get home. You've got a lot of knots and bruises on you and that eye doesn't look good" Helen said. "I've got some cuts in my head, Brook helped me last night" "I'll get ya fixed up when we get to the house. But I need to stop by the grocery store on the way, I won't be long." We pulled off the highway on the east side of town then drove a while down NE 23rd till we got to the grocery store she was talking about. I went in with her but I was still scared to death that he would walk in that store. I put a hat on that was in the car and put it down low to try to cover the bruises on my face. I kept looking around every corner and if I saw a black man from a distance I would get scared until he was close enough that I knew it wasn't Chris. There were a couple of people who stared at me for a minute, I'm sure I looked terrible but they didn't say anything. We got the groceries and headed back to the highway to go to Maya's house. It was a long drive and I was able to relax some. I knew he didn't know where this was, I don't even think he was aware of the town let alone the houses in the country. When we got to the house and started down the long driveway I could see that Maya had come outside and was on the porch waiting for us to pull up. She ran over to the car when we stopped she about broke my neck as I was getting out of the car trying to hug me. I was just as grateful and wanted to hug her too but it hurt. "You're hurting me girl, let go" I said. "Oh, I'm sorry, I was so glad to see that you made it. I've been worried to death for the last couple of hours" Maya said. "Can you help grab my stuff please, Imma grab Greedy" I asked. "Sure can" she said. We went inside and Maya showed me the extra bedroom that was her little girls that would be mine and Greedy's now. I was so relieved but still very scared at the same time. When he realizes that I'm gone he's going to go to my mom's house. I didn't even tell her I was leaving because he would have gotten it out of her. We settled in for the night and Helen looked me over, cleaned me up properly and put a couple of butterfly Band-Aid's on. "Girl you're gonna be hurting for a while but eventually you'll be ok. You don't need a doctor visit but we do need to call the police and report the beating". "Helen, please don't!" I begged her not too because a police report would involve their address and I didn't want anyone to know where I was so she agreed and we didn't call the police. I was safe and I planned to stay there for a while so I could stay safe. I had nightmares about him finding me almost every night. I would wake up sweating with my heart racing. I'd go stare out the windows of the house making sure that he wasn't out there in the yard like he was in my dreams. I was on edge 24/7, I knew that if he found me this time he would surely kill me. The school year had already started and her Pops, Carl, said that I had to get enrolled in school if I was going to say out there with them but we had to at least wait until it was safe. I was all for it, I had barely finished 9th grade and ended up going to three different schools trying to make it happen so I was hoping 10th grade would be a little better. For the first couple of weeks I Just stayed in the house, plus it was Just 2 months or so to Christmas break so I was going to enroll in Jan when Maya went back to school. When they all left each morning they would take the phone with them so I didn't have a way to call Chris or anyone else to "accidentally" give away my location. I had my welfare check transferred to their PO Box so there wasn't an address for him to find and for the first time I had money of my own to spend on what I needed instead of what someone else decided I needed. When Christmas break rolled around me and Maya decided we were going out into the back yard, which was a couple of acres, to find a Christmas tree to cut down while her parents were at work so we could surprise them. We walked all over until we found the perfect tree with the perfect shape and height. We went to hackin away at that tree. There was only one problem. The tree was so low to the ground we had to work on our bellies and it wasn't working out. The more you moved the tree the more of the needles were falling into our hair and faces. We were sawin and hackin but it wasn't even barely putting a dent in it but we had to have THAT very tree. We didn't give up and after a good long while and some seriously sore arms and hands we got our tree. We drug it back to the house and it was at that point that we started thinking about how we were going to get it to stand up since we didn't have any kind of stand for it. We looked around for a while and then decided on a coffee can. We put the stump of the tree in and then added the rocks... all in the living room. Boy was there a mess. We were super proud of our tree and then we stepped back to see the mess. Whoa, we hoped that we would be able to get it all cleaned up before her parents got home. Anna, Maya's little girl and Greedy were playing with the needles from the trees so we took advantage of that made it into a game and started having them help pick up. This is one of the first normal, regular girl, my age kind of stuff I remember doing after I escaped. I was 17 and was finally able to do something a 17yr old should be doing. Getting a Christmas tree for mom and dad. I was happy and Greedy was happy, this meant everything to me. I still thought about Chris everyday wondering if he was looking for me, wondering if I would ever be able to go back to the city and see any of my family, wondering if Brook was able to get out and go back home. That was what I did most nights...wonder. One weekend right after Christmas it snowed and snowed and snowed for days. When it finished snowing it was waist deep and the drive way was completely closed off. Maya's parents were working that last day while it was snowing and we knew they weren't going to make it in if we didn't shovel a way for them. We bundled the kids and ourselves up and started marching through the snow. The kids loved being in the snow and at points it was taller than they were. We finally wore them out, took them in for a nap and went out to finish the driveway. Her parents were happy when they got home and the sense of pride I got from seeing them happy and pleased with us was something I wanted to continue getting. This was the kind of life I wanted to have this is the kind of life I should have been living the whole time and this is the kind if life I will continue to have and give to my children. After Christmas break was over it was time for me to enroll in school again. This was my second attempt at 10th grade. I had started the year in the city but was getting beat up too much to go all the time so I ended up dropping. I got enrolled out in the country and started going to school again. The first day was weird as usual like it is at any school but there was something I wasn't used to. In a school of over 500 there were only 8 black students…period. I wasn't used to that nor was I used to all the 4A farm stuff. I had all the regular classes and I usually excelled at any school work I was given, except in typing, I had problems talking with friends. That was my only C, all the rest were mostly A's. I enjoyed being at school, always have, it was my refuge in middle school and high school. I knew when I was at school there would be food and I would be safe, great combination. After being in school for a while and meeting different people I hung out with the hand full of black kids because that was what I was used to and that's where I was accepted. Kelvin, who was a local horse jockey, had started flirting with me. I didn't know what to do. We started sitting next to each other and going to lunch together and talking on the phone all night long. Of course I didn't tell him anything about my past, he thought I was sent out to the country because I was bad at home. Whatever he thought was fine with me as long as he didn't know what happened to me. I wanted to forget it ever happened and the easiest way was to not bring it up. Anyway he eventually asked me out on a date one night. He was going to take me to the movies and dinner and everything. I was so excited. This was my first REAL date. I was actually going to go out with a boy my age who is interested in getting to know me and this has nothing to do with the exchange of sex or money. I was soooo ready for this. I think I took more than 2 hours to get ready. His mom drove out and picked me up and she was our chaperone for the evening. She dropped us off at The Park Mall and said that she would be shopping and to meet her back at the same place in a couple of hours. I was excited the whole way but when she dropped us off and drove away my anxiety started rising. My hands started sweating and I started looking around to make sure Chris wasn't here. This was the first time I was alone in a public place where Chris could have access. I didn't know she was going to leave us, I thought she would walk behind us or something, but I was wrong. "Are you ok?" Kelvin asked. "Yea, I'm good, I Just get nervous around crowds, but I'll be fine, let's walk" as we walked I did my best to pull it together. We walked around to the food court and got some food while we waited for the movie to start. I felt much better inside the theater in the dark where I wasn't out in the open for anyone to see. We watched the movie and it was a perfect movie for my first real date. I was so excited about being on the date and with the other added anxiety, I couldn't even tell you what happened in the movie. Kelvin was the perfect gentleman though and didn't even try to kiss me, we just held hands. I didn't have much to add to the conversation because all my stuff was stuff you couldn't talk about so we spent most of the time talking about him and his horse riding, which he was totally ok with. After the date his mom took me back home and Maya was waiting at the door for me to tell her all about the date, and you know I did. We laughed and giggled like 17yr old girls were supposed to and it felt great. At school there was a group of us that had chosen to promote the democratic nominee for the Presidential election. That year Dulley was running and we were supporting him in the high school to give our fellow students a reason to start thinking about politics and voting. We made posters and hung them up all over the school. We also called the campaign office to tell them what we were doing. Just a few days later we get called to the office. There was a package there for us. It had campaign material in it including; posters, buttons, flyers, a couple of t-shirts and hats. This was really awesome. We talked to the counselor about letting us talk at half time in the game and throw out the prizes. They agreed and we did just that. One of the guys in our group started trying to date me as well. He didn't live far from where we lived in the country. I didn't want to break Kelvin's heart but I also wasn't trying to be in a full time relationship after all I had just gotten out of. Maya and I were sitting at the table doing our homework and passing a note trying to figure out how we are going to get over to Shane's house. We finally come up with the plan and head out. Helen watched the kids for us. We drove over in her Mom's car and were hanging out with Shane and the other teens who were there. We were having a great time. We noticed what time it was and had overstayed what we were supposed to. We ran out to the car trying to hurry back, already thinking of the excuse. Maya tried to start the car and it wouldn't start. She tried it several times and I tried it also. The guys came out and looked at the car but didn't have a clue about why it wasn't starting. Reluctantly we went back in the house to call Helen. Maya dialed the number and Helen answered. "Hello, Mamma, we can't leave because the car won't start. We don't know what's wrong but it won't start." "Ok, Momma" she hung up the phone. She just said "I know, because I found this note! It will start, go start it and bring your butts home right now! My Momma is really a witch girl, I've been trying to tell you. She knows things she ain't supposed to know!" "Your Mom is super spooky!" "Yea, girl! I know, let's go try this car" she said as we walked outside. We got in and the car started right up. Spring break was right around the corner so we were looking forward to that and didn't want to mess it up so we hurried home. Helen was mad about us making up a story, she said if we just told her we would have been able to do it if we had all our chores and homework done. We apologized and tried to keep her happy because we were afraid of her powers we thought she had.

Greedy's 2nd birthday was coming up and we started planning for the party. He didn't get to have a 1st birthday party because of Chris so I was going to make sure that this was a fun party for him. We invited all of our friends with their little sisters and brothers. Maya was the only friend I had that had a kid of her own. All my other friends were regular sophomores. I should have been a Junior but 9th grade and my life weren't mixing well. Kelvin was there with about 9 kids from their house. The trailer was definitely at maximum capacity. Greedy had a blast, I'd never seen him so happy. We were finally able to start having normal interactions with normal people doing normal things. It felt really good. His birthday was on a Sunday and we didn't have to go to school because it was spring break. I decided that I would take Greedy with me into the city so my sisters could see him for his birthday. Helen agreed to let me ride with her into the city that Monday. When we got there, me and Greedy took the city bus over to mom's house. I hadn't seen them in forever. I was extremely nervous because it had only been a hand full of months since I left and I knew Chris was still looking for me. I ran up the drive way and knocked on the door. I didn't tell her I was coming because I knew she would tell Chris. I stayed there for a couple of hours and made sure no one used the phone while I was there. I didn't have much interest in seeing my mom but I did want to see my sisters and they wanted to see Greedy. I called Helen at work and asked if my sister could come back with us for a few days and ride back home to the city with her on Friday to go home. Helen agreed and a little while later came to pick me and Lillian up on her lunch break. We spent the rest of the afternoon in the lobby of the place she worked at. When she got off we all rode back to the house in the country. Lillian really enjoyed being out there and I enjoyed having her. We talked a lot and I showed her all of the land and the horses. When it was time for her to go I didn't want her to but she had to. She was supposed to call me when she got home but she didn't and I was too scared to call the house. I went back a couple of weeks later and when I did, they had this girl living with them. Her name was Sammy, I didn't know why she was living with them but she was pretty cool. A guy showed up in a sports car with a bird painted on the hood and she left with him for a little while. When she got back she gave up just enough information that I knew she was sleeping with him for money, she was a prostitute too. I was curious, I wondered how she ended up at mom's house. And I wanted to make damn sure she wasn't trying to get at my sisters. I let her know in very clear terms that if she even thought about it, I wouldn't hesitate to make her disappear. She knew I was serious and promised me she would protect them. I went back home that afternoon when it was time for Helen to get off work. We went back to the country and I went back to school for the week. That weekend I asked Helen to take me on Friday and not pick me up until Monday. I knew it was risky staying there but I had to figure out some things. I couldn't keep staying at Maya's house. I loved it there, but Pops was starting to flirt too much and her Mom was starting to act weird. That weekend Tyana had a boyfriend over named Charles and we were all chilling at Mom's house. Sammy was out somewhere but her guy friend in the sports car showed up. He got out of the car and I was able to see who it was. There stood a short Asian guy. He was dresses to the nines and had his shades on. He looked to me like a cool version of Bruce Lee. We told him that she wasn't there and he took a seat anyway. When he sat down it was next to me and almost in my lap. We talked for a while and he was kind of funny. The guys decided that we would go on a beer run. I wasn't real big on beer or liquor because of Chris, which wasn't a bad thing. But I wanted to do different things, things I couldn't do before. After we got the beer we headed to his house instead of back to ours. He was staying in some apartments on May Avenue. We walked in and I was pleasantly surprised. It was a nice place with nice furniture, a big TV with a really nice and expensive looking stereo player with big speakers like Chris had. There were Asian pictures and calendars on the wall. We sat on the couch while Nam put the beer in the freezer to get it cold quicker. I finally got his name down, it took me forever. His name was Nam, pronounced like Pam but with an N. We decided to play quarters, a new game for me. Pretty soon I was starting to feel the beer. We kept going and soon none of us were doing great at walking or sitting up for that matter. We went to the room and there were two beds. Nam and I got on one and Tyana and Charles were on the other. We were all drunk and one thing lead to another. Pretty soon Nam and I were doing more than we planned on. We woke the next morning and were instantly a couple. We barely knew each other and he barely spoke English but we were willing to see what would happen. I called Helen and told her that I had a ride back to the house and not to worry about me. Later that evening Nam took me home. For the next few weekends Nam would come get me after school and bring me back on Friday nights. Well this all ended one day when Helen thought something was going on between me and Pops. It was Sunday night and Nam had let me have the car by myself for the first time. I had planned to drive me and Maya to and from school the next day and then take it back to Nam that evening. When I pulled up in the driveway I had no idea what was about to happen. When I got in the house I didn't see Maya. Helen was the only one around. I had just walked in the door when she said "Good thing you have a car because you are leaving here tonight!" and she meant it. I didn't have to ask her why, I already knew from the way she had been acting in the weeks prior. I walked to the room and started gathering me and Greedy's stuff. I continued to pack my things in the car while Greedy played on our bed. When I was done I went to Maya's room but I didn't get an answer. I walked out of the house and drove down the long driveway to the road. It seemed like it took hours to get back into the city. I wasn't finished with school yet. I didn't want 10th grade to go like 9th grade did. I'll never get to graduate. But here I was, headed back to the city. That wasn't where I was supposed to be and it was the most dangerous place to move back to. And where was I going to stay? I certainly didn't want to go live with mom. I pulled up at Nam's apartment and knocked on the door. He answered with a puzzled look on his face. "I thought you were keeping it for school" he said. "No, I got kicked out" "What do you mean?" "I mean I got kicked out, like I don't live there anymore, I'm homeless." I started crying which made Greedy start crying too. We went inside to his room and I explained to him what happened. He said I could stay there tonight and we would figure out the rest in the morning. That morning we moved all my stuff in and that was my new place. I was back in the city but at least I had a place to stay and hopefully someone who will protect me. I had only been there for a few weeks when I realized I was late on my period. I went to the drug store and got a pregnancy test and took it back to the house. I hurried into the house and hid it in the closet. The directions said to do it in the morning and that's how doctor's offices did it as well. If I was pregnant I wasn't going to be un-pregnant in one day. I watched him cook dinner that evening. He was always showing me something new. He was Vietnamese and the cuisine was delicious for the most part. That next morning when he went to work I was about to explode. I needed to pee earlier but couldn't so I was holding it. He seemed to take forever to get ready for work and leave. When he did I made a mad dash for the bathroom. I pulled out the stick and peed on it. I waited and watched. I finally see the fluid start running through the area where the lines were. One line means no, two lines mean yes. I was watching it crawl across and turn pink as the first line was saturated. Then I watched it go across the other line and slowly but surely the other line was turning pink, I don't mean a baby pink, I mean a, you can't miss this, all in your face pink. I didn't know what to think. I was scared, a little excited, and nervous about what he would think, I was all kinds of things. I waited until Nam got home from work and showed him the pregnancy test. When I showed it to him he didn't even know what it was. I explained it and his face lit up like the full moon. He opened the door and ran out talking in Vietnamese to his brother and cousin. He was very happy and I didn't want to ruin his happiness or for that matter my own so I got happy about it too. I didn't tell my sisters right away because I wasn't sure about this myself. I was told that after you have a miscarriage that you will have trouble having another baby so I was very worried about that. We had been living together for a couple of months and I was keeping his car while he worked so I went by my mom's house to tell my sisters I was pregnant. When I came in I said "I got something to tell y'all come on." As I walked us to the bedroom. We all climbed on the bed. They were all ears. "I'm pregnant!" "By Chris?" Lillian asked. "No, by Nam, not Chris, matter of fact don't ever even say his name again!" "Well then I won't tell you that he Just left about 15 minutes before you came here" My heart sank and my anxiety shot through the roof. I jumped off the bed, scooped up Greedy and headed for the door. When I opened the door and stepped outside he was right there. His car was parked behind my car and there was no way out. I froze where I was and the girls were in the door right behind me.

"Give me my boy Angel" he said with his arms stretched out. I brought Greedy in closer to me as Chris came near. "Go inside y'all" I said to my sisters. I didn't want them to get hurt and I also didn't want them to see me getting hurt. Greedy stretched his arms out to his Daddy and they embraced. I was happy to see it but frightened at the thought of what would happen next. He turned and walked back to the car with Greedy. I walked behind him "Please don't take him Chris, I need him. Please Chris!" I begged. He got into the front seat without even looking my direction and closed the door. "Follow me and I will kill you Angel!" was the last thing he said as he started the car. I watched as he backed out of the driveway with Greedy in the car with him. Tears started running down my face. I had no idea what he was going to do with him. This was his son, his first born, surely he wouldn't hurt him. I was trying to convenience myself I was right but I knew deep inside, it was all wrong. I went back inside and told them he had taken him. They were used to him having Greedy and didn't understand what it meant. I didn't have time or energy to explain. The only thing that was going on in my head was where do I think he would have taken him? I left in Nam's car and went to the all of the old houses. They were either empty or had new tenants living in them. I couldn't find him anywhere. When I had to pick up Nam I had to tell him where Greedy was. He had heard from others that I had a mean ex-boyfriend but he had no clue what he was really up against. He got real upset because he knew I was upset. We drove around for hours looking for Chris or anyone associated with him. It was after midnight and we were headed home defeated. I took a shower and went to bed. There was nothing I could do right now, I had cried out all the tears I could. Nam was beginning to get worried about the baby. "My ma said if you cry a lot when you have the baby in you it's not good. You need to stop crying for the baby" he said. The next morning I stepped outside and saw police officers and my heart started pounding. I ran over to the officers and asked "what was going on, was there a little boy?" They said no and asked me what was going on with me. I told them and ultimately said that they couldn't do anything. Because I acknowledge that he is the father and he left with his father and he has rights, so it's not kidnapping. There was nothing they would do. Days went by and I didn't know what to do. I had been everywhere and there was no one to help me. I would cry for hours on end and again started thinking of suicide. I had told myself that if I didn't find Greedy or if something bad happened to him that I was going to kill myself. I couldn't see living if he wasn't living. It didn't matter that I had another life growing inside of me. The only thing that mattered was getting Greedy back and knowing he was ok. I was sitting on the couch trying to think of new places to look for Greedy when the phone rang. It was Lillian, he had dropped Greedy off at her house. I raced over there, I didn't care if Chris was still there or not, I wanted my son. I pulled into the dive way and left the car running. I walked in and grabbed him then left as quickly as I got there. I didn't want to stick around for anything. I stayed inside the apartment for a few days to give things time to calm down. Nam and I were awake and getting ready for an appointment. He was going to have to be dropped off at work and I had a doctor appointment for the baby. We got in the car and headed to his job. We were coming up on 63rd street when I noticed that the breaks were doing nothing to slow down the car. I started panicking and looking around everywhere for something to do to stop it. I was screaming and pushing the crap out of the petal and it was doing nothing, in fact the car seemed to be speeding up. I was stomping on the pedal and nothing still. We flew thru the intersection and I jerked the car over to get it out of the traffic. I landed in the grass area right in front of a mechanic shop and ran into the sign post. I got out of the car with my heart going 90 miles per hour. I fell down to the ground with my head in my hands. Greedy got out right behind me and was trying to console me. I grabbed him and held him close to me, we could have been killed. He didn't know what was wrong but he knew his mommy was upset and scared. This could have killed us, I was pregnant with Nam's child and had my son in the car with me. Nam was walking around the car trying to figure out what happened. The guys had come outside when they heard me crash into their place. Nam told them the breaks stopped working and that's why we crashed into their sign. They pulled the car over to the bay and started looking it over. Nam was with them and I was in the lobby room with Greedy. He had mostly recovered and was playing with anything he could find. I was still in a state of shock. My children and I were almost killed. There were several cars in the interception that narrowly missed our car only because they swerved their cars away. The mechanics finished looking at it and the result was that the break lines on the front two tires had been disconnected. Not cut with some scissors or shears but unscrewed and removed from their connection. The mechanic wrote up a letter to give to the police, he said whoever did this was trying to kill me. I was scared to walk out of the apartment after that. He was really trying to kill me, Nam didn't have anyone trying to kill him. I was the only one with death threats on my head. Not to mention I had just seen Chris again, I hadn't seen him since I left him. What if he had April or Brook in another car somewhere to follow me and that's how he knew where to find the car. I had nine thousand things going through my head but the number one thing was to keep my son protected and to stay alive. We didn't go out much but when we did I was very cautious about my surroundings. I knew Chris could walk up at any moment and that he did. I was getting gas one day and before I realized that he had pulled up he was already out of the car. He opened the door and took Greedy from the back of the car. I ran around to that side but he wouldn't let me have him. He got in the car and left again, just as he did before and still the police would do nothing. I had to wait until I either found him or Chris would be gracious enough to drop him off at my mom's. This time he was gone for more than a few days, it had been a week and still no sign of him. I couldn't do anything while he was gone. I was a frozen person, life Just didn't mean anything if I couldn't have my son. I didn't want to but I still had to go on with things. I had a doctor appointment and had left early to get some gas. I pulled into the same station where Chris took Greedy and he was sitting there in the Cadillac. I pulled up beside him and he let Greedy out of the car. I opened my door and let Greedy climb in over me. I didn't even speak to him, I Just shut the door and pulled off. What would I say, I still didn't have control over the situation, I had no one to help me and it wasn't getting any better. When I got back to the apartment with Greedy in my arms, Nam was steaming mad. He didn't like that Chris still had so much control and I didn't either. We had started a new life and were having tons of fun together. Nam had gotten him most of the toys he ever wanted but I would make sure the educational one's were in there as well. We would make tents in the bedroom and use flashlights to read. Greedy was smart, much smarter than other 2 ½ year olds. He already knew his alphabet, not the song, he knew them and was starting to recognize words for reading. We would do crossword puzzles together and he would guess words he thought might fit in. I don't recall him ever getting one right but the effort he put in to thinking about what the answer could be was well worth listening to the answers. He was growing and so was my relationship with Nam.

I didn't go to Mom's house often but when I did I was always cautious. I would back the car all the way in so you couldn't see it from the street. You had to get up the driveway to see that I was there. Anything I could do to make it harder for him I was trying to do. Unfortunately it didn't always s work. We ran into each other again at my mom's house and this time it didn't go as he expected. He was trying to get me to come back to him even though I told him I was pregnant and he could see it. He wanted me to go make money for him and I finally refused. When I refused he grabbed me and I resisted him. I twisted and pulled away. "Go away Chris or I'll call the cops!" I yelled. He didn't want anything to do with the police so he got in his car and backed out of the driveway. I went into the house for a few minutes to give him time to drive away. I gathered our stuff and headed home. I took the long way around just in case Chris was following me and I didn't know it. When I got home and told Nam he started laying down the law now. I was coming up on 6 months and he didn't want me around any of that. He didn't want me to go by moms at all. I stayed away for a couple of weeks then mom called and asked me to come over. She said she needed to show me something. I called and told her I was headed over but couldn't stay long. I got to the house and did the usual, pulled all the way in. I had barely gotten out of the car when Chris pulled in behind me. I knocked on the door hoping she would answer and let me in before he got out of the car. She didn't answer. He didn't get out of the car though, he just rolled down the window. "Come here Angel, I'm not going to get out of the car." I walked over to him. "Me and April are moving to Tulsa, I want you to have the TV that my mom gave us for our first apartment." "Seriously, when are y'all moving?" "This weekend." I was apprehensive but I also wanted the TV. I didn't have very many possessions of my own and I wanted the TV. "Sure, where is it?" I asked. "It's at April's place she's over there off of May." "When do you want to do this?" "Tonight if possible." When he said that same day, I started thinking. What if he's just trying to get me over there to hurt me? "Are you trying to get me over there to hurt me? I'm bringing a gun!" I said with a strong voice. I was shaking on the inside but I didn't want him to know that. "No, Angel, I'm not going to do anything to you. Bring Greedy so I can see him before we go." "Ok, I'll meet you there at 6." He backed out and mom finally answered the door. "What did you need to show me?" I asked. "Nothing, Chris wanted you, that's why I called you over." "Mom, you've gotta stop doing that, he's going to seriously hurt me one of these days." She walked back in the house and I shut her door and got in the car. I went back to my house and made arrangements with a friend to use their truck. Later that evening I headed out and was playing the "what if" game all the way there. I brought my sisters with me just in case so if he did try to hurt me I would have a witness. I made it to April's house shortly before 6 and they were both there. I walked in the house and you could tell they were moving. Chris had already moved the TV close to the door. He looked outside at the truck then picked up the TV and carried it out. I talked to April briefly, she was in the room packing. "Hey, long time no see." April turned around to see me standing there. "Where have you been Angel?" she asked. "I've been here and there, you know trying to stay out of trouble. Where is Brook?" She shook her head no as if to not ask about that. It was obvious that I was pregnant, she pointed down at my belly and gave a look of question. "It's my new boyfriend's baby, we're going to get married, and he has a real job" I said. "Chris had me driving all over looking for you for months. That picture your mom gave him of Greedy, he had me looking for that address that was in the background of the picture, he was trying hard to find you. I'm surprised he's letting you go." "Well he doesn't have a choice, I don't want to do this anymore and I'm pregnant with another man's baby. I wish you guys luck in Tulsa" I said as I walked out of the house. I figured that would be the last time I would see him. Greedy said goodbye to all of them and we left. I got the TV home and Nam was not happy. I didn't discuss it with him beforehand because I didn't think it was necessary, it was a TV. What difference did it make where it came from, it was a TV. He was looking out for me and didn't want me to get hurt. I put it in the bedroom and Greedy used that TV to watch his cartoons and shows.

Things had settled down for a while and I spent all my time playing with Greedy or shopping for the new baby. It was late one night when Greedy and I were building with his blocks. 10 o'clock rolled around so he hopped up and headed for the TV. Each evening, he was doing nothing else during that time except watching the Head Bangers Ball. His watched for his favorite band "Gun's and Roses" he would wait for their music to play. He knew how to tell simple time and knew when 10 was rolling up. He would go and get his little red plastic chair from where ever it was and he would put it right in front of the TV to watch. He didn't want any talking either, he would shush you in a heartbeat. He stayed up late but Greedy was always up early and with tons of energy. I was turning 7 months and the pregnancy was making me tired. I tried to keep up with Greedy but it wasn't easy. We both took naps in the afternoon. It was the only way to keep up with him. The only problem was Greedy didn't always want to take a nap at the same time as me. One day after I had put him down I laid down on the couch to sleep. I was awoken by him screaming and running from the kitchen holding his hand. When I was able to get to him I could see that he had round burns on his finger like the ones the burner would make on the stove. I went to the kitchen to put his hand under cold water and help the hurt calm down. I could see that the front burner was on but in order for him to get it on he would have had to climb the counter. He was pretty much unstoppable, just like his father. If he wanted it he was going to have it, good or bad. Greedy was still screaming and I was starting to cry as well. I hated to see him hurt. I got him to calm down and let me get a good look at it. It wasn't looking good to me so I took him to the emergency room. We sat there for a while and finally got called back. The nurse cleaned it and put some cream on it. The doctor prescribed the same thing for continued treatment at home. I got the script filled and read all about it on the papers the pharmacy gave me. By the time we got home we were both exhausted. We climbed up in my bed and went to sleep. The next morning Greedy was up with the sun as usual. I got up and made Nam some breakfast before he had to leave. We were talking about the burners and not touching them when I was cooking. He was still sore and wanted to sit and watch TV instead of playing around. We watched a couple of movies and I made us some sandwiches for lunch. We ate and then went back to the TV, I looked over and he had passed out without even finishing his sandwich. I picked him up and carried him to the bed. I stood there staring at him for a while. We had finally made it out, we were really out and Chris was not even in the same city with us. I was finally free, finally able to live a life without fear every day, and without having to prostitute. Nam even said I should go back to school to get a business degree, things were changing and it was for the better. After tucking him in I went back to the couch and laid down. I was so exhausted. It was almost noon and I was watching one of the soaps when I dozed off. A statement from the Anchor on the news startled me right up out of my sleep. In fact, startled is a gross understatement. The breath was taken right out of my body by Satan himself. I heard the news anchor say "Chris Sharp has been arrested for the murder of Brook Appletree and her unborn child." I rose from the couch to see both of their pictures side by side on the screen. Her high school picture and his mug shot. I fell to the floor and started gasping for air. I couldn't breathe, this can't be real, and she can't be dead. I didn't even know she was pregnant but the news said she was 6 months. I began sobbing like a child, he had really done it. He had killed her. I couldn't move from the floor, I had no life in me to raise me up. "This can't be happening." I kept telling myself that over and over. I couldn't believe what I had just heard. "This isn't real, this isn't real!" I yelled. I crawled over to the phone, still on the floor. I called downtown to the police department to check the listings and make sure this was real and he was in jail. "Oklahoma County Jail, can I help you?" "Yes" I said between sobs. "Are you holding Chris Sharp and for what?" She said "Yes, and it's for murder." I dropped the phone and began to wail. There were sounds coming from my body that I had never heard before. My heart was crying out. "This can't be real, this can't be happening. Why did you do this?" I began yelling out. "Why, why, why!" I couldn't wrap my head around what I was hearing. I reached over to the remote and changed the channel hoping the other news would say different. Say that she's in the hospital or she's already safe at home with her mother, but they didn't. They were all saying the same thing. She was dead, he killed her and the baby she was carrying. I laid right where I was on the floor crying. As the tears streamed down my face, I began to think. I couldn't keep letting life happen, I had to do something. This time it had to be different.

In loving memory of

"Brook" and our unborn children.

Brook you are an unforgettable young woman. Your heart is as big as the ocean and your talents are as wide. I watched as you loved with all of your heart. I have no doubt that you are watching over every move we make. You are our Angel. You are deeply missed and our hearts will not be the same until we see your smiling face again. See you soon Brook!

Love Angel

Mom, I miss you so much. There are so many things to tell you. So many things to show you. I know you are watching over me. I can feel you, I need to be by your side. I'll wait patiently, like a Warrior Princess, standing at the gates of Heaven until they let me in to you. I love you momma.

Love Brooklyn

Silencing an Angel

~Chapter 1~

Frozen

I went to the room to wake my son Greedy from his nap. I stood in the doorway looking at him with tears running down my face. He wasn't even three yet, how would I tell him that his Dad did? Would he understand if I told him? What would I even say? What kind of words would you use with a three year old? I decided that saying nothing was best. I walked over, touched his face, and leaned down to kiss him. As my lips touched his cheek he began to arouse. "Greedy, wake up Greedy, we've got to go somewhere" I said as I pull him up to me. I put him over my shoulder and he started drifting back to sleep. I reached over and picked up his shoes and we walked out of the room. I grabbed my purse and keys and we went to the car. I still had a constant stream of tears running down my face, I had no control over my tears. This can't really be happening. I wanted the news report to be wrong. I wanted them to take it back, I didn't want it to be true. I put Greedy in his car seat and buckled him in. I tried to wipe the tears as I walked around to the driver's side. I had to get myself together to drive. I sat in the seat with the keys in my hand staring at the concrete wall I was parked in front of. I was frozen in that moment. Flashes of Brook were flying through my mind. Flashes of her and I riding in the Cadillac, flashes of her and I cooking together, of her laugh and her smile. Flashes of Chris beating her were there too. The news anchor hadn't said exactly how he killed her Just that he did. I was still in disbelief. This wasn't real and I was going to prove that it wasn't.

I started the car and backed out of the driveway and onto the road. I got to the stop light to turn on to May Avenue and was waiting for it to turn green. The voice and words of the news anchor kept playing over and over in my head. "Chris Sharp has been arrested for the murder of Brook Appletree" This could not be real. Honk, Honk. I Jumped and looked in the rearview mirror. There was a car behind me and the light had turned green. I pushed the gas pedal and made my way down the road. I stopped at the light on 50th feeling like I had already driven 13 miles instead of 13 blocks. It was like being in a time machine that moved in slow motion. I had the same images rotating in my head and time was slowing down each time they came around. I was startled by the car next to me leaving parked position because the light had turned green. I pushed the pedal again and continued down through lights to 12th street with tears streaming down my face. If it weren't for instinctively knowing how to get there I would have never made it to my mom's house in the condition I was in. I pulled up in the driveway and parked the car, leaving it running. I got out and reached in the back to get Greedy. He was still sleeping and I tried to pick him up as gently as possible. I laid him over my shoulder and walked to the door. As I shifted Greedy to knock on the door, my sister Lillian, opened it. "Did you hear?" she said with a frightened tone, I could tell she had been crying. I quickly raised my finger to my mouth to shush her, pointing at

Greedy sleeping. "Yes, that's why I'm here. I need you to watch him, I'm going to Brook's mother's house. I can't let this Just happen like this!" I said as I laid Greedy down on the couch. "What are you going to do?" "I don't know but I can't Just sit back and do nothing anymore, I've got to do something." "I thought you said before that they don't like you?" "I know, but they have to know the truth, they have to know what was going on, I've got to speak up for Brook." I walked out the door and over to the car. As I got in I started thinking about what I was going to say. How to you start that conversation. What would they think when they saw me at the door? Would they be angry with me also, since I was connected to Chris? Would they listen to me? After all, I was an ex-prostitute and pregnant teenager for the second time. I was high on the list of people they wanted to see. I thought about going back in mom's house and crying it out with my younger sisters. Then I thought about getting Greedy and going back home to cry alone. I thought about the possibility of him getting out of jail and killing me and my son. Chris had been arrested several times and they were never able to keep him. He always had an answer for everything and was able to manipulate anyone around him. To us he was the Alpha and the Omega. I was frightened and I knew, when he got out, he would kill me, Greedy, and the baby I was carrying. It used to be a question in my head but now, it was no longer a question. It became a statement, and I didn't want to die. He said it many times, now it was not Just words, now he meant it more than ever. I got out of the car and started to walk over to the door. As I got closer to the door I stopped. I will be dead either way, I thought to myself. If I tell the truth, he will kill me when he gets out of jail. If I don't tell the truth he will still kill me when he gets out because I know too much. It became a stalemate. I figured I was going to be dead either way so I was going to try to do the right thing. I wanted my last moments on earth to be worth something. Not Just stories of a used up teenage prostitute.

I got back in the car, started it and backed out of the driveway. I turned the car to the east and headed down Park

Place to Penn Avenue. I had no idea what I was going to say, what they would ask, or if they would talk to me at all. I didn't know how they would react to me showing up during all that was going on. I turned down 12th street and made my way down the few blocks to her mother's house. I noticed as I was getting closer that there was yellow police tape at a house a few houses before I reached her mother's. I slowed down in front of the house and parked the car. I looked across the yard and up the concrete sidewalk to the little red brick house. It looked so normal, so peaceful. A door in the middle with a window on each side. It was exactly the shape of the house that we all drew when we were kids. It didn't give Justice to the things that were going on inside. I took a few deep breaths and opened the car door. There were several cars around so I knew there were other family members there with her mother. I stood up out of the car and looked across the top of the car to the house. I shut the door as I walked around the back of the car to the yard. My heart was beating so loud I could hear it outside my chest. My palms and underarms were starting to sweat. Taking a leap of no return, a leap of faith indeed was not common place for me. But I was starting to give it some practice. I had enough of the life I was exposed to and wanted something different, something better, and Brook deserved my dedication to that. She died for the life we were living, I would not allow that to be silenced. I walked across the grass to the sidewalk and up the porch stairs. I stood there on the door step for a minute, afraid to knock. The questions started hitting me again. What if I'm here at the wrong time? What if I did it wrong? What if they hate me? What if they want to hurt me because I was involved with Chris? Before I knew it the door opened, I didn't have to knock. I was staring at her twin brother through the screen. I knew exactly who he was because I saw her face in him. She had talked about him many times and I saw pictures of them when they were young but I had never seen him in person. "Yea, what do you want?" he said in a protective voice through the screen. "My name is Angel, I'm here to help, to tell you anything you need to know about our life with Chris." "Hold on!" he said as he disappeared into the dimly lit house. I started to panic. Who or what is he going to get? Is he getting a gun or a knife? Is he going to hurt me? I wanted to run off the porch, Jump into the car and speed away. It was only a few seconds when a lady with long black hair appeared in the door. "You're Angel?" "Yes, I came to help in whatever way I can." She opened the screen door. "Come in, Angel." As I walked through the door I told her "My name is really Sarah, Angel is what Chris named me. I don't go by that name anymore." "Ok, Sarah" she said as she lead me through the unlit living room to the small dining area. There were several family members in the room. Her brothers and sisters were all there. You see the pain in their native faces, you could feel the heartache in the room. They were broken, looking for a way to find the pieces and put them together again. Her mother was sitting at the table, she was clearly broken. Her dark hair was what I saw first. She was in her 50's and on her good days she could hold her own, no doubt. But this day was not a good day, her baby was gone and the pain was screaming from her body. She looked up at me with her strong determined native face. "Are you going to help us Angel?" Her eyes were dark and strained from all the crying, but I could see her heart. I couldn't let her down, I couldn't let Brook down. She already knew who I was. She had spoken about me to Brook. "Yes ma'am, I am! You can ask me anything, I'll tell you what I know." "Will you talk to the detectives for me?" "Yes, I will talk to whoever you need me to. I'm so very sorry. I got away from him a few months back. Brook said she was going to go back to live with you, I don't know what happened?" I said as I began to cry again. She started telling me what they knew so far. My entire body was cringing. I was in disbelief. I couldn't back out of what was being said. The truth was staring me so hard in the face, there was no way out. I wanted to reverse her story. I wanted to change what she was saying and make it not true. Her daughters and sons were confirming the story and were taking over telling it when their mother would begin to cry. I could not and don't want to imagine her pain. Yes, I had lost a child also, and by his evil hand. But it was nothing like this. They were telling the story of her death, at the hands of our children's father. As much as I didn't want to believe it, I had to.

They were with her and they knew, they saw her last moments. We were all frozen souls, frozen from the inside out. God had given us no other choice, time froze.

Look for the newest in the "Angel" series to complete the story.

Thank You!

First, giving all honor and glory to God, giving thanks for his guiding power and strength. On my best day I couldn't orchestrate what he has put together. I can't thank enough the family of Brook, she is my Angel and guides my steps daily. I am dedicated to being a guiding force in the life of her daughter and grandchildren.

I give tremendous thanks to my children for putting up with my mess. I have 4 children by birth and 4 more by God. I'm thankful and in love with all of them. Thanks is not a word that would cover what my eldest did for me during this time. He was a grown little man, my rock, my reason for striving to make things right, my reason to care about life. I am thankful for every moment I have with him.

A thousand thanks to my ex-husband/in house therapist, he changed everything and showed me much more of myself than I ever knew possible. I wouldn't be the same person without his input. Much thanks to my family, my brother and sisters, it was never easy but we made it out alive. That's enough to make me shout! I'm so grateful and thankful for all of the brothers and sisters (friends) God placed in my path and created the huge family I have today.

I literally owe my life to my sister from God Maya. She stepped in not once, but twice. The path I was on was certain death and she was the light at the end. Maya I am forever indebted and in love with you. Thank you to Karen for putting the spark in that made a difference in my life.

Thanks to my editors and readers you helped turn blubbering stories into a readable book.

Thank you to April for the care you did show to me, you could have made it much worse for me and you didn't. I pray that you are freed from the past. Ignoring the past allowed it to hold me down. Dealing with it, talking about it, freed me from it. I wish the same freedom for you.

Finally thank you reader. If this book sets any emotion in you let it be anger, and let your anger turn to action, action that makes a difference and stops the world from allowing our "Angels" to be abused.